The
Best American
Movie Writing
1998

The Best American Movie Writing 1998

GEORGE PLIMPTON, EDITOR

JASON SHINDER, SERIES EDITOR

St. Martin's Griffin
New York

Design by Jennifer Ann Daddio

ISBN 0-312-18049-7

First St. Martin's Griffin Edition: March 1998

10 9 8 7 6 5 4 3 2 1

Peter Bart, "The Mob, The Movies, and Me," from *GQ* (June 1997). Copyright © 1997 by Peter Bart. Reprinted with the permission of The Robbins Office.

Donald Bogle, "Beauty and the Beast: Did Hollywood Destroy Dorothy Dandrige?" from *Essence* (May 1997). Reprinted with the permission of the author.

Edward Field, "Variety Photoplays," from *Parnassus* 22, nos. 1 & 2 (1997). Reprinted with the permission of the author.

Bonnie Friedman, "Relinquishing Oz: Every Girl's Anti-Adventure Story," from *Michigan Quarterly Review* (Fall 1996). Reprinted with the permission of the author.

Stephen Fry, "Playing Oscar," from *The New Yorker* (June 16, 1997). Copyright © 1997 by Stephen Fry. Reprinted with the permission of Harold Ober Associates, Inc.

Libby Gelman-Waxner, "Pretty Is as Pretty Does," from *Premiere* (February 1997). Copyright © 1997 by Libby Gelman-Waxner. Reprinted with the permission of Helen Merrill, Ltd.

Albert Goldbarth, "Square of Light," from *Parnassus* 22, nos. 1 & 2 (1997). Reprinted with the permission of the author.

Daniel Harris, "The Death of Camp: Gay Men and Hollywood Diva Worship, from Reverence to Ridicule," from *Salmagundi* no. 112 (Fall 1996). Reprinted with the permission of the author.

Evan Hunter, "Me and Hitch," from *Sight and Sound* (July 1997). Copyright © 1997 by Evan Hunter. Reprinted with the permission of Gelfman Schneider Literary Agents, Inc.

Barbara Maltby, "What Do Movie Producers Do?" from *The American Scholar* (Fall 1996). Copyright © 1996 by Barbara Maltby. Reprinted with the permission of *The American Scholar*.

(continued on page 268)

Contents

Thanks—

Foreword

$\mathcal{T}$he movies are arguably the most influential form of communication we have today. Films mirror the desires and fears, fantasies and conflicts at the heart of our culture, itself in the midst of celebration and crisis. We talk more frequently, perhaps more ardently, about the films we watch together than about our personal experiences with written literature. We look today for illumination not only from novelists, poets, musicians, and painters, but also from the panoply of artists—directors, screenwriters, actors, cinematographers—who contribute to the creation of a motion picture. And what we read and write about film has become a key component of our literature and culture.

Pulitzer Prize–winning novelist James Agee, one of the first distinguished American writers to focus his talent and energies on writing about film, declared in 1950 that screenwriting was "a new dramatic form." Today we can match his observation with another. Writing *about* the movies—a discipline in which Agee was a pioneer—is a new written form, an evolving form of criticism that offers a unique combination of opportunities and rewards for our most talented cultural observers. A recent informal survey of more than one hundred popular magazines, conducted by students at Bennington College, concluded that movies, movie stars, moviemaking, and Hollywood—past, present, and future—constitute the most frequently written-about subjects in magazines today (and more than sixty of the periodicals surveyed listed a full- or part-time writer dedicated exclusively to film). The growing impulse of writers of all kinds to put down their observations on the movies we all watch may be inspired by the chance the genre offers them to survey and comment upon a world of the sweeping scale and depth that film alone has the ability to conjure. The fictional characters, involving story lines, and directorial vision of our best motion pictures inevitably engage the imagination and intellect of our finest writers.

The art of motion pictures offers the dual blessing of being both intensely private and extremely public. In the same way, writers whose work transcends the assignment of a traditional movie review frequently use the forum of a longer or broader essay to reflect upon our shared cultural universe, or just as frequently upon what their personal perspectives bring to their reaction to a film. Essayists who take on motion pictures have the opportunity to appraise our world from as many directions as our most wildly imaginative filmmakers do: to consider particular years, decades, centuries; to honor the dead and the living; to document private and public illusions, perceptions, denials— all through the kaleidoscopic looking glass of what Arthur Miller has called "the single greatest invention of this century."

The Best American Movie Writing has been conceived as a way to collect, highlight, and preserve, in a single annual volume, the enormous growth, diversity, excitement, and quality of American movie writing, and, by extension, of movies themselves. Indeed, the series is a celebration of cinema's extraordinary influence and growth as it begins its second century. Film is a brazenly commercial business as well as a viscerally powerful art form; as a result, while many movies are profoundly moving and memorable, many, many others are not. But movies have a tremendous audience; almost everyone goes to the cinema with some frequency and watches attentively enough to form opinions about their story lines, their actors and actresses, even the unseen writers and directors ultimately responsible for so much of what ends up on the screen. The size and sensitivity of the audience thus dictates that almost all movies, whether serious or merely entertaining, are important, and nearly every one of them is a fit subject for interpretation. The writers anthologized here are participating not only in the development of a new genre of writing but in a kind of American sport, a kind of "movieball" that always begins with one person turning to another and asking, "So did you like it? What did you think?"

The guidelines of this new anthology series are simple. Each year the guest editor, a writer of distinction and stature, makes the final selections based on a wide survey of nonfiction writing about film published in American magazines in the previous year. For this volume, each and every issue of more than two hundred general and special-interest magazines published between November 1, 1996, and October 31, 1997, were surveyed by me, the guest editor, and several research and editorial assistants in search of writings that might merit inclusion in the collection. In addition to our own survey, we have solicited nominations from the editors of nearly every one of the magazines we reviewed. As word of the series spread, many authors sent us copies of their published work, or the work of others they admired: profiles, memoirs, historical pieces, extended reviews, meditations, academic studies, diaries, essays of all kinds. The final selections are in the following pages, while an equal number of finalists are listed among the Notable Movie Writings of 1997 in the back of this volume.

One of our most distinguished and influential editors and essayists, *Paris Review* founder and executive editor George Plimpton, is our first guest editor. Through such best-selling books as *Paper Lion, Shadow Box, Edie*, and, most recently, *Truman Capote*, he has taken us into worlds we might never have dreamed of entering. Through his extraordinary ability to rediscover and remake as fixed a literary form as the interview, Plimpton has demonstrated a singular understanding of the fluidity of nonfiction forms. His role in the development of "participatory journalism" is just one example of his remarkable gift for using the written word to help us reexamine other fields, as well as his gift for bridging the divide between reader and writer; his place in the world of contemporary letters is unique. I can think of no better guest editor for the debut of a series that recognizes an emerging genre of writing.

In addition to helping the series editor locate pieces for possible inclusion in the anthology and writing the introduction to the book, the guest editor is also given the opportunity to include a recent appropriate writing of his or her own and one selection from a source other than a magazine. For this first volume, George Plimpton has chosen a piece by Alice Walker from her book *The Same River Twice* as well as his own delightful "Warren Beatty" from *The Paris Review.*

Along with Mr. Plimpton, I wish to thank Dan Kunitz, managing editor of *The Paris Review,* whose great support of the series and help with the research and selection process were invaluable. Thanks also to Katie Adams, who spent many, many long days and nights in the library surveying hundreds of magazines. And thanks to my wise and insightful agent, Sharon Friedman, and to Cal Morgan, my editor at St. Martin's. His passion for the best movies and literature, and his insights as an editor, are essential elements in the creation of this series.

Finally, thanks to the writers and editors who granted permission to reprint the pieces in this collection. As with any anthology, the writings included here represent a small portion of a much larger (and rapidly growing) body of work. Indeed, I hope this series will encourage readers to seek out, and read, further writings by the commentators collected here, and by those mentioned among the other notables. The series was not undertaken to assert any single interpretation of a year's film history or film art. Rather, it was founded to offer a necessary forum for the new, exciting canon of movie writing, and inspiration for the growing audience of moviegoers everywhere interested in enlarging their insight into film and its impact on our lives.

—JASON SHINDER

Introduction

I realized the other day that I have been in more films than I have written books (well over twenty)—a disturbing thought for someone who is considered a writer. An equally disturbing (if not melancholy) thought is that no film critic has ever recognized my work in films.

Admittedly, my roles have been small. The least significant of them was in *Lawrence of Arabia*. I played a bedouin—one of six thousand encamped in the Wadi Rhum one hundred miles north of Aqaba, a bleak desert area fringed by red-tinged buttes as large as battleships. On a participatory journalistic assignment from a major show-biz publication, I was expected to write about what it was like being in a major film, perhaps even in a small speaking role—say a British subaltern once we'd moved back to Cairo. But when I toiled up a vast sand dune to meet David Lean, the film's director, it was evident he was having a bad day; quite summarily he banished his aspirant actor into a distant tent in the encampment. I changed into bedouin robes, except for my shoes, which were Brooks Brothers penny loafers. I played in one scene. It involved Aouda Abu Tayi (Anthony Quinn) arriving at the outskirts of the encampment with Lawrence, riding up a sand dune on a horse and firing a large pistol into the air to alert his followers that he had arrived. The cameras were to film his men rushing out of their tents to meet him. I was in a tent about a quarter of a mile from the cameras. Three bedouins were in the tent with me, smiling and nodding. On occasion I had said to them, *"Faen posta kreb?"* (Where is the nearest post office?), the only sentence of Arabic I could remember from a phrase book. Bedouins from nearby tents came around to hear me say it.

Our cue to rush out was the distant sound of an explosion. It signified the cameras were rolling. I looked at my fellow tent-mates and called out, "Auda's here!" I ran out of the tent, as indeed hundreds were emerging from theirs. I have looked in vain for myself in the film. The Brooks Brothers loafers would have been a dead giveaway. Recently, a video edition of *Lawrence of Arabia* has been issued including footage not included in the original. Alas, while I am willing to point at a distant dot and say it is me, I'm truly not at all sure. Nonetheless, I proudly list *Lawrence of Arabia* as the production in which I made my first film appearance.

I had much stronger scenes in Warren Beatty's *Reds* (an oily editor trying to seduce Diane Keaton) and as Tom Hanks's father in *Volunteers* (Me: "Oh, I rue the day your mother and I brought you back from the orphanage." Hanks: "Dad, I'm not an orphan!" Me: "Please let me indulge my fantasies").

From that point I moved on to a period spent causing problems for directors—most recently by having trouble remembering my lines. One wouldn't think that this would be a problem, since cameo roles tend to be very brief. But inevitably it cropped up in a film called *Just Cause*, starring Sean Connery. I played a lawyer debating capital punishment in front of a large audience. After the third flub in a quite long speech Sean Connery walked across the stage. "You have no oxygen in your brain," he said. "Take a deep breath." Though fortified with this suggestion, nonetheless I failed yet again and for the final takes had to rely on large cue cards set up in the back of the theater.

Next, I had my problems with Oliver Stone, who had offered me the role of one of Richard Nixon's lawyers in his film *Nixon*. My major scene involved walking down a red-carpeted aisle with the President

(Anthony Hopkins), General Haig, and another lawyer toward the East Room for a full-scale press conference. My lines to a somewhat abstracted President were something like this: "Sir, the charges against you are very serious: first, obstruction of justice; second, bombing of Cambodia; third . . ." Stricken with an obvious case of stage fright, barely able to put one foot in front of the other as we moved for the doors of the East Room, I said the following: "Sir, the *changes* against you are very serious . . ."

I heard Oliver Stone's voice: "Cut!"

Hard to imagine, but I did this twice, and Stone, less patient than Sean Connery, stalked over and demanded of me, "What the hell's wrong with you?" to which I could only murmur, "Sorry, sorry."

My fellow actors were far more sympathetic, telling me about flubs of their own. One of them described a friend of his who had a scene with Marlon Brando in *Missouri Breaks*. The friend was enormously excited about this—the chance to play opposite the legendary star. Then, just before he went out onto the set, someone pasted a Post-it on his forehead. On it were Brando's lines. It turned out his function was largely that of a walking cue card—Brando, notorious for his inability to remember lines, squinting slightly as he leaned in to read the words off the poor fellow's forehead.

Last year I had a close brush with motion picture honors when a film with which I was associated won an Oscar for 1996's best documentary. *When We Were Kings*, it was entitled—about the Muhammad Ali–George Foreman fight in Zaire twenty-four years before, often referred to as "the Rumble in the Jungle." I had covered the fight for *Sports Illustrated*. I was asked by the documentary's producers to reminisce in front of the cameras about the occasion—quite easy to do since it remains one of the more memorable events I attended as a sports reporter. They asked the same of Norman Mailer, who indeed wrote a book about the bout entitled *The Fight*.

It seemed evident from the exultant reviews that the documentary was going to win an Oscar. So on impulse I went out to the coast for the ceremonies—indeed with a glimmer of hope that I might be called up onto the stage to be handed the gold statue. After all, I knew from television that often a whole passel of people crowds up onstage to be handed out Oscars, all with brief statements thanking their families. But, alas, only two Oscars were handed out for *When We Were Kings*, one to Leon Gast, the filmmaker, and the other to David Sonnenberg, who provided the film's financial backing.

After the awards ceremony everyone of prominence goes next door to the Governor's Ball. I did not have a ticket. So Leon handed me his Oscar, which we presumed would be capable of floating an entire *platoon* past the ticket-takers. Not at all.

"Where's your ticket?"

"But look, the Oscar! The Oscar!" I held it aloft. I could just as well have been holding up a dead cat. I was waved away from the entrance, until eventually someone slipped me a ticket.

Inside, the winners had set their trophies in the center of their tables. Admiring friends leaned in to lift one and remark on how heavy it was. It made me feel slightly better about not having won an Oscar to realize how little influence the statuette actually carries in the material world, at least as a ticket to an Oscar-related event.

Film critics and writers ought to get Oscars as well—perhaps even larger than those given the professionals. A ten-pounder! Maybe something more—the winning critic moving his mammoth Oscar off the stage in a wheelbarrow. After all, it is the family of film critics who are largely responsible for the success of any given movie. An Ebert thumb is raised in Chicago, and executives in Hollywood dance in the studio lot. A first-rate review in *The New York Times* may mean more to the success of a film than the abilities in that same film of an Oscar-winning actress. Besides, in their infinite wisdom, the film critics are the first to inform us if such and such an actress is worthy of an Academy Award. So their power is considerable—certainly enough to ignite wrath from their targets. "I love every bone in their heads," Eugene O'Neill once said.

What follows are the works of the best of them—film writers, reviewers, and critics. Disraeli had it wrong when he complained that critics are those who have failed in art and literature. Not at all. The proof is here.

—GEORGE PLIMPTON

The next best thing to seeing movies is reading about them.

STEVEN SPIELBERG

The
Best American
Movie Writing
1998

Pretty Is as Pretty Does

BY LIBBY GELMAN-WAXNER

*T*here are films that can entertain or inform or even move us, but perhaps only once in a generation is there a cinematic effort that reaches out to all the peoples of the world, a movie that dives deep into your heart and your brain and clomps around, an auteuristic achievement with the power to give the entire planet a makeover. Such a film is *The Mirror Has Two Faces*, or, as I like to think of it, Barbra Streisand's *Triumph of the Will*.

In this movie, Barbra plays Rose Morgan, a charismatic English professor at Columbia University. When Rose lectures on courtly love, she knows every one of her many students by their first names, and they all laugh uproariously at her every quip; clearly, the course is Barbra 101: An Introduction to Worship. The classroom scenes reminded me of when I went to see Barbra at Madison Square Garden during her big tour, where she performed in front of an all-white set based on Monticello, presented a slide show illustrating her career

FROM *PREMIERE*

peaks, and read all of her lyrics and even her spontaneous patter from an enormous TelePrompTer hanging from the ceiling; all of her conversation, including her adorable pauses, was visible to the audience, in case we wanted to join in. At first I wondered, Gee, since Barbra's personally grossing at least a billion dollars from this tour, couldn't she learn the jokes? But then I remembered that Barbra was phobic about appearing live, and I repented for my crassness by running out to the enormous gift shop in the lobby and buying a mug, a key chain, and a huge silk scarf featuring impressionistic sketches of Barbra in all her greatest roles. I returned happily to my seat, wondering if Barbra would be back at the Garden next year, playing the Knicks.

In *The Mirror*, Barbra begins as a slightly overweight, mildly shlumpy woman, which means that she wears flattering oversize sweaters and schoolgirl berets; the other people onscreen keep insisting that Barbra isn't wearing makeup, a question that was later raised at the O.J. civil trial. Barbra still lives at home with her mother, played by Lauren Bacall, who favors Barbra's glamorous younger sister and has never told Barbra that she's pretty. In interviews, Barbra has claimed that her real mother never told her she was pretty; as Barbra told *Us* magazine, *The Mirror* is not merely a fluffy romantic comedy but contains "serious overtones about vanity and beauty, the external versus the internal." The film dares to ask the largest philosophical question possible, something even more profound than Is there a God?, Why is there evil?, or Why is this film shot in such soft-focus that sometimes the actors don't seem to have eyes? That question is, of course, Is Barbra pretty?

Barbra soon meets Jeff Bridges, who plays an adorably rumpled math professor who is so tormented by his affairs with beautiful young women that he longs for a sexless "union of souls" with Barbra, and they get married. Barbra falls in love with Jeff and wants a fully passionate, sexual relationship; one night she lights candles, wears a black negligee, and puts the moves on Jeff, who runs from the room, refusing to tell Barbra that she's pretty. For this he must be punished, and Barbra leaves him just as he's about to go off on a European book tour. Barbra returns to her mother's apartment, where she confronts Lauren, asking her what it's like to be pretty. Then she forces Lauren to confess that she's always been secretly jealous of Barbra. Watching a fifty-four-year-old movie star haranguing her mother onscreen is a very special moment; it's like seeing the perfect therapy payoff, where your mom writes a formal note of apology for your childhood and has it printed as a full-page ad in the *Times*. When Lauren breaks down, Barbra smiles a knowing half smile and nods sagely, and I'm sure that in Europe the subtitle will read, SEE, I'M PRETTY. TOLD YOU.

While Jeff is away, Barbra diets and works out, and she greets him with the results of her transformation: The camera travels up her body, revealing her newly slim figure, her manicure, her cleavage, and finally, her highlighted perm and her heavily made-up face. Jeff is stunned, and I waited for him to exclaim, "Oh, my God! While I was in Paris you turned into a nasty Beverly Hills divorcée!" Instead, Jeff just grovels and Barbra walks out on him, in proud moral victory. Then she teaches her class in a clinging low-cut top, and all of her students, even the girls, drool and ogle her. Everywhere Barbra goes, she is lusted after, as if no one in New York had ever seen a grizzled mafia wife with a Sassoon cut before. Barbra even has a scene with her plump best friend, Brenda Vaccaro, in which Brenda frets that they are no longer in the same pathetic boat, now that Barbra is a knockout. Barbra comforts Brenda, helping her to work through her selfish problem, and their chitchat is more hateful toward women than anything in *Hustler* or on *Baywatch;* Brenda's issue is, of course, Why can't I be as pretty as Barbra?

Finally, Jeff comes to his senses and stands outside Barbra's apartment building, howling her name. She runs downstairs in white satin pajamas, he confesses that he has always loved her, and they dance together ecstatically in the street, as the credits roll and Barbra sings "I Finally Found Someone" with Bryan Adams, although the song would be more appropriately performed by Barbra and that mirror. It's a truly gorgeous finale, as if *Sunset Boulevard* had been direct by Norma Desmond. It is simply the ultimate Barbra moment, where all the world tells Barbra it loves her and that she's pretty. It's like watching Clint Eastwood direct himself as a sexy, sixty-four-year-old shirtless stud in *The Bridges of Madison County;* it's like seeing Warren Beatty backlight himself like the Virgin Mary in *Love Affair;* it's like casting Barbra Streisand in *Nell*.

I left the theater in tears of joy, and I ran to meet my mother, Sondra Krell-Gelman, for a post-Hanukkah brunch at Sarabeth's Kitchen. I stood at the table with my coat on, demanding, "Why didn't you ever tell me I was pretty?" "Are you nuts?" my mom replied. "I told you that you were pretty fifty times a day. I told you that you were the most beautiful child who had ever lived, and that no man would ever truly deserve such a perfect jewel. That's why you're so healthy today." "That's true," I admitted, but then I saw through her little game. "But, Mother," I said, "why didn't you ever tell *Barbra* she was pretty?"

"I sent a note!" my mother insisted, but it wasn't enough. I was on a holy crusade. I ran into the street, aglow with my mission, and accosted a jogger by grabbing his fanny pack, his Walkman, and his mobile reading light. "Have you told Barbra she was pretty today?" I bellowed. "No!" he moaned, falling to his kneepads in shame. "I'm sorry, Barbra!" he cried out. "You're the most beautiful woman in the world! Your new boyfriend, James Brolin, isn't worthy—you should become a lesbian so you can date yourself!"

"Have *you* told Barbra she's pretty?" I asked a Hispanic woman with a grocery cart and two small children. *"Si! Si!"* the woman insisted. "She is the vision of Guadalupe! I have told my little ones, 'You must pray to Barbra, to make your grandmother well again!' Every day I kneel before her photo from *Funny Lady* and I sing along to 'Let's Hear It for Me!' " Soon the fever spread across the city, the nation, and the world; everywhere I went, people hung out of windows, chanted from rooftops, and intoned from that Vatican balcony: "Barbra, your mother was wrong! You may be fifty-four and completely self-obsessed with stuff even thirteen-year-olds get over, but you're right! You're pretty!"

Finally there was only one holdout: my cousin Andrew. Andrew has always been a Barbra loveslave; he has even claimed that during "No More Tears (Enough Is Enough)," Barbra's disco duet with Donna Summer, Barbra didn't pinch Donna so that she'd stop holding notes. But Andrew has disdained *The Mirror Has Two Faces;* he said that Barbra used to resist playing the standard ingenue, a nice girl, but that in *The Mirror* she'd betrayed her fans by playing a fifty-four-year-old twinkie, and that watching the scene in which Jeff is forced to call her "a pretty girl" is like watching Godzilla crush Tokyo. I said that no one ever accused Laurence Olivier of making a vanity film when he directed himself as *Hamlet,* but Andrew said that Hamlet wasn't just worried about making Gertrude tell him he was pretty.

Andrew said that Barbra is a brilliant actress with no interest in playing a character. He said that all of Barbra's onscreen pals now have to be played by increasingly older, nonthreatening actors, and that pretty soon she'll be hanging out with the cast of *Cocoon,* talking about boys and prom night. He said that at least in *Yentl* and even *The Prince of Tides* Barbra wasn't playing roles based entirely on her image of herself, and that watching *The Mirror* was grim, like reading one of Donald Trump's autobiographies as an inspirational text.

"But, Andrew," I said, "don't you think that Barbra is pretty?" "Barbra has been a legend since she was in her teens! She's a zillionaire! The entire world has told Barbra that she's pretty! What more does she want?" "*You* know," I said calmly. "I'll try," said Andrew, finally surrendering and sobbing at my feet. And with that he crawled off on his sacred mission, his grail: to kill Barbra's mother. It's the least he can do after how he's behaved, if you ask me.

A Century of Cinema

BY SUSAN SONTAG

$\mathcal{C}$inema's hundred years seem to have the shape of a life cycle: an inevitable birth, the steady accumulation of glories, and the onset in the last decade of an ignominious, irreversible decline. This doesn't mean that there won't be any more new films that one can admire. But such films won't simply be exceptions; that's true of great achievement in any art. They have to be heroic violations of the norms and practices which now govern moviemaking everywhere in the capitalist and would-be capitalist world—which is to say, everywhere. And ordinary films, films made purely for entertainment (that is, commercial) purposes, will continue to be astonishingly witless; already the vast majority fail resoundingly to appeal to their cynically targeted audiences. While the point of a great film is now, more than ever, to be a one-of-a-kind achievement, the commercial cinema has settled for a policy of bloated, derivative filmmaking, a brazen combinatory or recombinatory art, in the hope of reproducing past success. Every film that hopes to

FROM *PARNASSUS*

reach the largest possible audience is designed as some kind of remake. Cinema, once heralded as *the* art of the twentieth century, seems now, as the century closes numerically, to be a decadent art.

Perhaps it is not cinema which has ended . . . but only cinephilia— the name of the very specific kind of love that cinema inspired. Each art breeds its fanatics. The love that cinema inspired, however, was special. It was born of the conviction that cinema was an art unlike any other: quintessentially modern; distinctively accessible; poetic and mysterious and erotic and moral—all at the same time. Cinema had apostles (it was like religion). Cinema was a crusade. Cinema was a world view. Lovers of poetry or opera or dance don't think there is *only* poetry or opera or dance. But lovers of cinema could think there was only cinema. That the movies encapsulated everything—and they did. It was both the book of art and the book of life.

As many people have noted, the start of moviemaking a hundred years ago was, conveniently, a double start. In that first year, 1895, two kinds of films were made, proposing two modes of what cinema could be: cinema as the transcription of real unstaged life (the Lumière brothers) and cinema as invention, artifice, illusion, fantasy (Meliés). But this was never a true opposition. For those first audiences watching the Lumière brothers' *The Arrival of a Train at La Ciotat Station,* the camera's transmission of a banal sight was a fantastic experience. Cinema began in wonder, the wonder that reality can be transcribed with such magical immediacy. All of cinema is an attempt to perpetuate and to re-invent that sense of wonder.

Everything begins with that moment, one hundred years ago, when the train pulled into the station. People took movies into themselves, just as the public cried out with excitement, actually ducked, as the train seemed to move toward *them.* Until the advent of television emptied the movie theaters, it was from a weekly visit to the cinema that you learned (or tried to learn) how to walk, to smoke, to kiss, to fight, to grieve. Movies gave you tips about how to be attractive, such as . . . it looks good to wear a raincoat even when it isn't raining. But whatever you took home from the movies was only a part of the larger experience of losing yourself in faces, in lives that were *not* yours—which is the more inclusive form of desire embodied in the movie experience. The strongest experience was simply to surrender to, to be transported by, what was on the screen. You wanted to be kidnapped by the movie.

The first condition of being kidnapped was to be overwhelmed by the physical presence of the image. And the conditions of "going to the movies" was essential to that. To see a great film only on TV isn't to have really seen that film. (This is equally true of those made for TV, like Fassbinder's *Berlin Alexanderplatz* and the two Heimat films of Edgar Reitz.) It's not only the difference of dimensions: the superiority of the larger-than-you image in the theater to the little image on the box at home. The conditions of paying attention in a domestic space are radically disrespectful of film. Since film no longer has a standard size, home screens *can* be as big as living room or bedroom walls. But you are still in a living room or a bedroom, alone or with familiars. To be kidnapped, you have to be in a movie theater, seated in the dark among anonymous strangers.

No amount of mourning will revive the vanished rituals—erotic, ruminative—of the darkened theater. The reduction of cinema to assaultive images, and the unprincipled manipulation of images (faster and faster cutting) to be more attention grabbing, has produced a disincarnated, lightweight cinema that doesn't demand anyone's full attention. Images now appear in any size and on a variety of surfaces: on a screen in a theater, on home screens as small as the palm of your hand or as big as a wall, on disco walls and megascreens hanging above sports arenas and the outsides of tall public buildings. The sheer ubiquity of moving images has steadily undermined the standards people once had both for cinema as art at its most serious and for cinema as popular entertainment.

In the first years there was, essentially, no difference between cinema as art and cinema as entertainment. And *all* films of the silent era— from the masterpieces of Feuillade, D. W. Griffith, Djiga Vertov, Pabst, Murnau, King Vidor to the most formula-ridden melodramas and comedies—are on a very high artistic level, compared with most of what was to follow. With the coming of sound, the image-making lost much of its brilliance and poetry, and commercial standards tightened. This way of making movies—the Hollywood system—dominated filmmaking for about twenty-five years (roughly from 1930 to 1955). The most original directors, like Erich von Stroheim and Orson Welles, were defeated by the system and eventually went into artistic exile in Europe— where more or less the same quality-defeating system was now in place, with lower budgets; only in France were a large number of superb films produced throughout this period. Then, in the mid-1950s, vanguard ideas took hold again, rooted in the idea of cinema as a craft pioneered by the Italian films of the immediate postwar period. A dazzling number of original, passionate films of the highest seriousness got made with new actors and tiny crews, went to film festivals (of which there were more and more), and from there, garlanded with festival prizes, into movie theaters around the world. This golden age actually lasted as long as twenty years.

It was at this specific moment in the hundred-year history of cinema that going to movies, thinking about movies, talking about movies became a passion among university students and other young people. You fell in love not just with actors but with cinema itself. Cinephilia had first become visible in the 1950s in France: Its forum was the legendary film magazine *Cahiers du Cinéma* (followed by similarly fervent magazines in Germany, Italy, Great Britain, Sweden, the United States, Canada). Its temples, as it spread throughout Europe and the Americas, were the many cinematheques and film clubs specializing in films from the past and directors' retrospectives that sprang up. The 1960s and early 1970s was the feverish age of moviegoing, with the full-time cinephile always hoping to find a seat as close as possible to the big screen, ideally the third row center. "One can't live without Rossellini," declares a character in Bertolucci's *Before the Revolution* (1964)—and means it.

Cinephilia—a source of exultation in the films of Godard and Truffaut and the early Bertolucci and Syberberg; a morose lament in some recent films of Nanni Moretti—was mostly a Western European affair. The great directors of "the other Europe" (Zanussi in Poland, Angelopolous in Greece, Tarkovsky and Sokurov in Russia, Jancso and Tarr in Hungary) and the great Japanese directors (Ozu, Mizoguchi, Kurosawa, Oshima, Imamura) have tended not to be cinephiles, perhaps because in Budapest or Moscow or Tokyo or Warsaw or Athens there wasn't a chance to get a cinematheque education. The distinctive thing about cinephile taste was that it embraced both "art" films and popular films. Thus, European cinephilia had a romantic relation to the films of certain directors in Hollywood at the apogee of the studio system: Godard for Howard Hawks, Fassbinder for Douglas Sirk. Of course, this moment—when cinephilia emerged—was also the moment when the Hollywood studio system was breaking up. It seemed that moviemaking had rewon the right to experiment; cinephiles could *afford* to be passionate (or sentimental) about the old Hollywood genre films. A host of new people came into cinema, including a generation of young film critics from *Cahiers du Cinéma*; the towering figure of that generation, indeed of several decades of filmmaking anywhere, was Jean-Luc Godard. A few writers turned out to be wildly talented filmmakers: Alexander Kluge in Germany, Pier Paolo Pasolini in Italy. (The model for the writer who turns to filmmaking actually emerged earlier, in France, with Pagnol in the 1930s and Cocteau in the 1940s, but it was not until the 1960s that this seemed, at least in Europe, normal.) Cinema seemed reborn.

For some fifteen years there were new masterpieces every month, and one allowed oneself to imagine that this would go on forever. How far away that era seems now. To be sure, there was always a conflict between cinema as an industry and cinema as an art, cinema as routine and cinema as experiment. But the conflict was not such as to make impossible the making of wonderful films, sometimes within and sometimes outside of mainstream cinema. Now the balance has tipped decisively in favor of cinema as an industry. The great cinema of the 1960s and 1970s has been thoroughly repudiated. Already in the 1970s Hollywood was plagiarizing and banalizing the innovations in narrative method and editing of successful new European and ever-marginal independent American films. Then came the catastrophic rise in production costs in the 1980s, which secured the worldwide reimposition of industry standards of making and distributing films on a far more coercive, this time truly global scale. The result can be seen in the melancholy fate of some of the greatest directors of the last decades. What place is there today for a maverick like Hans Jurgen Syberberg, who has stopped making films altogether, or for the great Godard, who now makes films about the history of film, on video? Consider some other cases. The internationalizing of financing and therefore of casts was a disaster for Andrei Tarkovsky in the last two films of his stupendous (tragically abbreviated) career. And these conditions for making films have proved to be as much an artistic disaster for two of the most valuable directors still working: Krzysztof Zanussi (*The Structure of Crystals, Illumination, Spiral, Contract*) and Theo Angelopolous (*Reconstruction, Days of '36, The Travelling Players*). And what will happen now to Bela Tarr (*Damnation, Satantango*)? And how will

Aleksandr Sokurov (*Save and Protect, Days of Eclipse, The Second Circle, Stone, Whispering Pages*) find the money to go on making films, his sublime films, under the rude conditions of Russian capitalism?

Predictably, the love of cinema has waned. People still like going to the movies, and some people still care about and expect something special, necessary from a film. And wonderful films are still being made: Mike Leigh's *Naked*, Gianni Amelio's *Lamerica*, Fred Kelemen's *Fate*. But one hardly finds anymore, at least among the young, the distinctive cinephilic love of movies, which is not simply love of but a certain *taste* in films (grounded in a vast appetite for seeing and reseeing as much as possible of cinema's glorious past). Cinephilia itself has come under attack, as something quaint, outmoded, snobbish. For cinephilia implies that films are unique, unrepeatable, magic experiences. Cinephilia tells us that the Hollywood remake of Godard's *Breathless* cannot be as good as the original. Cinephilia has no role in the era of hyperindustrial films. For cinephilia cannot help, by the very range and eclecticism of its passions, from sponsoring the idea of the film as, first of all, a poetic object; and cannot help from inciting those outside the movie industry, like painters and writers, to want to make films, too. It is precisely this that must be defeated. That has been defeated.

If cinephilia is dead, then movies are dead, too . . . no matter how many movies, even very good ones, go on being made. If cinema can be resurrected, it will only be through the birth of a new kind of cine love.

Square of Light

BY ALBERT GOLDBARTH

Introduction

"But sir, my name is on a list. . . ."

"You think you're special, then? You're a lump. You're one more formless lump."

"The mayor's office they signed the list, sir. . . ."

"Mayor my ass. Four hours, not one minute more. You won't get paid here for those four hours, do you understand?"

"The list . . ."

"Do you understand?"

She does. She goes, she leaves the gates of Pryor's Manufactory Cottons with the note in her carpetbag purse. She is a formless lump. Her father is a formless lump, her mother is a formless lump, and seven

FROM *PARNASSUS*

siblings share two beds like pallid balls of dough that still await a baker's shaping touch.

I don't think we can be ourselves again—I mean our original selves, before the twentieth-century silver-screen-TV-and-magazine-ad-infonetathon provided its thousands of models for any possible emoting.

You were on the bed, your arm raised in an eloquent, skewed *L* that meant dismissiveness, but meant it in the language of an image of a gesture of dismissiveness picked up from this or that iconic figure which preceded us.

And I could almost envy, a moment, the neighborhood's singular mutter-and-spit old man we find on benches in the summer swatting demons off, his mumbles and his raw gesticulation unprovided for by anything—so, pure in a way; a shape outside ideas of succession.

I could see your mind's eye calling forth its stored range of celebrity dismissiveness, in microseconds selecting a posture from out of similar second-bests. . . . In an artist's sketchbook once, I saw the body of a woman with her left arm lifted, only it was dozens of rehearsal left arms lifted, she was waving like a hydra on the smudgy page.

It's this way: Say a woman wants to rent a cast-of-suntanned-thousands Biblical Epic video, something with sandals and shields and plumes and golden chariots and a love scene near a pyramid as the sky storms. And a man prefers to rent the story of four *echt*-pensive people at a table, talking, talking.

Then the mode of what they're arguing about instructs the arguing itself. The hothouse thespian hauteur of Nefertiti; and the generated chill from a man who has studied shoestring-budget portrayals of auteur emotional freon.

"You will simply climb one side of the ladder until you reach its top, at a natural speed, don't hurry, and then at the top pose—*so,*" and Eadweard Muybridge, in his graying frowzled garden-of-a-beard and eternally-on-him-whether-out-of-doors-or-in black crumpled Amish-look surveyor's hat, swings one leg grandly in back of himself, and lifts his arms and puffed-up chest aspiringly upward, with the full effect of a ballerina's kick cum Viking dragon prow, "and count to five, and then simply climb back down. Do you see?"

"And I will be undressed?"

"And you will be undressed."

There's silence now in this building on the well-trimmed Pennsylvania University grounds. He fancies he can hear the light in its ceaseless lap against the outside walls—*his* light, his wrought gold that he captures and condenses like an alchemist in an alembic.

"Elsie—" What to say? She's new. A friend of a friend of the provost's daughter. She's the only model who's shown so far today, and the cameras he'd swear are lowly purring in impatience to be used.

He nods at one of them now, his lovely four-foot box with its thirteen Dallmeyer lenses. "I will be here with the camera, Elsie, fully forty-nine feet away from the ladder."

If this reassures her, there's no visible sign. She *knows* this is "important," that it's "Art" or "Science" or some such term come down to touch her life from where it's been carved on a marble entablature, and yet . . . and yet. . . . What tale will she tell them, when she returns to her day at the folding line of Pryor's Manufactory Cottons?

"Dozens have preceded you, Elsie, women, men, all—" He has an idea. "*This*," and he unties the leather cover of an album, and removes two sheets of developed images, "*this* will either send you fleeing in horror, or convince you of the . . . *naturalness* with which we view the project."

One is eighteen sequenced shots of *Athlete swinging a pick,* and one is forty-four of *Model No. 95, ex-athlete, aged about sixty, ascending and descending incline,* and bearing a fifty-pound weight in twenty-two of these snaps. The man is naked. The man is Muybridge, chuckling now over his sixty-two tiny selves.

"You see?"

"But Mr. Muybridge," she says—is there a nascent twinkle in her eye?—"when you was a-posin' for these . . . ?"

"Yes, Elsie?"

". . . sir, *I* wasn't behind the camera." And then the both of them, chuckling. She milks the joke of her sly observation. "*I* never made no such photygraphs."

"Elsie. . . ." he fully undoes the album, and then two more, and fans a hundred sheets across the table, selecting some, pointing in rapid succession at his astonishing serial studies, naked men at cricket, boxing, fencing, horseback riding, naked women running, somersaulting, rolling hoops with sticks, a trotting camel on loan from the Pennsylvania Zoo, a greyhound, a milk-white parrot in flight, more naked men (one pugilist feigns a knockout), a deer, a woman performing jumping jacks, and all of them immediately blinking out of themselves and into their next selves. . . .

". . . nobody, *nobody*, has ever made such photographs."

If you run beside an ancient Egyptian temple mural, skimming your vision linearly along those beaked and snouted anthrobodied gods, and the captives taken in war, and the stately parade of geese at the Nile's shore . . .

Does it "move"?

It's "motion" pictures.

Yes, or if you take a vase, a cayenne-red Greek vase with its circular frieze of courtesans or wrestlers in flat black profile, if you spin it, if you place it back on its potter's wheel and spin it . . .

"For Claude Monet, there are a hundred thousand images," art historian Elie Fraue declares, "in the space of a second." How to separate them into single painted moments that maintain their continuity? It's 1891: Monet is painting "frames" of what could be a continuous "reel" of haystacks aging over—*aging into*—time. . . .

But let's go back to May 4, 1880. Eadweard Muybridge tonight is lecturing at the San Francisco Art Association Rooms, he's introducing his quaint invention by which his sequenced photographs of a horse in motion are set around the circumference of a glass disc, and projected by a lantern onto a screen, while a handle is turned and the disc is rotated.

Kevin MacDonnell: "To Muybridge belongs the honor" (not that it isn't debated) "of inventing the movie."

In 1888, on a lecture tour that brings him to Orange, New Jersey, Muybridge meets Thomas Alva Edison, who received a demonstration of the "zoopraxiscope," and who "purchased a set of Muybridge's horse pictures. When he invented his revolutionary cine-camera, using the long perforated films we know today, he is said to have made his first movie by copying these photographs." By 1910, the Edison Company's already publishing *Edison Kinetogram,* announcing "Edison Films to Be Released," including *Frankenstein.*

Imagine for your first time seeing the battle of love and monstrousness in a form that subsumes you entirely. It's said that people continued to sit there, demanding not the movie again, but just the square of light itself—as if even that were instructive.

This isn't an easy confession to make, but I'm the kind of guy who leaves at the end of a Jerry Lewis movie duplicating Jerry Lewis's wacky ham abrasiveness for a day—it gets inside me, like a hand inside a puppet. I'm suddenly honking the noses of friends. James Dean: that beestung sneer. James Bond (the Sean Connery Bond): that killer haut monde eyebrow arch.

Weight lifter Gordon Scott was the Tarzan of my childhood (*Tarzan's Hidden Jungle* appeared in 1955; Scott stayed with the role through 1960): rugged good looks, a touch more pretty than craggy. Forty years go by, I'll still startle up from the work at hand (a poem; or the drone of committee work; or the fussy upkeeps houses require, and love) and I'll have the half-subliminal flash of that immense heart-whanging parabolic sweep-through-air on a jungle vine: a single green and graceful scallop.

It's this way: Fifty years before that day when Muybridge redefined the gallop of the horse for us (*renumerated* it, actually, with photographic proof that all four hooves are off the ground at once, a refutation of centuries of equestrian depiction in the fine arts), sheets of plate glass came to the streetside windows of snooty shops in Regent Street and Oxford Street; some, nine feet tall by five wide. Now the idea of "display," of spacious, elegant interiors. And now the idea of shop assistants selected for certain paradigms of physical appeal. With all-night lighting installed, pedestrians would gather in enormous knots before these windows, learning what they wanted to become.

Today, when the tonier big-bucks fashion models strut their ramps in versions of otherdimensional-sci-fi-funk-punk-faery-fireman-shepherdess-hookerapparel, it's harder to remember, but these *are* "models"—these are paragonic structures—and their trickle-down will fill our common psychic air, will determine the mall-talk of Omaha.

The most stellar of these, of course, will even try "making it" in the movies.

We think of Hollywood as "the land of dreams": It's one of Hollywood's favorite self-descriptions. But the reverse is true. The movies *are* our lives—writ large. And if they're often wish-lives, if they're nothing but otherdimensional fashion . . . still, our minds try on those giants' clothes, those clothes consisting of shadow and light, and for better or worse we wear them into one another's days and nights.

The ancient High Myths, with their cycles of gods and hellspawn, have deserted us (or we, them). Religion is a thin shell, not an infrastructure. And yet we hunger for precepts, modes of conduct and social assurance ("The name is Bond . . ." *pause-pause,* then turn and give her a javelin star full tilt, oh, fourteen-year-old manboy lost in the wilds ". . . James Bond"). We *need* a world larger than we are. No—we need a world larger than we are *that addresses* what we are.

I have to ask now: Did I love my father? Irving Goldbarth, weary, decent family-minded peddler of Metropolitan Life Insurance through the penny-ante living rooms of Cicero, Illinois, at ten P.M., who never lied to me, not once, whose voice in the blessing over the Hannukah candles wavered like the flames, who danced in his underwear in the kitchen (*"hoochiekoochiekoo"*), who embarrassed me (he'd never read a book), who worked the weekends so that *I* could lead a life of reading books, who walked the dog and waited patiently for it to pee on its signature trash can, even in winter, even when Dr. Steinitz said that in winter he'd have to wear the breathing mask, for his heart . . . did I love him? Yes. Did I learn the rudiments of what it is to walk this planet from him? Yes.

But I wouldn't have spent ten minutes trying to emulate my father. I could be Tarzan or Bond in my head for a month.

She's placed a thumb in each of her ears and spread her fingers apart, like wiggling, cockamamie antlers.

"See? Like this? And I can spin around like a toy top." Both of them giggling—she and Muybridge.

"Or so?" She pulls her mouth grotesquely wide, then squats and hops like a frog—assured her audience will be won, assured by her eighth time back to pose for Art and Science that she can clown this way and still retain the composure of a professional conspiring in hi-jinks with a coworker. This is the ambience he's created for her, and she's risen from out of some beat-down, bottom shapelessness to make herself over, into the image this newfound world has seeded for her and that she's continued to lavishly nurture.

"Or simpler, sir?" She pairs her hands beneath her chin, as if for prayer, and bows elegantly from the waist, in slow repeated clockwork fashion.

"Elsie, Elsie. You're as frisky today as a pent-up cat. *Relax.* I need to bring more lenses over, from the shed outside. When I return, we'll think of some proper posing." They both laugh: *proper!* The day be-fore she spent her four-hour session juggling a pear and an orange, then climbing the ladder with a circus parasol held in either hand.

He leaves her standing before the project's standard backdrop, a floor-to-ceiling grid of two-inch squares created of taut white cord against black. He lingers amid a pile of Carbutt's Keystone Dry Plates, checking the shipment. When he returns . . . She's cut a cat—*a pent-up cat*—from a roll of butcher paper, and set it clawing its way up the grid.

She's inventive that way, and she notices he's appreciative of her gamin creativity, and this inspires more. She milks her jokes. Just to see what will happen, he thinks up another excuse for leaving the hall. It's a game now: He returns to find she's papered the *X*'s and *O*'s of tick-tacktoe into nine of the squares.

"Enough. Here's a pan and some sawdust. Go, pretend that you're feeding the chickens."

It *is* enough—perhaps too much. The truth is, they've created an Elsie so aware of her bearing (after all, these are supposedly photos of people caught in common, candid motion) that her modeling sessions are some of the least productive. While her "Elsieness" strengthens in charm and durability, it translates into something artificial on the proof sheets. Anyway, the project is nearly over. He likes her, they all like her, he could see her on his arm, with a foamed-over pail of beer and a platter of iced raw oysters . . . hmmm. . . . Regretfully, though, they ease her out of the schedule. Her note is not renewed.

And from then on . . . ? Muybridge in Paris, Muybridge in London, Muybridge addressing the gathered grandees of the worlds of Art and Science, Muybridge, opening Zooproxological Hall at the World's Columbian Exposition in Chicago (1893). "On 8 May 1904 he died and was cremated in Woking."

No, I mean Elsie. Back to the folding line. Back to the twelve-hour days of spirit-vitiating labor. Although there's this:

"You! Havercomb! Elsie Havercomb! Step from the line!"—a loutish assistant manager. "Production rate for your section is down, and I swear that if you don't—"

Something about the set of her jaw, the unexpected aliveness in her eyes now. Lamely, letting it dwindle: "Havercomb, just get back to the line." And she turns from him like royalty.

The same year that the most fashionable of plate-glass windows opened up its opulent realm of furs and buttery leather goods on Regent Street, and started its work commercially mentoring people into gaining newly elevated concepts of themselves . . . that same year, a Dr. Horn from Salzburg reports that, in the infirmary, there was "a girl of twenty-two years of age . . . who had been brought up in a hog-sty among the hogs, and who had sat there for many years with her legs crossed. She grunted like a hog, and her gestures were brutishly revolting."

The annals are filled with the various mewlings of humans-raised-by-animals stories, from (the first of contemporary record) the wolf-boy of Hesse, who was found in the woods in 1341 "and growled, and beshat himself naked in public, and raw meat only would he eat; and this while on his knees," through (for example from 1971, in the London *Daily Mirror*) the gazelle-boy of the Spanish Sahara near Río de Oro, seen leaping with the herd, and according to anthropolgist Jean-Claude Armen, "I have watched him approach gazelles and lick their foreheads in a sign of recognition."

The monkey-boy of northern Ceylon (1973, in the London *Sunday Times*) "is speechless, grunts in a half-wolf, half-goat way, and bites and claws at anyone who shows him affection." The bear-girl of Fraumark was found in a den, a woman/girl of about eighteen, asleep on a floor of bear scat: "She refused to eat anything but raw meat, roots and the barks of trees."

Those for whom Another Kind is precedential.

So much of us, inside us, is innate. As for the rest . . . Somebody hypnotized at that furrier's gold-and-ruby-highlighted, easeful, splendid family of mannequins: a schematic display not only of adornment, but of the rules of a possible life.

And somebody (just as "happy"? how are we to judge?) on her rump in a mire of pigness.

How could she have been otherwise, without a god or a guide or a single scene from *Casablanca*? Without, essentially, a window: into the world of what and how to be.

"Heroes? *Heroes?*" asks one of the likably nasty midget-rapscallions in the classic camp-adventure flick *Time Bandits,* almost spitting the words. ". . . What do *they* know about a day's work?"

And it's true. For example:

The sun in Sumeria savages the everyday afternoon air, as you'd expect. As you'd expect, sun makes a burning mote in the center of every sweatbead. Gilgamesh cuts down a tree. Gilgamesh, whose father was a *lillu*-demon, King of Uruk who founded civilization in the Seven Cities, fells a great *huluppu* tree with a dragon's nest at its base and the terrible *Zu*-bird in its crown "and in its midst the demoness Lilith had built her dwelling."

I wouldn't say he doesn't strain. I'd say he doesn't sweat. Exertion is never that intimate for him. I've looked at the cylinder seals, I've read the cracked, translated tablets, and the sweat isn't there, no, not at the lip of the Well of Immortal Life, not in the wrestle pit of lions or by Humbaba's mountain, and not at the tree, and not at the one great swing or at the one clean bite it requires.

But look at flipped-through pages from *The American Photographic Postcard, 1900–1920:*

Here above the mill at Loleta "Mr. Gibson is the 3rd from left and Harris our son is the 4th from right"—nine men are ready to pole a background of hundreds of ton-jumbled fifteen-foot logs. It always looks like fifty men's work, a hundred. There are always nine. I come back often, and count—there are nine, their heavy faces say their easy poses have nothing to do with their work, which is hard, too long, and depleting; and the small empty corner up in the right says: Air has been converted today, into just a new place to hold wood.

And the light in the simple sky and the cumbersome cameras of

1910 is saying, flash by flash, and ice delivery truck by hod by plow by shovel, that twelve men in Ohio are halfway up a frame for "Duncan, the Round Barn Man." I close the book. Days later I open it. Yes: There's still halfway to go. They wake up every morning and know it, and there are overalls here so rumpled, they carry permanent shadows in places no matter where the sun or how strong.

I won't suggest that Hercules was ignorant of effort, in the stables, "diverting the course of a river" to cleanse their waist-high filth. But on the white-ground jar and the red-figured platter, the sun pours down in a column behind him, a clement and almost sculptural sun. He doesn't pant. The stables are newly fresh, and here he is now, busy posing as if for a calendar featuring surfer boys. Later there will be bonfire feasts, a speech, a green wreath, and some nubile dancers.

And later there will be, and there will always be, "Mrs. Adeline Havercomb Maggody and sister, Mrs. Elsie Havercomb Atkins. During their thirty-five years of service at Pryor's Manufactory Cottons *Pennsylvania's Very Finest* they have boxed and folded 71,280,000 sheets of Pryor's excellent products." (Elsie's the one with the elfin cockiness.)

Seventy-one million, two-hundred-eighty thousand.

Smile. Hold it. (flash)

Seventy-one million, two-hundred-eighty thousand and one . . .

Perhaps you have seen me. I know well, my purpose was merely that of a symbol, "equals," "times," or that of the person drawn as a code, with sticks for limbs and a circle for a head. I could be anyone. I was specifically asked to be anyone. I do know what a "portrait" is; and mine are not. I could have been the woman on her toetips just as readily, or the woman lifting imaginary laundry from a real tub. I could have been a man fencing the air, or a bicyclist. I was, we all were, series of connected dots upon the graph we posed against. Our flesh it was, that connected the dots, our own insistent flesh; but what it said, for all that, was identityless: a kind of live geometry.

And yet when I look at myself here thirty-five years back, I take my individual pleasure; this, I think, was the moment I first understood that a pleasure could be an autonomy, that I was something more than a human unit inside a human machine. You see?—here?—these are the sturdy, wheaten haunches that Tallow, the manager, couldn't bring to his bed like trophies although he threatened dire consequences every week for a decade until the shearing engine one day went off track and ate him up to the waist; and these are the sassy breasts that brought the haughty Lemuel Atkins to his knees; and here, your finger can trace the strength of this back, that never gave out, and supported—once father had disappeared into too many brandywine cordials—a mother and six unappreciative ne'er-do-well brothers and sisters, bless them anyway each one (excepting Henry perhaps, the rotter).

You see?—in this one, here, I smile, and Lemuel won't be thrown from the spook-eyed strawberry roan for another twenty years. Time stops here. Nothing can take away this smile.

I patterned myself, for the rest of my days, on the form you see here making itself completely in eight four-hour modeling sessions. I never regretted it.

And these are the ones in which I posed with Isabella, my friend, the contact who recommended me to the mayor's offices in the first place. Here—the badminton ones, and the sillier ones with the pillow fight. Perhaps you have seen the ones in which she splashes me with a pail of water, its contents entirely flung in the air and caught there forever uncurling like a fern; or like the silvery train to a gown at my coronation.

Nobody really argues over which video to rent. They argue over lassitude-versus-retentiveness, they argue over God and no-God, immediate-gratification-or-future-security, they argue over money, over seemliness. The video is only the mask for this, the key, the lever.

Soon, they compromise: They watch the video *she* wants. But she has to feel indebted for a while.

They watch it—something alternately steamy and deific, about a slavegirl's rise to queenship through the (overgilded, technicolor) pharaonic bed—they watch it sleepily and chatter, easy and sweet but with a small glint of the squabble's after-edge, and when it's over and rewound they chatter sweet-and-squabbly more, until his sentences grow scratchy and distracted, yes, and her attention warbles like a song on the whipping tip of a thread-thin wavelength on the radio when the car speeds ever out of range, it's here now, what's she thinking, reed in a slipstream, now it's gone. . . .

She walks outside . . . the night sky feels as snug as a headdress—in a way; and in a way she's aware of its limitlessness, its dizzying outward-onward. She's been given—since the royal eye has declared her a sexual favorite—a break this evening from her line work in the stuffy deeps of the House of Folding the Sacred Cloth. It's fold-and-fold-and-pile-it, and fold-and-fold-and-pile-it, and the gossip of Takh-te and Natra-tiy beginning to harden like plugs of glue in her ears. . . .

Out here, away from them, and away from the lusty touch of He Who Is the Shining Lotus of the Two Lands, she can be a whole number again—before the duties all resume, and so refraction her—can be a number feeling that it might rise to a higher power.

A laggard breeze from off the river reaches her skin. . . . The cries of the compound's geese . . . She looks up at the sky, at its fiery diagram of connection points—the Nurturers and Warriors and Devils and Martyrs and Shapers who have always burned up there no matter who we were down here, and always will. We *are* those elements—in mortal combination. She flexes her nostrils. If she had a wish . . . So simple:

She wants to be like the stars.

Note: This essay gratefully adapts material from the following books: *Eadweard Muybridge: The Man Who Invented the Moving Picture* (MacDonnell), *Pheonomena: A Book of Wonders* (Michell and Rickard), and *Prairie Fires and Paper Moons* (Morgan and Brown).

Me and Hitch

BY EVAN HUNTER

SNOWBALLING

"Tell me the story so far."

These are the words Hitch would say to me every working week-day morning.

"Tell me the story so far." And every morning, after we'd had our coffee, he would sit back in his big black-leather chair with his hands folded over his belly, and I would tell him the story to date, ending with wherever we had left off the afternoon before.

In the beginning, there *was* no story to tell.

Day after day, we grappled with vague ideas and ephemeral notions, doing what the cartoonists call "snowballing," but the only recurring approach was the kernel of the Stranger-in-Town idea I'd brought from New York. The schoolteacher was gone, of course, an early casualty. What remained was the concept of a woman coming to a strange town that is attacked by birds shortly after her arrival. Do the townspeople have something to hide? Is there a guilty secret here?

Do they see this stranger as a messenger of revenge? Are the birds an instrument of punishment for their guilt? All very heavy stuff.

We toyed with this approach for days on end, stopping only for lunch taken in Hitch's office, when he invariably ordered a minute steak, and I ordered tuna and tomato on a hard roll. After lunch, and before we resumed work again, I would take a brisk walk outside the studio while Hitch spent half an hour or so with Peggy and Sue, dealing with the accumulated details of running a production company. It was on one of my solitary strolls that the idea came to me. I take full credit— or blame, as the case may be—for what I suggested to Hitch that afternoon: a screwball comedy that gradually turns into stark terror.

The idea appealed to him at once. I think he saw in it a challenge equal to the one the birds themselves presented. I think, too, that he saw in it a way of combining his vaunted sense of humor with the calculated horror he had used to great effect in *Psycho*. Moreover, the concept had two other things going for it.

We both realized that by the time the movie opened, the audience would know well in advance that birds would be attacking people. If not, then a multimillion-dollar promotion and advertising campaign would have been a failure. So there would be a built-in suspense similar to that in *Appointment at Eleven*. Here the title and all the preopening hoopla would tell us what would be happening—birds were going to attack—but not *when*. Suspense. And if we could start the audience laughing in the early part of the picture, and then suddenly cause them to choke on their own laughter, the suspense would turn to shock.

During his lifetime, Hitch explained the difference between suspense and shock so often that I'm reluctant to repeat it now. But let me do so hastily.

A meeting is taking place in a boardroom. Men sitting around a table discussing business. We cut away to below the table. We see the businessmen's trousered legs and shoes. Sitting on the floor, unseen by them, is a ticking clock wired to several sticks of dynamite. As the board meeting progresses, we keep cutting away to that ticking clock. Will the bomb be discovered? Or will the dynamite explode when the minute hand and the hour hand are standing straight up? That's suspense.

Same boardroom. Same meeting. Same discussion of business matters. One difference. We never cut away to the ticking clock and the sticks of dynamite. The audience never knows a bomb is sitting under that table and that it is set to go off at high noon. Suddenly an explosion tears apart the room and everyone in it. That is shock.

Hitch was no stranger to either, and had used both in combination in most of his movies. The difference in *The Birds* would be the goofy humor. Once we got them laughing, we would be leading them down the garden path. And once the early comic scenes turned frightening, then whenever there was a lull between bird attacks, we could hope for a sort of nervous laughter that would lead to further screaming even if we photographed an innocent feather duster.

My own reference points were the black-and-white comedies I'd grown up with in the forties: Cary Grant and Irene Dunne, Cary Grant and Katharine Hepburn, Cary Grant and Ginger Rogers. Hitch's more personal reference points were the scenes he'd directed between Grace Kelly and Ray Milland, Grace Kelly and James Stewart, Grace Kelly and—yes—Cary Grant. There is no doubt whatever in my mind that as we began discussing the characters who would set our screwball comedy in motion, we were both thinking of Grace Kelly and Cary Grant. This was in September. By November, Grace Kelly had turned into Tippi Hedren, and sometime later Cary Grant became Rod Taylor. But for now, we were casting platinum.

BRITTLE DIALOGUE

Grace Kelly goes into a bird shop to buy a mynah bird for a prissy aunt of hers. She intends to teach the bird some profanities that will shock her aunt. Cary Grant comes into the shop, mistakes Grace for a salesperson, and inquires about lovebirds he wants to buy for his young sister. Ever the prankster, Grace pretends she does indeed work there, and Cary goes along with the masquerade, even though he recognizes her as the madcap socialite daughter of a prominent newspaper publisher. The brilliant brittle dialogue between them sets the tone for all that follows, paving the way for uncontrolled laughter that pervades until the first of the bird attacks.

Even though there was and continues to be a sometimes wild blend of humor in the *87th Precinct* novels—and even though I later wrote two unabashedly comic novels (*A Horse's Head* in 1967 and *Every Little Crook and Nanny* in 1972)—back then in 1961 I was not particularly known for my antic comic flair. Moreover, as I was soon to learn, screwball comedy demands a very special kind of writing that derives more from situation than it does from character. The funny lines in my novels were not gags. The humor came in the innocent utterances of people who didn't know they were saying anything funny. But just as the pulp magazines were the forerunners of today's genre fiction, so were the screwball comedies of the forties the ancestors of today's television sitcoms. Blithely unaware, fast approaching my thirty-fifth birthday, and earning five grand a week, I confidently proposed—and Hitch enthusiastically accepted—a concept I had no idea I could actually bring off.

PICKING HOLES

Melanie: (*solicitously*) Yes, what was it you were looking for, sir?

Mitch: (*deadpan*) Lovebirds.

Melanie: Lovebirds, sir?

Mitch: Yes. I understand there are different varieties, is that true?

Melanie: Well . . . yes, sir, there are.

Mitch: These are for my sister's birthday. She'll be eleven. (*lowering his voice*)

Frankly, I wouldn't want a pair of birds that are too demonstrative.

Melanie: I understand completely, sir.

Mitch: At the same time, I wouldn't want birds that are aloof, either.

Melanie: Of course not.

Mitch: Do you have a pair that are just friendly?

"When does he realize she's not a salesgirl?"

This from Hitch. Sitting in his big leather chair, eyeing me like a wise old owl. I had not yet written a line of dialogue but I had just told him the story so far, and now he was picking holes in it. This would become our working routine. I would tell him the story, and he would ask questions about it, and I would try to answer them and then accommodate them. In this way, he edited the script before any of it was actually written, commenting on character development and comic effect in these early scenes of the film. We knew that once the bird attacks started, the audience was ours. But would we be able to keep them sitting still while a Meeting Cute romance between an impetuous young woman and a somewhat staid San Francisco lawyer developed?

From the beginning, Hitch had decided that he would shoot the picture in Northern California. He had shot *Shadow of a Doubt* in Santa Rosa, and was familiar with both the chicken-raising country around Petaluma and the little coastal town of Bodega Bay. He thought, too, that San Francisco would make a sufficiently sophisticated hometown for The Girl. He invariably referred to the Grace Kelly character (whom I had temporarily named Melanie) as "The Girl." Later, when Tippi Hedren was cast for the role, he referred to the actress herself as "The Girl." In an odd coincidence, Tippi's then infant daughter was named Melanie. I vaguely remember seeing her at a cocktail party Tippi gave for the Hitchcocks. I had no idea she would grow up to be Melanie Griffith. Neither did Tippi, for that matter.

"Has The Girl called her father yet?"

"Well, no, she hasn't."

"Well, does he know she's gone up to Bodega Bay to deliver these lovebirds?"

"No, he doesn't."

"Shouldn't she call him, then? So he won't be worried?"

"Yes, she should."

"Good. You have to remember, Evan, that even though it all goes by too fast for them, they *notice* little things like that and start wondering about them, and stop paying attention to the story."

In much the same way, Hitch questioned The Girl's *every* move. He said in interviews later (when he was trying to justify the film as a great work of art) that The Girl represented complacency. "Generally speaking," he said, "I believe that people are too complacent. People like Melanie Daniels tend to behave without any kind of responsibility, and to ignore the more serious aspects of life. Such people are unaware of the catastrophe that surrounds us all. The birds basically symbolized the more serious aspects of life."

This was utter rot, a supreme showman's con.

While we were shaping the screenplay, there was no talk at all of symbolism. There *was* talk about character depth, but Hitch's real concerns about the shallowness of the people we'd chosen did not emerge until after I'd delivered the first draft and he'd solicited opinions from everyone but his barber. The inherent problem, of course, was that the characters in a screwball comedy *have* no depth. They merely represent conflicting attitudes. We were trying to tell a story lighter than air. The irony was that the terror later comes from the air. As far as I was concerned, everything that preceded that first gull hitting Melanie on the head was pure gossamer.

Hitch had a different agenda. Hitch wanted respectability.

Beauty and the Beast: Did Hollywood Destroy Dorothy Dandridge?

BY DONALD BOGLE

*I*t was Oscar night, March 30, 1955. A limousine pulled up in front of New York City's Century Theater, and Dorothy Dandridge stepped out. As she smiled and waved, the crowd went wild, screaming and shouting her name. Photographers rushed to snap pictures while reporters pressed her for a comment. She was a dazzling sight, every inch the movie star, and the crowd that had gathered that evening scrambled to see the famous face up close: the dark eyes, the sensuous mouth and the color—usually described in the press as café au lait— that set her apart from Hollywood's more traditional beauties.

She had worked hard all her life to reach this point. She'd performed since she was a little girl, when her mother, the comedienne Ruby Dandridge, had put her and her sister, Vivian, onstage in an acrobatic act called The Wonder Kids. Believing both her children might become stars, Ruby, a stern disciplinarian, had pushed them at every opportunity.

FROM *ESSENCE*

There had also been a marriage to Harold Nicholas, half of the famous Nicholas Brothers dancing duo, and a daughter named Harolyn, born severely brain damaged. When the marriage failed, she resumed her career to support herself and her beloved daughter, becoming famous in the country's top nightclubs. Her hot-cool style—the sexy voice, the sensual, dramatic, dancelike movements—drove patrons wild. Never had there been an American nightclub performer quite like her.

Weary of the club scene, Dandridge sought to move her career in a new direction and won the movie role every black actress in Hollywood wanted: the fiery Carmen Jones in famed director Otto Preminger's all-star black musical of the same name. Her performance stunned and captivated everyone, including director Preminger, who by now was in love with her. It was also a historic breakthrough, as Dorothy Dandridge now became the first black woman to be nominated for an Academy Award as best leading actress.

In an era that celebrated Marilyn Monroe, Elizabeth Taylor, Grace Kelly, and Audrey Hepburn, Dorothy Dandridge was Hollywood's first full-fledged movie goddess of color. Throughout black America she was not merely a glamorous icon but also a symbol of a new day. Her triumph couldn't have come at a more socially significant time. Nineteen fifty-four was the year of the Supreme Court's ground-breaking decision in *Brown v. Board of Education,* in which it ruled that segregation in public schools was unconstitutional. A year later, seamstress Rosa Parks refused to take a seat at the back of a Montgomery, Alabama, bus. Dorothy Dandridge held a place—alongside Jackie Robinson—as a symbol of the future. Her presence was a sign that the movie industry, like the rest of American life and culture, had to finally make way for men *and* women of color.

SEX SYMBOL

"Ella Fitzgerald is one of the most talented people in the world," Dorothy once told her close friend Geri Branton. "And it embarrasses me that she cannot work the rooms that I work. She's not sexy. The men in the audience don't want to take her home and go to bed with her. Yet she's up there singing her heart out for one third the money they're paying me. And I resent being in that [sex-symbol] category."

Dandridge was never comfortable with so much media emphasis on her sex appeal. In the past, black women like Josephine Baker, Billie Holiday, Lena Horne, and dancer and choreographer Katherine Dunham were seen as powerfully sexy and desirable women. Yet the American press rarely openly acknowledged them as such. They simply weren't considered female ideals to be fawned over as were Rita Hayworth, Hedy Lamarr, and Betty Grable. In the dominant culture, the Negro Goddess was only to be appreciated or desired on the sly. In the fifties, things began changing as black women like singers Eartha Kitt and Joyce Bryant and, most especially, Dorothy Dandridge found themselves openly saluted as sex goddesses. Most people chose to see that as social progress. But the constant emphasis on sex was as disturbing and damaging to Dandridge as it was to that other sex goddess of the era, her old acting-school pal, Marilyn Monroe.

"Dorothy really loved dignity and elegance," Vivian Dandridge once recalled. "Almost to a fault."

CARMEN JONES

The story of how Dorothy eventually won the leading role in *Carmen Jones* reads like a press agent's dream. The morning of her appointment with Otto Preminger, she carefully dressed and made up. "I saw her leave the apartment," Vivian said. "She had on a navy-blue dress with a white Peter Pan collar. It fit through the waist, then flared. Her hair was pulled back in a ponytail." Vivian remembered thinking her sister was dressed inappropriately for an actress about to discuss the role of the fiery Carmen.

After Dandridge arrived at Preminger's and cordialities were exchanged, the discussion turned to the role of Carmen. Preminger looked directly at her and asked, "Now, Miss Dandridge, what makes you think that you can do Carmen?"

"Well, Mr. Preminger, what makes you think I can't?" she answered.

"You're very sophisticated. You're the epitome of high fashion," he replied. "But this Carmen is an earthy girl who's entirely different from you. Every time I look at you, I see Saks Fifth Avenue."

Dandridge later recalled, "Mr. Preminger told me that I seemed too sweet and too regal and that he didn't think I'd do."

Though angry, Dandridge controlled her temper and decided on a new approach. At her next appointment, Preminger sat behind his massive desk, again expecting a demure, girlish Dorothy. This time she walked in with tousled hair, dark makeup, a tight skirt, revealing blouse, and the sexiest swinging hips in town. She didn't even have to open her mouth.

"My God," said Preminger. "It's Carmen!"

AFTER CARMEN

Dandridge was offered the part of Tuptim in the movie version of the Rodgers and Hammerstein hit Broadway musical *The King and I*. But she balked at the idea of playing a rebellious slave girl. Preminger also advised her against taking the part because he felt strongly that after *Carmen Jones* she should play only leading roles; if she accepted the part of Tuptim, she would forever relegate herself to nothing but supporting roles in films with white female stars. Preminger considered Dandridge in the same league as Elizabeth Taylor and Marilyn Monroe. Had either of these women just been nominated for an Academy Award, neither would have played a secondary role, no matter how big the production. He refused to believe that Dandridge might be limited in the movie industry because of her race. Preminger was in this instance blind to movieland realities. She turned down the role of Tuptim, and plans for every other major production fell through. Three years would pass between *Carmen Jones* and Dorothy's next big-screen appearance.

THE MEN IN HER LIFE

In the media there was a growing perception that Dorothy was no longer attracted to black males. For a while she had a close but largely clandestine romance with British actor Peter Lawford. The taboo against interracial dating also led her to keep secret her romantic relationship with Preminger. But that didn't keep the press from speculating. Both black and white publications linked her to such white leading men as Tyrone Power, Michael Rennie, Farley Granger, and scores of others.

It seemed as if she lived in an exclusively white world, which was partially true, but never to the extent that some imagined and never without complications and contradictions that disturbed Dandridge herself.

"Sometimes people thought that Dottie was prejudiced against black men," Vivian said. "She discussed it with me many times. She would say, 'What can I do? I'm earning so much money, I don't want to feel I'm keeping them.' My sister would have been very happy to have married someone like a Harry Belafonte or a Sidney Poitier. But those men were already married. Dottie just didn't meet black men in her world."

HER LAST YEARS

Her involvement with Jack Denison, a white Las Vegas maître d' turned nightclub owner, marked the beginning of the end for Dandridge. He was reckless with money, running up bills that she found herself paying off. He also had laughable pretensions and grandiose visions for himself. In Hollywood, Dandridge conferred status and relevance on Denison. At the same time, she diminished her own.

Once they married in 1959, Dorothy grew to fear her husband's violent temper. He sometimes struck her. Yet she stayed with him and numbed herself with alcohol. Finally, after three years, when she could endure no more of his tirades and incessant demands for cash, she told Denison to get out of her life.

With no reserve to support herself—because of Denison she had gone through it all—Dandridge found herself deep in debt, behind in her mortgage payments and the fees for her daughter's care. At night, her mind raced. Engulfed in her fears, she could sleep only with pills. Then she learned that the IRS was demanding payment of $8,500 in back taxes, a large sum in those days, especially for her. Soon afterward, she discovered that some oil-well investments that she had expected to provide her with lifetime security had dried up. Dandridge was penniless.

On September 8, 1965, in the midst of a nightclub comeback and after signing a new movie contract, Dorothy Dandridge was found dead on the bathroom floor of her Los Angeles apartment. The autopsy concluded that the cause of death was the result of an overdose of drugs used to treat depression. The coroner's office refused to determine whether her death was accidental or a suicide.

Polanski's Inferno

BY JILL ROBINSON

*R*emember, it was the sixties. We were doing everything. It was free love. You know what it was like. It was Utopia. Society was moving forward on the hopes of young people. We were the young people then." I am listening to Roman Polanski's voice from Paris, where he has lived since fleeing the U.S. before sentencing for unlawful sex with a thirteen-year-old girl. Some of us who were part of the sixties era might not use the word "Utopia" to cover it. But Roman grew up in Poland during World War II; the Nazis killed his mother. He had probably never felt young in his life before he came to Los Angeles.

I remember Roman from canyon parties and smoky clubs as hungry like a wolf. Yet the fringe was never really his scene. He spoke French, which south of Sunset meant he was intellectual, but he learned how to work the Hollywood room. In Beverly Hills, he knew which fork to use and didn't come off like one of us ungrateful

FROM *VANITY FAIR*

industry kids who didn't get the business. He had seen too much to be naive.

Like a lot of people who came to Hollywood from back East or from Europe, he wanted to suck it up, ride it fast. Outsiders arrive here and look at the mountains and surf and forget the limits because their seasons are gone. They don't catch our rhythms right off.

I was born in L.A. From 1948 to 1956, my father, Dore Schary, ran MGM. I longed for stars, but even more for directors like Polanski, who seduced the magic out of you. Richard Brooks, William Wellman, Joe Mankiewicz, the Europeans: I watched them as they straddled benches by our pool, hoping they'd be interested in me, interested in that adult way. I was burning. I wanted to feel like a star.

Maybe the girl felt that way.

She had spent her thirteen years on the outside in a company town. Then he appeared. A man her mother had invited in.

On a day in February 1977 Roman Polanski drove a rented Mercedes to the far end of the San Fernando Valley to meet her. He was by this time only a visitor to Hollywood, where he had first tasted youth and freedom, a forty-three-year-old nomad with a suite at the Beverly Wilshire and a doctor's prescription for 150-milligram quaalude tablets. He was a man in transit, buffeted by war, death, and the rock music of changes. Since the murder of his wife, Sharon Tate, his life had been numbed and fragmented. He had skied frozen slopes in Gstaad and traveled in the company of stars, users, and an opium-smoking prince. He had wandered the world, trying to escape new sorrows and old shadows—Kraków, the war, the face of his lost mother.

Seed money for movies was tight, certainties were in limbo—tough for an autocratic little man who had learned the necessity of control. On the set he was Napoleon, dominating a world of light, action, color, and sound. He could perfect it all his way. Yet his career was fluctuating erratically between highs and false starts, despite the success of *Chinatown* a few years earlier.

He had wasted too much time on an aborted project called *Pirates* and then turned to a bizarre little film called *The Tenant*, in which he himself starred opposite Isabelle Adjani. His character, Trelkowski, was, in Polanski's words, "a shy, Polish-born bank clerk whose creeping schizophrenia culminates in transvestism and suicide." Not a career move.

The memories of the home he had found with Sharon, the radiance of their California evenings filled with the sound of vintage records such as "Baby, It's Cold Outside," had been shattered first by Charles Manson's murderers and then by the recriminations and the sensationalism of the press. Utopia was smashed, youth extinguished again by loss. "Sharon's murder and the landing on the moon changed everything," Polanski tells me. "When man walked on the moon, some romantic idea of the moon was over. I believed in romance when I was with Sharon. It was happening! I mean, *why it cannot be?* But the magic illusion of romance was gone."

In Munich he had met fifteen-year-old Nastassia Kinski. ("My friends call me Nasty.") After a threesome with Polanski and a second young girl, Kinski had grown on him, despite the fact that "her makeup and hairdo and clothes were all wrong."

He had remade her his way when—as part of guest-editing an issue of French *Vogue*—he supervised a photo shoot with her in the Seychelles. He described Kinski to *American Film* as "woman and child at the same time."

After the shoot he had returned for the first time in fifteen years to Kraków, where he had lived from age three in a house marked with a hybrid—part dragon, part eagle—carved in stone.

He had never taken Sharon to Kraków, where the dark tones of the streets had become a kind of counterpoint for Polanski to the Technicolor world of the movies, in which Jeanette MacDonald, "attired in a vaporous white gown, descended a staircase to the strains of 'Sweethearts.' "

For Polanski, Kraków remained the symbol of all the things he could not control. It was still the place where day after day he and his parents had rehearsed what he, who could pass as a Gentile, should do if they were taken away to the camps.

His proud and glamorous mother died in a Nazi gas chamber. In *Roman,* her son's autobiography, she is portrayed as resourceful, elegant in fox fur. Polanski's descriptions—"the precise way she drew thin lines over her plucked eyebrows, the equally careful way she applied lipstick to alter the shape of her lip in keeping with contemporary fashion"—summon memories of Faye Dunaway in *Chinatown*. The actress, whom Polanski had hired for "the same sort of look I remembered in my mother," enraged him with her close attention to her makeup, a fixation which may have seemed too familiar. After a period of hostility, war broke out when Polanski, concerned with perfecting a shot, abruptly plucked an errant strand of marcelled hair from Dunaway's head.

In the ads for the picture, the face of Evelyn Mulwray, Dunaway's character, rises from the smoke of the hero's cigarette like a ghost.

In L.A. he had heard about a "fabulous-looking teenager" whom he would later describe as "a would-be model who had already appeared in a TV commercial." It is not clear whether the girl had actually appeared on television. Or whether she had acted or modeled professionally. She was open to the idea of being, as we used to say, "discovered," but it was her mother—whom Polanski had once met briefly, at an L.A. club called On the Rocks—who seems to have held greater expectations.

On the day when he first visited the girl's home in Woodland Hills, anyone watching from a kitchen window would have noticed Polanski as an arresting presence in the neighborhood, one of the subdivisions that had sprung up in the late forties along the hills overlooking the ranchland of the San Fernando Valley. "Roman's a difficult and passionate man," his old friend and admirer the director Bob Rafelson says in his wry way. "He's obsessed by his work. . . . Plus he's small, plus he's twisted."

Polanski saw the girl when she walked into the living room with her bird and her dog. He was showing her mother the French *Vogue* he had guest-edited. He asked if the girl would like him to take her picture.

The girl, whose parents were divorced, did not exactly live in isolation from her time. Her mom's boyfriend, who lived with the family, worked for a magazine called *Marijuana Monthly*. The girl, thirteen, was not a virgin. She had made love with her boyfriend twice. In her testimony, she appears tentative, embarrassed, and somewhat passive. Her reactions are muted and basic, presented flatly without detail. She seems to lack the sophistication of "professional" children.

Today, she is a housewife in Hawaii, the mother of three. She doesn't want her identity revealed, even after twenty years. She is worried about the effect of the publicity on her children. But her lawyer tells me she wants to bring her kids to Disneyland and is willing to meet with me, perhaps for a formal interview, if *Vanity Fair* will help pick up her expenses.

When I mention my article on Polanski during a telephone conversation, she gets upset. "I thought you said this story was all about me." She reminds me of the Unsinkable Molly Brown, still longing, in her way, to be "up where the people are."

On the night that Polanski met the girl's mother at On the Rocks, the woman was out with her older daughter, the daughter's boyfriend, and his buddy. Someone introduced her to the director. According to one Polanski biographer, the mother slept with the director that night. In court the mother insisted that the meeting was "just to say hi. That was it."

Months later it was arranged that Polanski would come see the girl. In his autobiography, he describes arriving at the family's "typically suburban middle-income" house and points out "the ill-kept lawn, the mother's boyfriend in the living room lounging in front of the TV set without really watching it."

Polanski emphasizes the fact that the mother "kissed me in the overly demonstrative way so many American women have." He says she commented on his cologne, Vetiver, which she remembered from before. He claims that the mother told her daughter "to get a load of my aftershave. . . . [The girl] sniffed my cheek."

As they scanned the French *Vogue,* the mother described Kinski as "stylized," pointing out that her daughter was a good contrast, so "spontaneous." In her testimony, the mother said that Polanski said his pictures were of girls "seen through his eyes." When he asked her daughter's age, the mother said thirteen. "I thought maybe she was too old," the woman testified, "I thought he might want younger girls [for the shoot]."

Polanski says he described the planned layout as beyond "pastel, romanticized nymphets," and recalls that he mentioned the work of David Hamilton. " 'You know Hamilton's pictures?' I asked," recounts Polanski. "The mother said yes, but only," he suspects, "because she didn't want to betray her ignorance."

He says that the girl kept leaving the room and returning. "Simply a way of getting herself noticed," he writes, not thinking she might have been nervous.

According to Polanski, he and the mother discussed the mother's getting a foothold in films. "She asked if I knew a good agent. I gave her Ibrahim Moussa's number and said I'd have a word with him. She invited me to have dinner at The Yellow Fingers, a local restaurant, but I made an excuse."

Just before Polanski left, he asked the girl if she wanted him to take her picture. She did.

Polanski, it was eventually decided, would return for the shoot on the afternoon of February 20. During one phone call, the mother said she wanted to come along and take pictures of the two of them. She was, she told Polanski, sort of a photographer herself. He said no; the girl would respond more naturally on her own.

When I mention Roman, Howard W. Koch Sr., a Paramount producer, advises: "In Hollywood you have that story every week. . . . It's just you don't know about it." My friend Guy McElwaine, formerly ICM's vice-chairman, says that his father was known at MGM as "the bag-man."

"We had no money," McElwaine remembers, "but Dad had this big black bag, filled with cash, and he'd run out in the middle of the night getting people out of trouble. One big star—and I'm not telling you who—was caught in the bathtub with four girls."

Most of the other industry people say something else when the subject of Polanski is broached. They talk about "the times." A young friend of mine calls that period between the invention of the pill and AIDS "the Golden Age of Sex."

I know about that time. I spent most of it addicted to speed. My habit had started when I was a kid with asthma. The doctor gave me some white powder to breathe when I had an attack—there was no other way I could breathe in those days. But the powder kept me awake and I stayed up all night coloring with my crayons. When the powder wore off, I went out to the kennels to sniff the dogs—to bring on another attack. By the '60s, I was on heavy speed. I kept my children home from school for peace marches or, just as often, because I needed them around. I am telling you this because I want you to understand that this was a time when a lot of us found something that was not like freedom at all.

It was the era of "Love Me Two Times," LSD, and late parties in the hills where huge tripping crowds spilled out on the grass. Roman and Sharon were the center of a hip, glamorous set. *Rosemary's Baby,* directed by Roman, had become a hit; no one was saying no now.

While Roman obsessed about his career, the rest of us talked about drugs and sex and *The Doors of Perception.* But what had started out sunny got heavy, dark, and complicated; the energy changed. Things began to get strange, surreal. Paul Petersen, a former child actor, tells me a story of the fallout of changing times. His first wife, a soap actress, got involved in a coven in Malibu and left him for another performer, the late Bill Bixby (*My Favorite Martian, The Courtship of Eddie's Father*).

"They had a son who died in her care when he was six. After divorcing Bill she shot and killed herself. Our coroner in Malibu said she was the most beautiful corpse he had ever seen. She was gorgeous, Ava Gardner pretty."

The murders came—on a night so unnaturally still that one of the killers would remember hearing ice rattling in cocktail shakers in the canyon. The heat in the basin would not break.

Helter Skelter. For anyone alive in 1969—on August 9, to be precise—the words from the Beatles song that, according to myth, inspired Charles Manson's tribe of homicidal maniacs, still bring a shudder. The word PIG scrawled in blood, the smears on the French louvered doors between Sharon and Roman's bedroom and the pool. Tate, stabbed sixteen times, begging, pleading for her unborn baby's life. No detail was overlooked. The Texas-born actress who had appeared in *Valley of the Dolls* and as a bumbling spy opposite Dean

Martin in *The Wrecking Crew* was found, after having been hanged from a ceiling beam, near the body of Jay Sebring, a Hollywood hairdresser who had once been her lover. The other three bodies were scattered around the grounds of the ranch-style property on Cielo Drive off Benedict Canyon Road. Manson, a man who would carve a swastika into his forehead, loomed large. "I am what you have made of me," he raged. "In my mind's eye my thoughts light fires in your cities."

Rumors blossomed out of each other. Everyone had a tale, a bit of gossip, someone to blame. Polanski himself, working in London during the tragedy, became a citizen suspected of lasciviousness, excess, even witchcraft.

Mike Sarne, a director close to Roman who had dinner with Sharon at a Japanese restaurant on the night before she died, says it was all nonsense. "Roman is not magical, not religious, has no truck with anything mystical. Sharon was a wonderful cook. We'd gather at night, she'd make pasta dinners for us. I once saw her packing a trunk. She laid tissue paper between the layers. She was from Texas, but she had the kind of sophistication to appeal to Roman. They were perfect for each other. Roman's into cold showers every day, deep knee bends, hours and hours of skiing. People who didn't know Roman got so paranoid that police were around them all the time. And local residents in Malibu, where he was staying, said, 'We object to these people being here.' "

Wally Wolf, Polanski's attorney, says he had trouble introducing Roman at a press conference after the murders. "People think they see more in Roman's films than they do. They also have a preconception of what Roman is."

Cielo Drive is a winding street of eucalyptus trees and right angles; the city spreads out below in a cleavage of palms and ferns. Joseph Stefano wrote the screenplay for *Psycho* here. Another neighbor, Betty Freeman, lived about a half mile from the Polanskis. "You'd usually hear Porsches racing down that street," she says, "but not on the night Sharon was killed. There'd been an eerie silence that night. For days to come they were searching up and down the canyon, and we knew no doors or windows or locks would ever feel safe again."

The murders seemed the consequence of everything all of us had done. We had gone too far, done all of the things our parents warned against—and more. But Polanski, it was believed, had gone farther than anyone.

"It's not like it came from out of the blue," recalls Bob Rafelson. "If someone said, 'Guess which house this took place in,' and if you had to sit down and think, first you would have thought of Polanski. Because something was associated with his name that made people feel uncomfortable. . . . Something he had done had tempted the Fates. . . . The point I'm trying to make is that these people were outsiders before any news event took place."

Not surprisingly Polanski began what would become his era of hostility and embitterment. He hated the idea of being reduced in the media and in people's minds to the man who lived in *that* house. "These were the films you made," he said in 1992, paraphrasing his public trajectory, "so this was the life you lead—and the death you died."

Sharon Tate had married Roman Polanski in London in 1968. She wore a cream-colored baby-doll mini. Though he loved her, Polanski admitted to some reluctance. "Personal ties," he wrote, "made me feel vulnerable. This fear was a hangover from my childhood, from the insecurity I had experienced at the age of five or six, when my family began to disintegrate. The only way of not getting hurt, I'd always felt, was to avoid committing myself deeply in the first place."

The Polanskis used drugs—mostly pot and a little acid—but probably no more than most of their peers. Sharon and Roman had done acid on one of their first dates. It was Roman's second trip. The first, not altogether pleasant, had included a vision of a woman who "looked like a princess in a children's story book. Gradually, the face was transformed into a Lotte Lenya face, extravagantly daubed with mascara and black lipstick. To my horror, her eyes and mouth became three spinning swastikas."

Tate's final legacy to Polanski, which he found after she left him in London to sail for America and her death, was Thomas Hardy's novel *Tess of the d'Urbervilles*. It is, fittingly, the story of a girl whose life is ravaged by uncontrollable fate.

Polanski would film it in 1979 with Nastassia Kinski, his lover. He had never hidden his preference for being the older member of a couple.

"I always liked them young, romantic, innocent," he told *The Guardian* in 1992. But after Sharon's death, the preference seemed a necessity. "I don't know what his life was like, post-Sharon, how many other young girls he was seeing," says Toby Rafelson, Bob's wife. "He couldn't have been with older women, because I don't think that appealed to him. . . . I think what he could not do was get involved again with someone like Sharon. In other words, her age group, her looks—that sort of thing. That was too painful. . . . But a young girl, one he would not have to be serious about, one that he could just have a good time with, who was full of life and promise . . . seems like a possibility. Someone who was just going to look up and adore him."

Polanski was candid about what he was no longer capable of. "I doubt," he conceded, "that I will ever be able to live again on a permanent basis with any woman." In the course of an evening everything had changed. The house on Cielo where the music had played became, in Betty Freeman's words, "a monument to murder."

On February 20, 1977, Roman Polanski returns to the Valley and begins sorting through clothes which the girl's mother has set out. (According to court testimony, he chose a white shirt and a patchwork blouse for her daughter's modeling session. In Polanski's more elliptical account, he chose the mother's long white Indian-style dress.)

Polanski says he wants to shoot her in Benedict Canyon, over the crest of the mountains behind the house where the girl lives—over on the southwestern side, below Mulholland. But the light is fading, and the mother suggests that they go to some hills behind their house—about a block away. The two drive there and climb through the dry brush about halfway up the hill. The girl poses as he clicks off instructions: "Sit this way." Or "Don't smile."

Polanski writes that as he began taking close-ups, he noticed "a bruise, or rather a love bite," on the girl's neck. "I asked if it was the result of taking karate lessons from her boyfriend. She laughed. 'It was

Chuck [the name is a pseudonym] all right,' she said, 'but it wasn't karate.' "

She says she changed shirts in front of him. ("She removed her blouse," according to Polanski. "She wasn't wearing a bra but seemed entirely at ease. . . . She had nice breasts.")

They move farther up the hill; he asks her to remove her top again and she complies. In court, the girl would testify that she believed this was for "the shots [where] you don't have anything on your shoulders." She wasn't sure about telling her mom of these pictures.

According to Polanski, "I took pictures of her changing and topless. Then I asked her to unzip her jeans a couple of inches and hook a thumb in her waistband. She posed with professional aplomb. Motorcyclists had clustered around a pickup twenty or thirty yards away and were gawking. I thought she should put her blouse back on. 'They don't bother me,' she said. 'I don't care.' I insisted, feeling that her indifference to the boys was a pose—an attempt to appear worldly and sophisticated beyond her years."

They quit around six-thirty, when the sun goes down. Back at the house he draws her some pictures of pirates, makes some calls, and goes. She doesn't tell her mom about taking her top off. She doesn't say she doesn't want any more pictures taken. But later, in court, she would say that she did not want another session. I think, from what I have been able to learn, that she did not want to provoke a confrontation between Polanski and her mother. She did not want to be the center of a battle. And besides, Polanski was a famous director.

You can make a lot of arguments here about what she should have done. But remember that this was a child who, whatever her sexual history, had believed, not so many days earlier, that the visiting director might be interested in meeting her pets. When I was thirteen my parents took me to a party at Sinatra's. I asked for a drink. Humphrey Bogart sized me up, told me I was the only virgin in the room, and ordered my parents to take me home. This girl's mother was raising her daughter on her own in a Hollywood where Bogie wasn't around. Havoc had been wreaked in many of our lives. Before I sobered up, I lost my money and had to send my children away for a while. It was the worst thing that could have happened to me, to be in a position where I could not protect my children. I don't want to judge anyone.

By 1973 Roman Polanski was in Los Angeles working on *Chinatown*, to be produced by Robert Evans from a screenplay by Robert Towne. He was about to turn forty, an event which he termed "a depressing moment in any man's life." The city lowered his spirits further. The place had shed its sixties skin. "Beverly Hills," Polanski wrote in *Roman*, "had changed. . . . The relatively innocent use of psychedelics and grass was on the wane. Cocaine and quaaludes were now the rage. Nearly all of my friends were dead or long gone, their houses shuttered and deserted. I'd even lost my agent. Bill Tennant had simply walked out of his office one day, not bothering to empty his desk drawers, and never came back."

Polanski reworked the script, concentrating on the ending. Towne wanted Evelyn Mulwray, the Dunaway character, to live, and her father, the evil tycoon played by director John Huston, to die. But Polanski left an unmistakably personal signature at the close of his smoky noir drama. The film ends, as the director wrote, with Evelyn—who has borne her powerful father's daughter—being shot through the eye as she attempts to rescue her daughter from the desirous old man. In one of the closing images, the young woman is taken away from her mother's body by the grandfather, whose freedom to provide the most tender attentions is now, presumably, unlimited. Corruption reigns. The hero, Jack Nicholson's character, watches powerlessly as a friend puts his hand on his shoulder to advise: "Forget it, Jake, it's Chinatown."

Polanski goes to see the girl for the third time on March 10, around four P.M. In his autobiography, he writes that he had been "rather disappointed" in her appearance when they met. "She was about my own height, slim and quite graceful, with an unexpectedly husky voice for her age—a good-looking girl but nothing sensational."

But he keeps coming back.

In her testimony, he tells her, "Let's go. . . . Hurry up."

Again, he chooses her wardrobe—a blue dress, Rugby shirt, and T-shirt. She is wearing panties of a rust or copper color, no bra. When the mother asks Polanski if she can see the photos from the first shoot, he says later.

Polanski tells the girl that they are going to his friend's. At the house they visit (actress Jacqueline Bisset's), he introduces her to some friends—three men, two women—and takes a few shots.

Then he says, "I'm going to call up Jack Nicholson and see if we can go down to his house." She hears him talking on the phone. (Apparently he does not speak to Nicholson. The star of *Chinatown* is skiing in Aspen after his latest breakup with Anjelica Huston, who is moving out.)

Nicholson's sprawling home is on the same road as Bisset's. When they arrive, Polanski presses the button at the gate. Someone asks, "Is this Roman?" And he says, "Yeah." When the gate opens, the girl sees a woman with black hair and two dogs. (Polanski identified her as Nicholson's associate Helena Kallianotes.)

Polanski gets his camera, puts the lens on, and chats with Kallianotes.

When the girl says she's thirsty, Polanski goes into the kitchen and gets out a bottle of champagne. (Cristal, according to Polanski.) "Should I open it?" he asks. And the girl says, "I don't care."

After the drink, the girl just stands by the pool. Kallianotes says she has work.

Finally, Polanski and the girl are all alone by the beautiful blue pool at the movie star's house on Mulholland Drive. Even the street is famous.

"Look at the Shirley Temple movies, you see it here. She was in diapers and then dressed like a trollop from the waist up. A critic once said something like: What you have in movies, in the dark, is a rounded little innocent girl, sitting on a man's lap and making the world's troubles go away. It's in Hollywood and in biology—an adult male mammal who has his maturity is forever breaking in girls who are coming into their first season. That's the way it works."

The speaker is Paul Petersen. Of those I spoke to in Los Angeles about Roman Polanski and the girl, he is the one I cannot get out of my mind. When he was a kid he starred as the son on *The Donna Reed Show*; today he is an advocate for child actors, the founder and president of A Minor Consideration. Petersen has no regrets about giving up acting. He says that he got started in the first place "because my mother was bigger than me."

I think of the face of Roman's mother in a circle of smoke and Roman, all those years later, plucking the hair which distorted his perfect memory from the head of Faye Dunaway.

"Did you hear what the interviews were like for the new *Lolita?*" Petersen goes on. "Thousands of girls attempting to be teenagers and their parents sat for hours. This has to do with the desire to get it at any cost, at any age. . . . [In the Polanski case] what was being held out was the opportunity to be famous. A person in power can corrupt even the bond between mother and daughter."

After taking pictures by the beautiful pool, Polanski and the girl go inside. Standing at the big silver camera box, he starts choosing lenses. She changes into the blue dress, right there in the living room, and walks into the bathroom.

They go out to the Jacuzzi. She's still in her dress. He says he wants to take pictures of her in the Jacuzzi, but wants her to call her mom first. It's about six P.M. She says she's at Nicholson's, and when her mom asks her if she's okay, she says she is. "Do you want me to come by and pick you up?" the mother asks. She says no.

Polanski gets on the phone while the girl goes back out and gets into the Jacuzzi.

In her testimony, she says that later, when she is back inside, he shows her this little yellow thing from the bathroom. In it is a quaalude—a drug that she admits having seen before. It has three parts. "Is this a quaalude?" he asks.

She says it is. And he says, "Oh, do you think I will be able to drive if I take it?" She says, "I don't know." And he says, "Well, should I take it?" and then she drinks some champagne. "Well, I guess I will," he says, as he takes part of the pill. "Do you want part?"

She says no. Then changes her mind.

(In court the girl did not deny drinking the champagne, but she said she must have been pretty drunk to have taken the pill. The court decision makes note of the fact that she was "not unfamiliar with the drug quaalude, having experimented with it as early as her tenth or eleventh year." Polanski wrote that the girl said she had stolen the quaaludes she had used in the past—from her sister.)

With a swallow of champagne, she takes a little less than half of one section of the pill. As the camera clicks she keeps sipping from the glass.

Then she enters the kitchen. She thinks she should eat; she's been drinking too much. So she takes something from a dish in the kitchen and goes into the bathroom to take off her dress. Then, according to her testimony, she goes outside and Polanski says, "Take off your underwear." She does. Then she gets back into the Jacuzzi. With the champagne in her hand.

He doesn't take many pictures. She just looks at him. He's wearing tan pants, a sweater. He says he's going to get in, and goes into the bathroom. When he returns he is naked. He goes down to the deep part of the Jacuzzi.

She goes to the other end.

"Come down here," he says.

"No. No. I got to get out," she says.

"No, come down here."

She tells him that she has asthma and that she has to get out. Because of the warm air or the cold. Or something like that.

"Just come down here for a second," he says. And she does.

"Doesn't it feel better down here?" he says, holding her up with his hands on her sides and around her waist.

She tells him she'd better get out—and does, wrapping a towel around herself.

Then he goes into the large pool and says, "Get in here." She dives in one end, swims a lap, and gets out.

She is drying off in the bathroom when he comes in and asks if her asthma is bad. She says she wants to go home to take her medicine. "Yeah," he says. "I'll take you home soon."

He tells her to lie down. There are no lights on in the bedroom, which has a bed, couch, and TV. She says she wants to go home now. She's afraid. She's wearing just underwear and a towel. She'd put on the panties. She's having trouble with her coordination, walking and stuff.

When she sits down on the couch, he sits beside her and asks if she's okay. She says "No." He answers, "Well, you'll be better."

She says she has to go home. Again.

Then he kisses her. And she's saying, "No, keep away."

He pulls off her panties. She just keeps saying, "No. Come on, let's go home." And then he starts doing what she referred to in court as "cuddliness," placing his mouth on her vagina. He is just licking and she's ready to cry. She's saying, "No. Come on. Stop it."

And he isn't saying anything that she'll remember.

She's kind of dizzy, blurry. Then he starts to have intercourse with her. (She said she didn't fight that much; she thought no one was there to help.)

"Are you on the pill?" he wants to know, and she says she isn't. "When did you last have your period?" he asks.

"I don't know. A week or two. I'm not sure."

"Come on, you have to remember."

And then, she said, he sodomizes her without saying anything. She pulls back a little bit, but not really, she recalled; she was afraid.

A woman knocks, calls out: "Roman, are you in there?" He says yes. "I just got out of the Jacuzzi and I'm getting dressed." He opens the door a crack. The woman is Anjelica Huston, who can see that Polanski—whom she has never liked and later reportedly called "a freak"—is nude. Apparently angered that he is using the house for sexual purposes, she demands to know what is going on.

As the girl listens, he says he is doing a photo session. Then she puts on her underwear and walks toward the door.

But Roman sits her back down, takes her panties off. And then, she says, he starts having intercourse again. When he stops suddenly she kind of senses that he's finished. She feels that he has ejaculated.

She puts on her dress, combs her hair. "Now wait for me," he says—but she doesn't. When she goes out, she sees Huston on the phone. "Hello," Huston says. "Are you the girl Roman is taking pictures of?"

The girl says yes, walks out to the car, and begins to cry. He comes out in ten minutes. On the way home, she testified, they don't talk much. He says, "Oh, don't tell your mother about this, and don't tell your boyfriend either," and then later he says, "You know, when I first met you I promised myself I wouldn't do anything like this with you." And he adds: "This is our secret."

At home the girl's older sister notices that the girl is "glassy-eyed." When the sister sees the slides of the photos Polanski took the first day, she just walks away. And then, according to the mother, there is a shot of her daughter "bare to the waist with just her jeans on. . . . And I kind of stepped back. And the dog peed on the floor . . . and she doesn't do that. It must have been some kind of energy thing, because she doesn't do that."

"Roman gave me a big speech on how to take care of dogs," the sister said. Then, after a phone call, he leaves.

Later, Philip Vannatter of the Los Angeles Police Department (who will play a role in the O.J. Simpson case) arrives at the Beverly Wilshire Hotel with a search warrant, which he serves on Polanski in the lobby. The director asks the policeman to come back to his room. "As we walked through the lobby going toward the back portion of the main lobby toward the elevators," Vannatter later testified, "Mr. Polanski was slightly to my front and right side. As we were walking I observed Mr. Polanski reach into his left coat pocket with his left hand, side pocket of his coat, remove a small white object from the pocket that looked to me like a tablet. Was holding it in his left hand. And it appeared that he intended on dropping the tablet to the floor."

It was a quaalude, Rorer 714.

After a six-count grand-jury indictment, Roman Polanski's trial was set for August 9, the eighth anniversary of Sharon Tate's murder. But lawyers on both sides immediately began negotiating, and on the day before the trial, in a plea bargain arrived at by the prosecuting attorney, the director's attorney, and the girl's attorney and family, Polanski pleaded guilty to the charge of unlawful sexual intercourse, the least serious of the six counts against him. The judge, Laurence Rittenband, agreed to dismiss all other charges. He acknowledged the girl as "not inexperienced" or "unsophisticated," while emphasizing the fact that this was not "a license to the defendant, a man of the world, in his forties, to engage in an act of unlawful sexual intercourse with her." He also noted that "the part played by the prosecutrix's mother in permitting her daughter to accompany the defendant to the Nicholson home, unchaperoned, is to be strongly condemned although there is evidence that the mother asked to go along on that venture."

Rittenband set a sentencing date of September 19 for Polanski and ordered the director to undergo examination by two court-appointed psychiatrists who would report back on whether he was a mentally disordered sex offender. Many observers expected Polanski to receive probation after these tests. But several days before the scheduled hearing the judge dealt a wild card, announcing that he intended to send Polanski to Chino state prison for more extensive (ninety days) psychiatric assessment. The judge then granted a stay of incarceration to allow Polanski to complete the picture he was working on, *Hurricane,* produced by Dino DeLaurentiis. On December 16, 1977, Polanski reported to prison, where he served forty-two days (the sum total of his jail time). On January 27, 1978, after completing the required testing, he was released. On February 1, Rittenband said that he intended to send Polanski back to Chino for another forty-eight days, and pressured Polanski to agree to voluntary deportation.

Early in February, Howard Koch was in the shower room at the Hillcrest Country Club, listening to Rittenband (who had presided over highly publicized trials, including Elvis Presley's divorce and Marlon Brando's custody battle) "grandstand" about how he was going to put Polanski away "for a hundred years . . . for the rest of his life."

Koch called Polanski and told him to get out of town as fast as possible. Not long after, the Los Angeles police reportedly found Polanski's Mercedes abandoned at LAX.

Despite his vow to remain on the bench until Polanski returned to the U.S. for sentencing, Judge Rittenband stepped down in 1989, saying of the director: "I'll quote a Gilbert and Sullivan opera. I've got him on my list. I've got him on my list. He won't be missed. He won't be missed." Rittenband died of cancer on December 30, 1993.

Like Roman Polanski, I left L.A. many years ago. On my last trip back to finish this story, I noticed how much the city is returning to the family feel that the studios had tried to maintain before blacklisting, before the sixties. The conversations are about children and bringing them up the way we lucky Hollywood kids were brought up. Implicit is the sense that at some time things had slipped and are now being put right. As Polanski himself told me, "Now when you speak to the ingenue on the phone, you hear the baby crying."

Around the time of my visit, a made-for-TV movie, *Bastard out of Carolina,* was dropped by Turner Network Television because of a graphic scene depicting the rape of a twelve-year-old girl by her step-father. The film's director had refused to modify the scene for Turner. Her name was Anjelica Huston. Artists have convenient ways to process their experience. Movies let them recreate old scenes and familiar faces. Sharon merges with Tess, and Nastassia ("Call me Nasty") smiles on screens from coast to coast. But in the real world, where a kid who didn't know what she was getting into found herself crying in a rented Mercedes outside the house of a famous man, memories are harder to put to use.

Polanski's name keeps coming back. John Travolta, the star of the director's new project, *The Double,* walked off the set and flew back to the U.S. after a heated and somewhat mysterious confrontation with Roman, who had asked him to play a scene nude. Ultimately Polanski was fired. "Sure Roman's arrogant," said columnist Army Archerd. "Some of the best talents in this town are tough to work with."

Mike Sarne remains loyal: "Roman's back to normal now. He's got a wife [Emmanuelle Seigner, whom he married in 1989] who has been able to replace Sharon. He has a new life." Polanski himself refuses to say much about the present or the past. He tells me, "The artist catches violence. If it's there in the culture, he'll reflect it." He says that he was "taken in by the ingenuous times of the sixties. It was free love. . . . We were doing everything. But we all did things we might regret."

Later, a friend of mine, a New York–based screenwriter, tells me something I think of as a fitting response to that. "Sometimes," he says, "a director might be led to believe that in life, like in art, you can do other retakes. You can't." And when you spend a lot of time in Hollywood this becomes very tough to remember.

When I talk to the girl again, she is torn between protecting her children and wanting to tell her story. "What if it becomes a movie," she asks, before deciding that for now she wants no formal interview. Because of the kids. Maybe, I think, it's "the times." Her court testimony will have to do. "I really want this to be over with," she tells me. "I want him to be able to come back and just let it all be finished. I've forgiven him and it's all over."

Sal Stabile, for Real

BY MARK SINGER

*B*ecause we're talking Hollywood, where the writer is that laughable *schmendrik* so low in the food chain he gets flossed after breakfast, the story alone counts for only so much. Hence the inclination to embroider the story *about* the story, the narrative of how the movie got made. Salvatore Stabile, an independent filmmaker whose driver's license says he'll soon turn twenty-three, began embroidering a couple of years ago, when he first smelled money. At that point, he'd completed a rough version of *Gravesend,* a dimly lit black comedy about four young men in Brooklyn and a violent Saturday night in their heading-nowhere lives. Would anyone seriously object if, to entice audiences of warm-bodied ticket buyers, Stabile perpetrated a little fable about who he was and where *Gravesend* came from? Was he not, after all, a natural storyteller?

The unembellished facts are these: Sal Stabile grew up quickly in a middle-income high-rise at Twenty-fifth Avenue and Benson Avenue,

FROM *THE NEW YORKER*

in a not very *Leave It to Beaver* neighborhood where Bensonhurst slouches toward Coney Island—a slice of Brooklyn called Gravesend. In 1992, he graduated from Catholic high school in Bay Ridge and immediately moved to Manhattan, where he shared with his maternal grandmother a one-bedroom apartment in Little Italy. That fall, he enrolled in New York University, intending to major in screenwriting. The following spring, his grandmother died and left him five thousand dollars. Along with what he was earning as a waiter in a restaurant on Mulberry Street, the inheritance was supposed to help pay his tuition. But after four semesters at NYU he dropped out. He had a shelf of books about screenwriting, plus a file cabinet filled with screenplays— by Francis Ford Coppola, William Goldman, Robert Towne, Paul Schrader, Paddy Chayefsky, and Richard Price, among others—and he'd written the draft of a script he felt ready to shoot. When his parents urged him to stay in school, he replied, "What should I do? Walk into Miramax with a diploma? Don't you think they might pay more attention if I walked in with a film?"

That he couldn't afford to pay actors didn't interfere with his presumption that he was entitled to work with professionals. In *Back Stage* he placed an ad announcing a casting call for a "trailer" for a feature film. "I was talking through my ass," he told me not long ago. "I didn't even know what a trailer was. What I meant was I was shooting a short part of a movie." Neglecting to specify the ages and sexes of the actors meant having to wade through seven thousand head shots. ("It was crazy. My mailman refused to deliver them. I had to go pick them up at the post office.") He invited forty young actors to an audition and selected three for lead roles; he found a fourth while waiting on tables. Miramax, Stabile assured all involved, had made a solid offer to finance the film, but first he had to deliver some footage—the sort of brazen bluff that would seen to suggest a bright future in the business.

Tony Tucci, who wound up with the role of Zane, a bullying psychopath and the story's protagonist—"Zane wasn't well liked. We were his friends, and we didn't like him," Stabile says in a voiceover narration—told me, "I hooked on to Sal because he talked shit, but I didn't realize that at the time. I thought he had something going for him." Friends, friends of friends, family members, and neighborhood acquaintances from Brooklyn and Manhattan were cast in minor roles.

At a New Year's Eve party, Stabile met a retired-cop-turned-cinematographer named Joseph Dell'Olio, who had walked a beat in Brooklyn and knew Gravesend from having lived there for ten years. Dell'Olio read the script, recognized the characters, and agreed to work gratis, with the understanding that he'd collect something if and when *Gravesend* turned up in a theater. The film would be shot with a hand-held camera in sixteen-millimeter color—plus eight-millimeter black-and-white flashbacks of the four main characters—and Dell'Olio could get by without a lighting assistant, because he had only two lights. Whoever happened to be available handled the location sound. Sal's girlfriend and his mother did the catering.

Stabile had written dialogue for disparate scenes that he hadn't quite determined how to thread together. The story, he knew, would begin with Zane and his pals Chicken (Tom Malloy), Mikey (Thomas Brandise), and Ray (Michael Parducci) hanging out in the basement of a house that belonged to Ray's brother. A gun would go off accidentally, and what to do with a corpse would drive the plot. There was no shortage of discussions with the actors about the characters and their "motivations," and no shortage of faith in the merit of improvisation. During the fall of 1994, they spent seven days filming in various Brooklyn locations: a house in Dyker Heights, assorted street corners, under the elevated tracks in Bensonhurst. The Stabile family car, a defeated Buick Regal with a screwdriver jammed in the ignition, hauled equipment and also provided the setting for several scenes. In early December, Sal borrowed a screening room at NYU and showed the actors and a few other people a less than fully gestated rough cut. By his own estimation, it was "pretty bad," but it stopped short of being hopelessly bad.

Next came two months of rewriting, followed by ten more days of filming. Stabile rented a Steenbeck editing machine in early March, installed it in his apartment, and cloistered himself through the spring and most of the summer of 1995, until he had seventy-five minutes of footage that he could transfer to videotape and submit to the third annual Hamptons International Film Festival, on Long Island. The festival directors accepted *Gravesend* as a "work-in-progress"—a designation that suited Stabile fine because he wasn't yet prepared for the scrutiny of reviewers or distributors. A couple of plot gaps still needed to be filled, and he figured that it would take sixty thousand dollars to pay bills he already owed and to cover the final shooting, editing, sound mixing, and printing.

Only about fifty people at the festival actually saw *Gravesend*—technical complications, never mind the details—but one of them was Toni Ross, who was the chairwoman of the event and was the daughter of Steve Ross, the late chairman of Time Warner. She agreed to become an investor and also enlisted her brother Mark and a friend, Dan Edelman, who had a background in film production and had helped finance the completions of the independent films *Roger & Me* and *Paris Is Burning*. Sixty thousand dollars entitled them to a joint credit as executive producers. Not the least of Stabile's challenges, once he had the money to complete the film, was coaxing the actors back to work, since a couple of them had made it plain that they weren't personally fond of him. The last scenes were shot in late February of 1996, and by Memorial Day weekend he was able to board a plane bound for the Seattle Film Festival, accompanied by a finished print "still wet from the lab."

Both in the Hamptons and in Seattle, Stabile embraced publicity interviews as opportunities to assume a persona that seemed straight out of *Mean Streets*—a tactic to divert the discovery that he was actually a kid from a solid family, with a father who worked for an airline and a mother who was a paralegal, an honor student who alternately wrote poetry and fiction and fantasized about playing catcher for the Yankees. "I wanted to come across as the least likely person ever to make a movie," he told me. "So that when people sat down to watch this they'd be expecting a total piece of shit, and then they'd see this great film and be blown away." He more than implied that, in its significant particulars, the movie script was plucked intact from his own life. The cleverly laconic narrator who identified himself as "Sal Stabile" had, in other words, fortuitously avoided the bleak destiny of the dead-enders in *Gravesend,* which had a primitive texture that radiated a documentary shimmer. For a couple of interviews, he trotted out a phantom older brother, David, who he said had died during a drug deal. Sal himself owned up to a string of misdemeanor arrests and a rotation through drug rehab at fourteen. He left home at seventeen, he said, because his parents "threw me out." He bragged about "beating the shit" out of a fellow NYU student. There were occasional lapses, failures to keep his stories consistent. One day, he'd say he made *Graves-end* with the five thousand dollars from his grandmother, and the next he'd describe having got the money from a drug dealer who was in jail. He claimed to have cut costs by not exactly paying retail for the film stock. How? "I'm Italian. That's how." His mother's maiden name was Gallo—did that ring any bells? He posed for one publicity shot holding a gun, and the caption said, "When I told my parents I wanted to be a writer, they called me a fag." All this was news to the folks at home, and they were less than amused.

The Cinderella myth has become a well-established leitmotiv of the independent-film world. In the familiar scenario, a nimble-witted, usually ethnic-flavored tyro bankrolls a movie using, say, the insurance settlement from a near-fatal motorcycle accident. After wowing them at, typically, the Sundance Film Festival, the director is anointed wunderkind du jour, thereby arousing the acute envy and resentment of thousands of film-school graduates: They pray for the nouveau auteur's imminent self-destruction. This is more or less the position in which Stabile now finds himself—the price he has to pay for having rendered in *Gravesend* an often perfectly pitched tale, both horrifying and laugh-out-loud funny, that explores a disturbed and disturbing segment of youth culture without ever resorting to pop-cultural name-brand dropping or Gen X hand wringing. Within a week of the Seattle festival, a review in *Variety* called *Gravesend* a "remarkable debut for self-taught Brooklyn helmer Sal Stabile." He was applauded for his "edgy sense of form" and "surprisingly original feel for film language." A scene depicting the four main characters, their gas tank almost empty and their trunk brimming with human slaughter, singing along tearfully as Louis Armstrong's rendition of "What a Wonderful World" plays on the radio was pronounced "an instant classic."

The phone started ringing, which Stabile recognized as a general summons to Los Angeles—his first visit. He schlepped the print of *Gravesend* in a plastic garbage bag and never let it leave his side. "If we went to dinner, I took it with me," he said. "That was all I had. I was almost twenty-two years old, and I felt like I had nothing else to show for my life." Dan Edelman agreed to escort him through the thickets, and quickly arranged two screenings. At the second, four agents from the Creative Artists Agency showed up, the most senior of whom was Robert Bookman. "I flipped over it," Bookman later said. "It couldn't have been more crude in some ways, but it was really brilliant." On the spot, he told Stabile he wanted him as a client. CAA, Stabile knew, was the most powerful agency in Hollywood. Instead of being cowed, however, he itemized a wish list. "They asked me what I wanted," he said. "I told them I wanted a distributor for *Gravesend*. They mentioned several directors—Jonathan Demme, Oliver Stone, Steven Spielberg, Marty Scorsese—and I asked whether CAA could get one of them to look at the film and agree to get behind it in some way. I said I wanted another filmmaker championing my career, I didn't want to become just another guy with a development deal at Paramount. And they said okay to everything."

Before long, CAA had delivered not one but two of Stabile's avatars—Stone and Spielberg. First, Stone lent his imprimatur to *Gravesend*—the words "Oliver Stone Presents" appear above the title—and then he helped guide it to a distributor, Island Digital Media. (*Gravesend* opens in New York on September 5.) Quid pro quo, Stabile plans to write and direct a film for Illusion, Stone's production company, though not before he makes a movie for the Spielberg factory, DreamWorks SKG, with whom he has a two-picture deal.

"I got this phone call at seven in the morning," Stabile told me. "It woke me up, and there's this voice saying, 'It's Steven.' I have a brother Steven, and I wondered what trouble he was in. I said, 'Steven! Where are you?' He said, 'L.A.' I said, 'Why are you calling me at seven o'clock in the morning?' He said, 'Who's *this?*' I said, 'Sal. Who's this? You sound so funny. You're Steven—Steven who?' He said, 'Steven Spielberg.' Now I realize he's up at four in the morning. I also realize I'm in my underwear. I said, 'Oh my God, could you hold on one second?' I started putting clothes on. Then I sat down on the bed, and the first words out of my mouth were 'I love *Jaws!*' Later, when I told my father that Spielberg called me, he said, 'Sal, you don't have to lie to impress us.' I said, 'No, Dad, he really did call me. I talked to Steven Spielberg. And I really have this deal with Oliver Stone.' "

Soliciting Stone's appraisal of *Gravesend*, I called his office one day recently, and he rang me back on a cellular phone during drive time. After a dramatic opening declamation—"Fuck! Shit! Hold on! I've got a bee on my fucking leg! There . . . it's a wounded bee. Christ, this is like having a rattlesnake in your car. . . . Okay, I'm back. Green light. Shoot"—he said, "*Gravesend* is a real, authentic, wonderful first film. It felt like it came from Sal's life. Parts of it look like it was shot on Kleenex. Watching it, you feel like you're dropping in as a witness on some very authentic-feeling dialogue. He has a knack for staging action that he knows—whether he knows he has it or not."

Was it true, I asked—this was a point of pride with Stabile—that Stone had called him "a really twisted guy"?

"Sure, I guess I said that," Stone said. "Probably that or 'a sick motherfucker.' I like him. He's a feisty little character. He understands the humor of impossibly awkward situations."

The encomium that I elicited from Spielberg was delivered with somewhat more restraint: "He is fluent in his own life, which makes him the most personal of filmmakers. Sal knows as much about behavior as I knew about lenses when I was his age."

Last month, in Los Angeles, I spent a couple of days tagging along as Stabile cruised in a rented Mustang convertible, dividing his time between a lab in Glendale, where a master print of *Gravesend* was being transferred to a video format, and appointments all around town with film-production executives. Stabile seemed to approach these encounters with an open mind and no illusions. "Certain people just want to take a meeting with you," he said. "They just want to schmooze. Everybody knows that nothing is sacred. They're hoping my next project with Spielberg falls through the loops, and I'll end up with them. Everybody wants to know what's next. Everybody wants your second picture. They want to create your career."

Perhaps on the advice of his consiglieri, Bookman and Edelman (Edelman has agreed to co-produce his next film)—or perhaps obeying his own instincts—Stabile has traded his street-punk pose for a low-key self-confidence leavened by an ingratiating self-effacement. Watching him in action, I was reminded of the adage "Hollywood is high school with money." Was Stabile's preternatural ease attributable to the fact that he had only recently escaped from high school? Or was he, as I often sensed, a middle-aged Tinseltown sage trapped inside a not-quite-twenty-three-year-old body?

One morning, on the Sony lot, he and Edelman arrived for a sit-down with Todd Black, the head of production of Mandalay Pictures, whose chairman is Peter Guber. The meeting, which took place in the so-called Burma Room—faux-antique map of Southeast Asia on one wall, glass conference table, brown leather-and-wood chairs, brown Oriental rug—began with Black gushing, "So, I'm really, really happy to meet you," followed by "Wow, you really are a baby."

"I'm a kid," Stabile confessed. "What can I tell you?"

The improvisational energy of *Gravesend,* Black decided, reflected the influence of John Cassavetes, and he mentioned having just come from a meeting with Sidney Lumet, where the topic of discussion was a remake of *Gloria,* one of Cassavetes' last pictures.

"The original film was very good," Black said. "But there were some missed opportunities, some ways it could have been even better."

"Didn't you have a director who just left that picture?" Stabile asked.

"We had a director we just had to let go. But it's fine, because now we have Sidney Lumet."

"What? You called Sidney—you didn't call me? I'm offended."

When the conversation turned to *Gravesend,* Black said, "Just take me through. Who's a real actor? How about the guy they asked to help them bury the body?"

"JoJo the Junkie? No. He's just a guy I know from Mulberry Street. The four leads are all real actors."

"Wow. That's pretty fucking impressive."

"And I worked with the actors," Stabile said. "The hardest part of making this movie was getting everybody to show up. It was tricky. They didn't necessarily want to be there. It was cold. I couldn't pay anybody."

"How did you incentivize them?"

"You just work with people. I got to know these guys. I worked with each one. I knew which buttons to push. And I let them interact. There were parts of the film where I was letting them tell me what the scene should be. I would just let them go up to the point that I didn't like what they were doing, and I'd step in and say no, yes, whatever."

"That's smart," Black said. "You realize what you did? You put yourself in a more powerful position by doing that. You *listened.* Just by listening, you made your role as a director more powerful. Sal, promise me: Whatever you do, don't ever let me or DreamWorks or

Scott Rudin or Joe Blow in any other studio force Hollywood ways onto your filmmaking. Because that would impair it."

"I think I realize that."

"I think it's just incredibly important not to be seduced."

"Look, I have nothing against making commercial pictures," Stabile said. "I want nothing more than to be able to walk into my agent's office on a Monday morning after we've grossed eighty million over the weekend. The difference is, I don't want to make the film for a hundred and ten million. And I don't want anyone on the set to get paid more than I do. Because I've been there since the beginning. I've worked harder than anyone."

A colleague of Black's, Ori Marmur, had joined the discussion, and now he launched into the sort of fawning hyperbole Stabile had become familiar with: "I hope you realize we screen a ton of movies here, and rarely does something stand out as much as your film. We wait weeks—months, sometimes—for a movie that we can respond to. It's very, very rare in our positions to see a talent like yours."

When Todd Black chimed in, Stabile said, "Please. Slow down. Say it one at a time. I want to take it all in." So they kept it up until he'd had enough. "I just want to hear what you have to say after my second picture," he said. "Let's see what happens then. You think you guys will still be willing to take a meeting with me?"

Last year, Stabile moved from Manhattan back to Brooklyn, and no one who has his best interests at heart has suggested that for the time being he should stray far from his home turf. Soon, he hopes, he'll finish a novel he began writing four years ago, and he's been polishing the screenplay of *Dancing with Angels,* his first DreamWorks project. "A black comedy about a family in Brooklyn dealing with the darkest period of their lives" is how he describes it, and when he's asked about his progress, he has a reply down pat: "It's going good. We're doing our fourth draft. Every time we do one, it gets ten times better. There's no rush. When it's right, we'll know it. When we're in production, we're in production. I mean, the movie's gonna be made, with or without DreamWorks."

Seated in his second-floor walkup in Bay Ridge the other day, he elaborated a point I'd heard him make frequently but wasn't sure I believed; namely, that, the Hollywood hierarchies notwithstanding, he would rather write than direct. "When I say that, people look at me strangely," he acknowledged. "They seem to be saying, 'You just did the impossible, and now you don't want to reap the benefits?' In fact, I do want to direct, and the movies I want to make are very personal. But directing is something I do as a job, and my whole goal is to be able to sit home and write.

"When I take these meetings, I tell everybody that, if they have a script they need somebody to rewrite, send it to me, I'll look at it. But one of the first things I told Bob Bookman was 'Please, spare me the gangster scripts. Send me a quality romantic comedy. Send me a thriller. Just don't send me another *Gravesend*.' And I never want to make a movie and have an audience go into the theater expecting anything in particular."

When the New York State lottery jackpot got up to $70 million a couple of months ago, Stabile had a scare. He and a friend agreed to go partners on a ticket, and the night of the drawing she called and told him they'd won. "She read me the numbers," he said. "I told her, 'Don't move. I'm coming right over.' On my way there, I couldn't believe it. But I didn't feel good, I felt guilty. I felt like my life was ruined, my whole career was over. When I got to her house, she showed me the ticket, and she had the six winning numbers, but they weren't all on the same line. I couldn't believe anybody could be stupid enough not to be able to read a lottery ticket. I told her, 'You really need help.' But I felt enormously relieved. Someone once asked me what my greatest fear is, and I said 'Success.' I'm not sure what success is, but one of the things that come with it is money. If, all of a sudden, this money was dumped in my lap, my career would become secondary. I wouldn't feel an urgency to work. I'm convinced that when people stop working, their lives end. When you retire, you lose interest, and the minute you lose interest you might as well die."

I studied Stabile's face as he said this—a slightly pudgy cross between Bruce Willis and John McEnroe, crowned with rapidly thinning light-brown hair—and found myself wondering all over again just how old he really was.

"A lot of people are afraid to admit they don't know what they're doing when they start something new," he continued. "The first time I walked on a film set, I thought I had to know everything, all the answers. I was afraid to let things happen. You understand that I never really expected to be a director. And I certainly didn't learn anything about directing at NYU. Technically, all I knew was there was a camera, there was film, and you put that in the camera. I never knew how to record sound. I didn't know that the clapper on the slate was for synching up the sound. You should see the outtake of the first shot we ever did. You hear the sound guy say, 'Speed,' and Joe, the cameraman, says, 'Set.' The guy reads the slate, Joe says, 'Mark it,' the slate bangs, and then there's silence. Everybody's just waiting for about seven or eight seconds. I go, 'Come on. The camera's running. We're wasting film.' And Joe said, 'You're supposed to call, "Action!" ' So we tried it again. I called, 'Action!' and everybody started moving."

The Mob, the Movies, and Me

BY PETER BART

A span of twenty-five years wreaks great change on individuals. When I first met Al Pacino, a quarter century ago, he was clean faced and hungry. Today he conveys the gravitas of a grizzled veteran. James Caan, the tough street kid, has mellowed into silver-haired benefocence. And Francis Ford Coppola, once tentative and unkempt, with his scruffy black beard, has become the prototypical padrone, his demeanor suggesting a man who has seen it all and has surely shot it all, from the vineyards of the Napa Valley to the rice paddies of Vietnam.

These impressions swept over me not long ago as I attended a commemorative twenty-fifth-anniversary screening of *The Godfather.* Invited to the old Castro Theater in San Francisco were most of the movie's principals, including cast members Pacino, Caan, and Robert Duvall. Marlon Brando had also been invited, but always the glutton, he had demanded a $100,000 "appearance fee," which no one intended to pay. Also on hand were the producer, Al Ruddy, and the two Para-

FROM *GQ*

mount executives who had patched the movie together, Robert Evans and I, as well as representatives of present-day Paramount, led by the steadfastly ebullient Sherry Lansing.

If Brando's grandeur was missing, Coppola's was very much in evidence as he embraced his guests, exchanging reminiscences about the shooting of a film that has achieved cinematic immortality. The astonishing legacy of *The Godfather* has been a mixed blessing in his life, Coppola acknowledged. It brought him wealth and power but also wrenched him from the career he had scrupulously laid out for himself—one devoted to making small, experimental films like *The Conversation* rather than big Hollywood star vehicles.

Coppola, the world-weary patriarch, stood in sharp contrast to the naive and very straight young man I'd first encountered twenty-five years earlier. Working with Evans at Paramount, I had acquired an option on Mario Puzo's novel, and while others were trying to corral big-name directors, I became fixated on Coppola. Though Coppola had never made a hit picture, he excelled as a screenwriter, and his early directing efforts showed great promise. Most important, Coppola saw the movie as a great family saga, not as just another shoot-'em-up Mafia flick.

Initially, there were two problems: (1) his reluctance to direct a big Hollywood movie and (2) his lack of worldliness and total ignorance of Mobdom. His family was middle-class Italian. His father was a musician and a composer, not a Mafia capo. In fact, the only person who knew less about the Mafia than Coppola was Mario Puzo, the rotund, kind-spirited novelist. "Everything I know about 'the boys' I learned from books," he told me at our first meeting. Having written two novels that were embraced by critics but not by book buyers, Puzo had decided to write a commercial novel on a subject he knew nothing about.

Paradoxically, the innocence of Puzo and Coppola worked to their benefit. What distinguished their work was their focus on family and character. Others had held forth on the intricacies of Mafia tactics, but until then no one had so effectively scrutinized the bonds and traditions of a family like the Corleones.

What neither Coppola nor Puzo knew at the time was that, even as they were inventing their vivid Mafia power players, the company that was financing their movie, Paramount Pictures, was rife with real-life prototypes of characters in their movie. One of the most influential members of this group would later die in an Italian jail in a rigged suicide. Another would rise to infamy as a Mafia front man. The Paramount lot itself would ultimately become a beachhead for the Mob, a substantial piece of it owned by a company with shadowy connections to "the boys."

While Coppola and Puzo were prepping *The Godfather*, did they sense that, with the melodramas being played out in Paramount's corridors, they could have done their research simply by keeping their ears open? I'm convinced they didn't.

But the evidence suggests that, years later, Coppola decided to do some retrospective fact-finding. There are remarkable similarities between the plot of *The Godfather Part III* and some of the incidents that took place at Paramount and Gulf & Western (as its parent company was then called). Even the name of the bad guys' company in that movie, Immobiliare, struck a chord: Charles Bluhdorn, who ran Gulf & Western and Paramount, sat on the board of a real-life company called Immobiliare alongside Michele Sindona, a Sicilian financier who was also a key financial adviser to the Gambino family and other Mafia clans. Bluhdorn was fascinated with his Sicilian ally, who seemed to have total access to Europe's rich and famous as well as a remarkable knowledge of the Vatican Bank's convoluted finances.

My own insight into all this advanced in stages. When Paramount recruited me for a senior production job in 1966, I'd been working as a reporter for *The New York Times* and so could hardly plead terminal naïveté. I knew Bluhdorn was a highflier—a dynamic, utterly reckless Austrian-born wheeler-dealer who had come very far, very fast. The corporate environment was so volatile I was convinced that within a year Bluhdorn would crash and burn, or I would be fired along with Evans, who was as inexperienced at studio management as I was. Hence, in accepting the job, I promised myself I would keep careful notes so that, in a worst-case scenario, I would be able to write an incisive insider's account of studio life in the fast lane.

At the end of the first year, I realized that Evans and I were becoming adept at our jobs and had begun preparation on some formidable movies (our term in office ultimately lasted eight years). I also realized that the single most prudent thing I could do with my notes was not simply to discard them but to incinerate them. They were quite accurate; they were also quite dangerous.

In looking through these notes, I'd finally started to put together an assessment of Bluhdorn and his company. It was at first amusing to scan the vignettes: Bluhdorn secretly meeting with Fidel Castro, trying to persuade him to join in launching the ultimate capitalistic caper, a global sugar cartel; Bluhdorn boasting how he could make huge losses from the Julie Andrews movie *Darling Lili* disappear into thin air by shuffling the numbers into a phantom subsidiary (the SEC later tried to throw him in jail for these maneuvers); Bluhdorn declaring that new European friends, like Sindona, now gave him virtually limitless funding for expansion, even to the point of allowing him to launch hostile takeovers of A&P and Pan American Airlines.

In retrospect, it's easy to see that Bluhdorn was over the edge—a maverick bent on self-destruction. At the time, however, the perspective wasn't so clear. Raucous and ill-mannered, Bluhdorn presented himself as a spirited outlaw who was raiding the sanctum sanctorum of the entrenched corporate power players. While the CEOs were playing golf at their country clubs, Bluhdorn was stealing their companies out from under them.

Besides, Bluhdorn was operating in New York and Europe. Evans and I were out in Los Angeles, working with a skeletal staff and supervising a program of twenty-five pictures a year. In the frenzy of Hollywood deal making, it was easy to overlook Bluhdorn's corporate machinations.

And there was more than enough to consume my attention at the studio. *Rosemary's Baby* was in production, with Roman Polanski directing Mia Farrow—an inexperienced young actress who had just become the bride of Frank Sinatra. Polanski was stretching Farrow to the limit, putting her through as many as thirty takes in an effort to elicit an appropriately tortured performance. Early in the shoot, I received a visit from a Sinatra consigliere, who urged me to intervene with the director. The number of takes must be limited to two or three, he instructed. He even offered me a strong incentive to take action—namely, that neither of my legs would be broken.

My retort was that I had no intention of passing that message on to Polanski and that, even if I did, he would ignore it. The incident brought home to me, however, the Wild West atmosphere that permeated the studio.

The reasons for this atmosphere went beyond Paramount and Bluhdorn. The entire industry was in a sad state then. Television had robbed the movies of much of their audience, the blockbuster hadn't been invented yet, and video was still in the laboratory.

Paramount in particular had been a pathetic invalid. Now, suddenly, Bluhdorn was pumping in big money. Since he was an outlaw, all sorts of fellow outlaws descended on the studio. It was both exciting and hairy. And there I was, taking scrupulous notes, keeping track of the players and their demands.

It was a vivid character named Sidney Korshak who indirectly made me decide to burn my notes. Always immaculately attired in a dark gray suit, the tall, somber Korshak had become a fixture at Paramount, constantly on the phone with Bluhdorn and visiting Evans almost every day. I always found Korshak to be impeccably polite but also utterly humorless. I don't think I ever saw him smile, but I was keenly aware of the folklore surrounding him. He and his brother, Marshall, had come of age in the Chicago of Al Capone, and he clearly felt at home in a number of power circles—not only big labor and big business but also "the boys." Korshak could settle a nettlesome labor dispute with a single phone call. Indeed, he could shut down Las Vegas. He never raised his voice, but seated each day at his favorite restaurant, the Bistro, two phones at his table, Korshak had extraordinary reach.

One day he dropped by my office to tell me that his son would be producing a movie at Paramount. I had never heard of the project, but Korshak assured me that it would be starting immediately. "Peter, my son has not produced anything before," Korshak confided. "I would be greatly in your debt if you kept an eye on him. He doesn't have your savvy."

When Sidney Korshak asked a favor, it wasn't smart to decline, especially when it was such a reasonable one. Korshak seemed relaxed that day. He started chatting about the state of Hollywood. His comments were, as always, clipped and discreet. At one point, he glanced at his watch, then excused himself and dialed a phone number. "Hello, Lew," he began. It soon became clear that he was conversing with Lew Wasserman, then chairman of MCA and the most powerful man in the entertainment industry. It was also clear that Korshak had accessed a private line, bypassing the customary secretarial intermediary.

After hanging up, Korshak praised Wasserman, noting how effectively and prudently the MCA boss ran his affairs. "Peter, do you know what's the best insurance policy in the world that absolutely guarantees continued breathing?" he asked. I shook my head. "It's silence," he said. He peered across at me as if he had just imparted great wisdom. In a way, he had. After all, how often did one receive advice from the man who was arguably the world's best fixer?

It was an especially persuasive reason to go back and burn my notes.

Inevitably, there have been times when I've regretted not having a journal to remind me of my years at Paramount. A myriad of books and articles have been written about the making of *The Godfather*. Indeed, the movies of the late sixties and early seventies have achieved near legendary status, and Paramount made some of the best—*Chinatown, Paper Moon, The Conversation,* Franco Zeffirelli's *Romeo and Juliet, Rosemary's Baby, True Grit,* and *Goodbye, Columbus.* These movies were created amid promises and threats, blandishments and epithets, which by now have all blended together. The in-house detonations and the Bluhdorn tantrums have merged with those of the stars and the star directors with whom Evans and I interacted each day.

It would be fascinating to re-create precisely who did what to whom. On *The Godfather,* why was Francis Coppola almost fired after the second week of shooting? It would be great to have a record. On the other hand, I have felt a sense of security over the years, knowing that I took out Sidney Korshak's recommended insurance policy.

Korshak himself is permanently silenced now, having died quietly of heart failure. In his final days, he still put on his dark suit every morning, walked into his den and watched television. He told family and friends he couldn't remember things anymore. Maybe he was simply acting out his code of silence.

Bluhdorn, noisy and rambunctious to the end, died of cancer in the Dominican Republic, though his associates put out the official word that he'd had a heart attack while flying back to New York.

Francis Coppola has outlasted them all, still directing movies and buying up wineries in his beloved Napa. Whenever he makes a star vehicle, the critics say it's not as good as *The Godfather.* And whenever he goes back to his original plan and directs a small movie, the critics admonish him for not aiming high enough.

For him *The Godfather* is at once his greatest accomplishment and his greatest curse. At the start of Mario Puzo's novel, Balzac is quoted: "Behind every great fortune there is a great crime." Part of Francis Coppola regards *The Godfather* as his greatest crime.

Superstars of Dreamland

BY GERALD PEARY

MARY VIVIAN PEARCE

*J*ohn Waters loathes sports metaphors, so I'll use one instead for Mary Vivian ("Bonnie") Pearce, Waters's great pal since high school. She's the Lou Gehrig of Dreamlander cinema, with the longevity record of eight straight Waters films. Her string began when she danced sexily in 1964's *Hag in a Leather Jacket,* and it concluded with her poor, harassed princess in 1977's *Desperate Living.* (Later, she's somewhere about in 1994's *Serial Mom.*) On screen, Pearce is the ditsy, paroxided Jean Harlow who moves lithely as a silent movie apparition, even as she (often) removes her blouse. Or has her toes sucked—who can forget the eye-popping scene?—in *Mondo Trasho* (1969). In *Female Trouble* (1974), she plays a fascist beautician. Normally, she's Waters's ingenue-in-residence, his neurotic "nice" girl who, alas, gets molested and defiled. Something's ever seedy in Waters's blighted Baltimore.

FROM *PROVINCETOWN ARTS*

Acting in *Pink Flamingos* ("I was with the good guys, of course"), Pearce is proud to have led an actors' revolt over the fact that cast and crew weren't fed. "John sneered when I complained to him," she recalled. "But the next week there was cheap wine for lunch and bologna sandwiches."

Pearce lives in a downtown Baltimore apartment with two cats. That's where I interviewed her. She's no longer a dyed blonde, though she's certainly got her Dreamland superstar, good-breeding looks. For years Pearce worked at the racetracks. This spring, she retired to become . . . a bicycle messenger. When she asked Waters for a reference, he replied, "What should I say if they call? That you can ride a two-wheeler?" Pearce is completing an MFA in Creative Writing at Johns Hopkins University, specializing in short stories, one of which is published in this issue.

In 1965 I had a Baltimore apartment with Pat Moran, when John went to P'town with Mona and came back impressed. "It's really cool. Everyone's gay or they're 'head,' or they're gay heads." The next summer, I went with John and Mona.

I was eighteen, and it was three months after I got married. My husband was a jockey at Saratoga, and he told my father I'd left him and run off with beatniks. I was so pissed at him for telling! As far as I was concerned, it was a fake marriage to get me out of the house. I'd taken all our wedding presents back and bought books and records.

We got to P'town before Memorial Day, and it was freezing. But we wanted to be at the opening day of restaurants and get free food. We'd go to art openings and guzzle the wine. Later, we'd go to Piggy's or the A-House, and as soon as people went to dance, we'd snatch their beers. There was a restaurant across from the A-House. I'd go there and snatch people's food. We had a basement apartment, and I'd cut through the backyard. We got thrown out because a guy complained to the landlady that I hopped his fence.

I'd been dying my hair blond since I was fourteen. In P'town, I cut it short, began wearing red lipstick and looking like Jean Harlow. It was kind of harsh, not as pretty as Marilyn Monroe, who I really wanted to look like. But I remember I had a really good time. Dr. Hiebert gave me speed, "black beauties." I told him I wanted to be a model, for an acting part. He said, "Okay, do you want the strong pills?" He was very old, and fell asleep examining people.

Speed was easily available. You could go into any doctor's mailbox and get free samples, or get it prescribed: It was either for depression or obesity, and everyone was fat or depressed. You didn't have to spend money on food, and speed gave you a lot of energy. For example, it would take us about ten hours to get dressed and put on makeup for our movie premieres. We could start at ten in the morning with a couple of hits.

Because I'd worked at the racetrack and knew how to ride, I got a job at the stable taking people horseback riding through the trails and dunes. But I got fired because of too much P'town night life. I'd be out until two or three in the morning. I'd have to get to the stable at nine, but I was showing up for work at noon.

So I was a chambermaid at a hotel. They'd pick me up, in this carpool of other maids, local girls. I was hideous. I lay around on beds watching TV. Then I was a waitress at the Flagship and had to get this outfit that was supposed to look like a peasant. I didn't last long. I poured coffee in someone's lap. One person gave me a nickel tip I gave him such bad service. The owner said I had a mental block.

Then I had a job at Bridge's Breakfast. I lasted a week. Then I worked in a dress shop, and they liked the way I looked. I didn't do *anything*. Sometimes children screamed when I moved because they thought I was a mannequin. Then I was at the fish factory. There, they found out that I was a movie actress because I tacked an article about it next to a clipping about the record for packed lobster tails.

Something happened during the time I was at the Buttery washing dishes. I was interested in joining the Venceremos Brigade in Cuba, and I was reading *Ninety Miles from Home* in my room. There was a knock, and I was afraid: Someone had followed me from a bookstore and caught me stealing. I opened it—and this guy had a gun. I pushed the gun and he ran away. I told the P'town police he looked like a used-car salesman. So the next day they drove me to a used-car lot!

My reaction was that I went out and got dead drunk, though the rumor about town was that I'd kicked the gun out of his hand.

I rode an old Schwinn bicycle covered with rust, but I almost got caught selling a stolen bicycle. The police took me in and questioned me. Somehow they believed me when I told them I'd bought it from a dishwasher.

Did I go to the beach? Oh, no. Jean Harlow with a tan? I wanted to keep my nightclub pallor. I'd wear No. 50 in the shade to watch the sun set.

Some Dreamlanders almost never had sex. We shoplifted and took speed, yet we all got crabs one summer. There was John, boiling his underwear! And John and I got scabies, too. The doctor told John he hadn't seen a case since migrant workers in the 1930s.

MINK STOLE

John Waters calls her "one of the most talented members of my film repertory group." She's been in his films since 1966, when she appeared in the *Chelsea Girls*–influenced (three 8mm films shown simultaneously) *Roman Candles*. She's notorious as the lesbian rapist administering a "Rosary Job" to poor Divine in *Multiple Maniacs* (1970), but she's most internationally famous as the repulsive pre-Yuppie, Connie Marble, in *Pink Flamingos* (1972). Her greatest acting job (if only there were Oscars for tasteless John Waters indies) was as the woe-ridden mad housewife in *Desperate Living* (1977).

Stole has lived in L.A. for seven years. Nobody from the East Coast believes her when she says, "I love California very much." She told me on the phone, "I'm sitting in a beautiful apartment with a lovely backyard. I don't mind if I never see another snowflake, except when I've chosen to go on a winter vacation."

Alone of living Dreamlanders, Stole has pursued acting outside of Waters's movies. There were dry times she blames on herself: "I was clueless, believing in my 'natural' quality, that acting classes would spoil it. And I had a grandiose sense of my own importance, that, instead of having to audition, theaters should call me. Well, they never called."

Still, she's had a colorful career. She did off-off-Broadway plays with the Theater of the Ridiculous's Charles Ludlam, dinner theater back home in Baltimore, and lots of alternative plays, including the dramas of Tom Eyen, while living in San Francisco. "Divine and I did shows there with the Cockettes." Since Stole moved to L.A., she's done voiceover work (she's the off-screen voice of the head juror in David Lynch's *Lost Highways*) and played a recurring role as a teacher on the Nickelodeon Channel's children's series, *The Secret World of Alex Mack*.

Stole has an independent film about to come out, *Pink As the Day She Was Born*, in which, she said, "I play the proprietor of a highly stylized S&M bordello."

I'd always wanted to be an actress. When I met John in Province-town it was fortuitous, though then he was more a friend of my sister, Sique.

My first summer there was 1966, when I lived in the Silva A-frame on Bradford Street. I moved from there to Prescott Townsden's place, separate units got together by gangplanks, and Prescott and I got engaged. He was homosexual and seventy eight years old, and he bought me a diamond ring. There was speculation he might want children. The next summer, we broke our engagement, an amicable separation. I hooked up with Chan Wilroy in one apartment at Prescott's. There were four or five units, and John lived there, and my sister.

We could all kick ourselves: There are no photographs of the tree fort. It burned down in 1969 or '70, and the town was so pleased that it was gone. The Moors restaurant leveled the hill and put in a parking lot.

In the summer of 1969, Sue Lowe, Cookie Mueller, and I found a shack to stay in on Bradford, in the low-rent West End. It used to drive me crazy: I'd come back from work at the Toy Store, the shop I worked in, and the two of them would be drinking jug wine and giving each other tattoos. Sue was a drunk, Cookie took lots of drugs: an equal-opportunity consciousness. We were all high on something, and wrecked. MDA and quaaludes! The speed years! I remember going to bed late at night and taking a "black beauty" so I'd get awake. I remember John delivering "black beauties" on his bicycle. (After some years, John had a car; the rest of us were still on bicycles.)

I remember going out to Long Nook Beach on acid. I could stand on the cliff, lean into the wind, and not fall. And the A-House! When I first came to town I was under age. I hung out in the alleyway desperate to be older. Sometimes they'd take pity on me and let me in for a Coke. When I was twenty one, I had a beer at the A-House. It was a momentous occasion.

Sue left town, Cookie and I stayed. We had a pet, Hans the clam. I got hepatitis, which I always attribute to bad shellfish, the little clams we'd pick. I got quite ill, and Cookie had to take care of me.

In the summer of 1970, John and I had a big apartment on Franklin Street. That's when Vincent Peranio came up from Baltimore and stayed on. We had a torrid love affair, and it was my first experience playing house. We had a wonderful Thanksgiving dinner, and I made a heart-shaped cake. Sappy! We were so poor we had to give up cigarettes. In winter, we took LSD and walked on the dunes. There was no sliding; the sand was frozen solid.

Divine had a thrift shop; the town closed it, and we had a hearing at Town Hall. I spoke up for the shop: "We need stores like this in town for people like me."

I'd worked at the Inn at The Mews as a hostess. That winter, I worked in the schools as a library aid, in miniskirts and high heels. The teachers were horrified, but the kids laughed. And I thought I looked beautiful. That's what Vincent told me.

It was a tumultuous relationship. Vincent had a deaf dalmatian named Pete that hated me because I'd usurped his place in bed. Then Vincent was planning to leave for Christmas. I said, "You can't leave!" Then he would not have a tree, and he would not play Christmas songs on his accordion.

Winter in Provincetown? I remember the harbor freezing. There was nothing to do except drive into Orleans for a second- or third-run movie. Social life consisted of the Fo'c'sle, maybe a few more bars, and it centered on alcohol. I've never been much of a drinker. When the weather got warm, Vincent and I both ended it. I left Provincetown in the summer of 1971. I didn't live there again, just came for a few days, a week, through the seventies. I had a summer there in 1981, when I had time to do it. But I haven't been back to Provincetown since 1988, almost ten years.

I do remember walking around town handing out flyers for *Multiple Maniacs* and *Mondo Trasho*. Were we movie stars in

Provincetown? Before *Pink Flamingos*, we were completely taken for granted. We were the next-door neighbors, the people who worked in shops.

SUSAN LOWE

Susan Lowe came to Baltimore in 1966 to study at the Maryland Institute College of Art as a seventeen-year-old, and soon met Divine, Howard Gruber, Van Smith. "I became a fag hag and fell into things: nudity, drinking, pot, and sex. Fun!" Her infamous attempt to hitchhike to P'town with Mink Stole and Cookie Mueller is immortalized in Mueller's essay "Abduction and Rape—Highway 31, Elkton, Maryland, 1969," in the 1997 posthumous collection *Ask Dr. Mueller.*

I met the very cool, quasi-punky Sue Lowe when I visited Baltimore, and we ate dinner with Bonnie Pearce in a cheapo Asian restaurant. Our interview was by phone weeks later. Interestingly, Lowe was cautious about implicating others in her wild adventures of the sixties and seventies, taking the blame herself for any indiscretions. Simply, she was a hopeless alcoholic then, out of control. "I was crazy, or having kids," she said.

Lowe has been one of Waters's people forever, as much for her off-screen friendships and Dreamlander nightclub acts as for his movies. She took small roles in his films, but her one substantial role is among the best-remembered, WaMole McHenry, in *Desperate Living* (1977). (Her part, I assume, is a splendid homage to duck-tailed, leather-jacketed Mercedes McCambridge in Orson Welles's *Touch of Evil.*) "Sue's so convincing," Waters told me, "that people always assume she's that butch role in real life."

Not at all. Lowe has long given up liquor, but, these days, she's got piles of boyfriends. She's also a university art teacher, finishing an erudite master's degree, and an extremely accomplished painter. She's represented in Provincetown by the Bangs Street Gallery.

In the summer of 1969, Mink, Cookie, and I hitched to P'town. We got a little house off Bradford Street, and I got a job at the fish factory. I was like a bum, hanging out with Howard Gruber, David Lochary, and Divine, and playing canasta. That was me on a calmer day. I was very drunk all the time, hardly ever dressed, crazy, hustling customers in the bars for drinks.

All the businesses went to Town Hall to complain about me, that's what I remember. Town Hall people came to my door and told me I disrupted the town. So I decided to hitch home. I ended up in Pittsburgh on a fishing trip, where these guys were going to rape me. Then I met these hippies, we tripped all night, and they gave me a ticket back to Baltimore. Then John Liesenring and I hitched to New Mexico to live on a hippie farm. After a month, we hitched back to Baltimore. I was tired of traveling, and I was eighteen!

The next year, I was on the rebound. I was modeling at the Maryland Art Institute, seduced this drawing teacher. We went to Ireland, got married, and I got pregnant. The next year, we were in Provincetown. My husband (we were married for seven years, two children) was building houses. He built one in Truro. I worked at Town Hall, selling 250th anniversary tchotchkes. Nobody noticed it was me back in town again. I didn't do much drinking: "It's time for cocktails and a bike ride."

I had children! Then my husband left me when the youngest was three. I was on welfare. I always had boyfriends and girlfriends, and I was back in P'town in 1976–77. I had a biker boyfriend, Kenny Orye, who played Eater in *Desperate Living*. He owned a bar in Baltimore's Fell's Point, used to run guns to Ireland. Everybody in P'town loved him. He was funny, and we were all crazy and dysfunctional. He played guitar, sometimes sat in on my band. He died about ten years ago of substance abuse.

I had a cabaret review, the BB Steel Revue and the Fabulous Stilettos. We played Max's and CBGB's in New York, and they loved us in P'town. I was the lead singer, Cookie and Sharon Niesp were backups. Also, Edith Massey played with us, and she did "Fever," "Over the Rainbow," and "Rhinestone Cowgirls."

Edith came to P'town twice. Howard Gruber treated us to dinner at Front Street, and Edith couldn't get over the gourmet food. She couldn't eat. She wanted chicken wings, or something like that. The Back Room gave me and Edith a room for free and a bar tab. They gave *me* a tab! Edith was mean when she got drunk, so she knew she shouldn't drink.

She wouldn't have been comfortable staying in P'town. She liked her little Baltimore shop. I traveled with her in the car from Baltimore to P'town and, let me tell you, she never was quiet! She'd count Volkswagens out loud.

In 1976, when I played the Back Room, they thought I was a drag queen. I'd tell them I was. I had a flamenco gown, red and glittery, and I'd do birdcalls. That's how I'd open up. I'd do Tina Turner songs, then rip off my clothes and be there in a miniskirt.

Though I'd started out in art school, in those days in P'town, I was more interested in being a movie star and being connected with theater people. I knew where the galleries were, but that's it. If we saw Robert Motherwell, we couldn't care less.

After the end of a second marriage, I've learned to live with myself. And I'm long sober. In the summer of 1996, I was in P'town for three weeks because the Bangs Street Gallery was including me in a group show. John was going up, Dennis Dermody was going up, and I had the best time. I stayed with Chan, whom I love, who bought some land and turned it into a circle of cottages. Now P'town is mostly a relax place: hang out and enjoy the water. Being with John, we always get a place in a restaurant. Everybody knows who we are.

But P'town has changed a lot. It's been built up. I miss the Fo'c'sle. I was a Fo'c'sle hag! Growing up Catholic, I miss the Blessing of the Fleet. They don't have it anymore. No more ritual. And I rode by Front Street and said "Hi" to it in my memory, but I didn't go in.

SHARON NIESP

In the early seventies, before they lived together, Cookie Mueller had a house on Railroad Avenue, and Sharon Niesp would visit. Gregory Corso would come by for breakfast after stopping at a liquor store for a bottle of Flame Tokay. One time, quite early in the morning, Niesp was sitting at the kitchen table, wearing men's silk pajamas that Cookie had bought in a thrift store. She had left her bridge upstairs. John Waters materialized. "John loves to say that the first time he met me, I sat there 'glowering at him with no teeth.'" She lived yearround in Provincetown until 1976, when she and Mueller moved to New York.

Niesp had already met Waters in 1972 when she performed in a production of the Provincetown Theater Company, *The Killing of Sister*

George. After the play, so effective was her acting, Waters said, "You know, Sharon, I didn't recognize you for the first ten minutes." He asked her to be in his next movie, *Desperate Living,* and in those years, making a movie meant she would go to Baltimore and live with the group for weeks. "Seeing the cast out of character, and then in character in the movie, sometimes there was very little difference!" Other roles followed in *Polyester, Hairspray, Cry-Baby,* and *Serial Mom.* As the films got bigger, her roles got smaller. "I'm not union. I just don't click that way. I'm too busy dealing with life in general."

VINCENT PERANIO

It feels like Poe's Baltimore, that tiny alley with abandoned, decrepit homes in the Fell's Point area. Here Vincent Peranio, John Waters's perennial art designer, lives with his wife, Dolores Deluxe. But what a property! Behind their gingerbread-sized house is a gothic castle's worth of dark gardens, hidden staircases, deserted buildings, all of which Vincent and Dolores plan to reconstruct. Their enthusiastic tour is alone worth a visit to Baltimore.

"I met John in Fell's Point," Peranio said. "Susan Lowe brought him into our house, which housed Maryland Institute of Art students and Johns Hopkins students, and we all hit it off. At one point, I lived with David, John, Cookie, and Mink at one time. I was an artist, and liked all kinds of people."

Peranio is the designer for the Baltimore-shot TV series, *Homicide.* But his greatest achievement was designing *Pink Flamingos* on a two-hundred-dollar budget. The legendary film title was inspired by the plastic lawn ornaments that Peranio decided to put into a shot. "*Pink Flamingos* is the only work of art of mine that has shown at the Museum of Modern Art," he said.

Deluxe, who was art director of *Polyester,* admitted, "I missed the Provincetown thing," though she traveled with her friend Cookie Mueller to a California commune. "But Vincent took me there on a nostalgic trip. I remember going to the Café Blase. And I was surprised about how much more beautiful things were in P'town then I had imagined."

*   *   *

John came back to Baltimore with stories about how wonderful P'town was, how crazy. "You'd love it as an artist," he told me. I visited once, and then had an affair with Mink, between *Multiple Maniacs* and *Pink Flamingos*. That had to be '70–71. I'd missed the summer madness and moved to P'town in October. We stayed with Cookie and Sue Lowe, who were roommates, on Bradford Street. Divine lived three doors up with Howard Gruber. They had a big house and threw big parties. Divine worked in a gourmet kitchen shop and had the best kitchen in town. He stole like crazy from these people, for his fiestas.

Mink was a high-school secretary and dressed like *Pink Flamingos'* Connie Marble: the cat-eyed glasses, the high heels. It says something about P'town that they hired her.

There were a million leather shops at the time, and I started working in one opened by Gus Gutterman on Commercial Street. I made belts, though I didn't have a traditional leather upbringing. I stayed on for several years, including winters. My apartment was seventy-five dollars a month, year round. Thank God for food stamps, which they passed out Labor Day. We needed them, we were so poor. With food stamps, Divine had a fabulous party, and Mink made a steak. Divine cried. He hadn't seen a steak in so long! Our Christmas tree was a scrub branch from the dunes. The decoration was Mink's and Divine's clip-on 1950s jewelry.

There's no bleakness like P'town winter bleakness. I can recall: Way down in the distance on Commercial Street, there'd be a little dark figure walking toward me, and then he'd turn off! One winter, we were so bored we did backup for these poor guys in a band. I guess they were desperate. My other memory is tripping on the dunes, which was a gas! I remember a wonderful February: LSD stops the cold.

Mostly, we'd go dancing at Piggy's, and also pick everybody up. This was before AIDS, and the worst fear was gonorrhea. There was a Puritan law of no dancing on Sundays. At midnight Saturday, there was music but no dancing. On Sundays, dancing started at midnight. We were avid dancers, and this may be the first time a lot of crazy outsiders spent the winter. We went to a town meeting and voted out this two-hundred-year-old law. We outvoted the townies, and that's my great legacy to P'town: Let them dance any night of the week!

Mink was a star, especially in P'town. She had this long scarf and did an Isadora Duncan: Her scarf got caught in the spokes of her bike. Mink and I had a rather torrid, storybook romance. After we would scream in the streets. She'd come into a coffee house and say, "I wish I could have a child named Vincent and kill it." How can you break up in P'town and not see each other? I moved for a month into a tent.

I bought a '54 station wagon and drove it back to Baltimore to do *Pink Flamingos*. In traffic, the brakes failed, and I crashed through cement steps. I was instantly in debt for damaging property. I've been pretty much encased in Baltimore since, including paying off that debt, though I hold P'town dear in my heart.

CHANNING WILROY

Channing Wilroy is the only Dreamlander who still lives in Province-town. In 1979, he bought a cottage colony on Pearl Street, between Henry Hensche's and the Fine Arts Work Center. He fixed it up and rents it out. "I was on P'town radio, playing fifties R&B on WOMR. 'The Night Train,' that was me. And I make telephone art."

Originally, he was a teen TV star in Baltimore, dancing rock 'n' roll for three years on the legendary *Buddy Dean Show*. The pro-totype of Dick Clark's *American Bandstand,* the program provided the inspiration, and chief setting, for John Waters's 1988 rock com-edy, *Hairspray.*

In a way, Wilroy was the first celebrity to appear in a Waters movie. Waters had admired him jitterbugging on TV. "I never auditioned for *Pink Flamingos,*" he said. "John asked me if I wanted to be in it. I played the Marbles' chauffeur-impregnator. In *Female Trouble,* I played the prosecutor who sends Fatso to the electric chair. In *Desperate Living* I played the Captain of the Queers Goon Squad. And I was music coordinator for *Cry-Baby,* using my 1950s R&B records."

He laughed when asked to comment on the capabilities of Wa-ters's friends/actors in the films. "Some are better than others," he said, "but the fact that some suck adds character. We've got to give credit to Divine and Mink as the best. Otherwise, I really don't know how to judge. I do know I've gotten a lot of feedback. And we must have done something right if *Pink Flamingos* is around after twenty-five years."

I came to Provincetown in 1966 with Pat Moran and her husband at the time. John was here, and we'd all known each other from Baltimore. P'town is where we got to be very good friends. I'd been coming to summer resorts to work, but I thought that P'town was an unusual place. My summer season got longer and longer, and I decided to stay. I've been living permanently in P'town since 1969.

In 1969, 1970, and 1971, I lived with Divine, and there was never a dull moment. He pulled a number of capers, and we always had to move because there was no rent money. We lived with George Tamsitt, also from Baltimore. I don't know which of them, George or Divine, was more full of shit and pulled the wool more over the other's eyes.

You've heard about when Divine auctioned off all his furniture? His landlady was Carey Seamen, a lawyer–real estate agent, quite old with lots of money and cheaper than shit. Divine was no longer here when the warrant was issued, but it lasted for seven years!

Divine ran a thrift shop, Divine Trash, on Bradford Street. Downstairs was the Penny Farthing Restaurant. He worked in his store and sold old clothing, china, bric-a-brac, collectibles. Some of the stuff came from the Truro dump. But he got in trouble because he didn't have a permit for a shop. Cookie Mueller was living with us at the time. That was the year she got pregnant and had Max.

I was a chef at the Inn at The Mews in 1969 and 1970. Then I owned my own restaurant, Channings, where The Commons is today. Then I went back to manage The Mews. David Lochary lived with me in 1975, when I had my restaurant. How would he spend his day? Picking out his outfits for the evening, or sitting in front of a makeup mirror wondering how he should present himself.

David was doing lots of LSD. We all were. David reveled in it more than the rest of us. Also, he was a star, and liked to be treated as such. He went to New York and died, most likely an angel dust casualty. And he was drinking. He was still alive when found in his apartment. He had fallen on a glass and cut himself.

I go back to Baltimore occasionally and visit, but those great days in P'town are a while ago. They're becoming a blur.

DENNIS DERMODY

Dennis Dermody is John Waters's best male friend, and he's not from Baltimore. "I was appropriated by the Baltimore people," he told me when we talked on the phone. In the seventies, he met the Dreamlanders one by one when he lived in P'town. Since, he's been to Baltimore as a house guest many times, and he lived there during the 1980 shooting of *Polyester*. He assumed the management of Pat Moran's Charles Theater so that she could work on the movie. A longtime New Yorker who doesn't drive, Dermody took a bus to work every day in Baltimore. Also, he was on the *Polyester* set for key days of shooting, like when four-hundred-pound Jean Hill bit a bus tire. He even appeared in one shot (his only appearance in a Waters movie): "I'm the last pervert coming out of the theater showing the film, *My Burning Bush*," he says proudly.

The one-time off-off-Broadway ticket-taker met Willem Dafoe through the Wooster Group, and Dermody started his long-held job as nanny for Dafoe's son, Jack. He's also senior editor and, for ten years, film critic for the spunky New York–based magazine *Paper*. Dermody's movie reviews are knowledgeable, irreverent, genuinely hilarious, and share Waters's adoration of the absurd and bizarre.

I was working in Connecticut with retarded children, and I decided, "I've got to get out of here!" I came for the summer to P'town in 1972 and was there outside of John's opening of *Pink Flamingos*. The actors arrived in cabs! I went to the theater that week and saw it, and said, "Thank God, there are people as fucked up as I am."

I met Cookie first, and she said, "Let's make a date to go to the movies." When I went over there, she was in the kitchen peeling potatoes, and her son, Max, was sobbing. "Potatoes are my friends," she said. "Max loves potatoes."

The movie we saw was *Executive Action,* and we got friendly. Cookie said to me, "You've got the same crap on the wall as John, you've got to meet him." She meant horror posters, similar kinds of books and artifacts. We read the same books—Grove Press publications: *The Naked Lunch,* John Rechy's *City of Night.* There was a murder in town that summer; a woman was found without hands. John got it into his head that I had the hands. He'd bug me, "I know you've got the hands. Show me! I'll give you twenty-five dollars!"

I worked in a record store, then I started spinning records at Piggy's, and it was really bizarre. You had two turntables, you weren't in a booth, and people literally would come up and rip records out of your hands. But you could mix anything. I remember on some JFK memorial day I played a John Kennedy speech, and then Junior Walker's "Shotgun" could be heard coming up in the background. People laughed!

I saw David Lochary at Piggy's, and he had a cool way of dancing. He had a great look: the Hawaiian shirts, the beard, the white-bleached hair. He cut quite a figure. We were in a play together, *The Man Who Came to Dinner.* I was Henderson, the ax murderer, with one line: "Yes!" David was the all-American gentleman caller! Can you imagine! Actually, David did lots of theater, and he was inimitable on stage, with his special charm.

I worked at The Movies, and eventually, for about five years, I was the manager. It was funky fun—old films, art films—and we'd yell at the customers. We showed *Pink Flamingos* and *Desperate Living* at midnight. I was always obsessive about movies. I'd hitch into Boston, see four movies, then hitch back. I remember one winter when we all went into Boston to see Robert Altman's *Thieves Like Us.*

I became close to John, and we corresponded in the winters. I was in Provincetown from 1972–1981, almost ten years year-round. I'm glad that actor Ron Vawter dragged me out of there. Otherwise, I'd be a four-hundred-pound alcoholic at the Old Colony. I remember a showing of a video of John Huston's *The Bible* at the Governor Bradford. The bartender said, with no irony, "The book was so much better." I thought, "I've got to leave!"

In New York, I lived with Mink Stole for a little while. That didn't work out. I love her, but not as a roommate! I was screaming for her when she won fifteen thousand dollars on TV on *Scrabble,* appearing three days under her real name, Nancy Stole. She is fabulous!

I've known John for more than twenty years. I go to his house in

Baltimore for Christmas, and, in the summer, we drive to P'town together. What do I do there now? Go to a disco? I'm fifty! I never went to the beach. I do have friends there, but they are "reclusive," to put it mildly.

PAT MORAN

She's tiny, tough, and Jeanne Moreau good-looking. I talked to Pat Moran on Baltimore's waterfront, in the production offices of TV's *Homicide*, for which Moran is casting director. Before that, she ran Baltimore's premiere arthouse, the Charles Theater. She's also John Waters's three-decade very best friend, and confidante, and right-hand/left-hand person on the set of every one of his films. "My Siamese twin," he calls her.

"John and I have been hanging out for more than thirty years, and we talk *constantly*," she told me. "If he's on his way to New York, I'll call to make sure he gets there. Or he'll call me and leave a message that he's arrived. And after being together so many years, I know when he walks in the door that it's him!"

Moran is tremendously smart, and down-to-earth, and remains a sixties political outsider from the left. Before we discussed Provincetown, Moran railed articulately against American government policy, then we talked old movies. She's an expert, adoring Bette Davis especially, and making me promise to see a French film called *Baxter* about a murderous dog.

Why did I first go to P'town? Have you been in Baltimore in the summer with the humidity? It's like living in the Mekong Delta. But in those days, the sixties, people were footloose and fancy-free. Times were different, and you could pack up a car and take off. P'town was reasonable enough to work and live there. The guy I was with there first had a job as a bartender at the Provincetown Inn.

In later years, after I had kids, we'd vacation there for two or three weeks. It's the greatest place in the world for kids, who can run around and everybody looks out for them. I have two—one is twenty-nine, the other twenty-four—and we started to bring my oldest son when he was six. I went there always with Chuck, who's been my husband for twenty-six years. He's a contractor who has nothing to do with the movies.

We never shared an apartment with John, Mink, and the Baltimore gang. My husband would find us a place in the East End. Or we'd stay with Howard Gruber, or a lot of the time we'd stay at Poor Richard's Landing, which was perfect for my family. It was almost all gay people except for us. Poor Richard's had no sign, so you'd have to swing a gate. But when you're in there, you can sit in back and watch twenty-thousand million stars. What's the sense of P'town if you can't be right on the water? And why would you need to go to Truro? If you'd been to Poor Richard's before they filled in underneath, it was just great.

John and I have had an odd relationship with the scripts. Even though I always kind of knew what they were about in P'town, and when he was on to something, I didn't ask him what he was writing. Even today, I don't ask him.

If John is working on a screenplay, I won't talk to him from seven in the morning until twelve. Then I'll give him a few minutes until maybe twelve-thirty. In P'town, I was always an early riser. If John was writing, I was walking up and down, looking out my window, maybe heading down to the Portuguese bakery. My husband might go shop at the fish market. Then we'd all meet up at the beach, usually off of the Landing.

On a typical day, we'd actually sit in the sun, though with five hundred newspapers and maybe a trashy book, some great summer read. It was also great when a news story would break. Everyone would have an opinion, a big deal.

Sometimes, people would want to go off to Race Point, which was too athletic for me. And why would I want to go dancing? Why the hell was I at the beach?

For dinner, Chuck would cook sometimes, or maybe we'd go out, though in those days it took forever to dress, to finally see Howard at Front Street, his restaurant. Chan Wilroy was cooking at the time, and Dennis Dermody would meet us there after he got off work at The Movies. After Front Street, we'd sit on The Benches gabbing, or we'd walk up to Spiritus. Or five or six kids would go up to Spiritus alone, even if it was ten o'clock, and get a pizza. Or there were three movie theaters we could go to.

And we'd do the same thing the next day. Basically, the day was busy doing nothing. It was getting used to doing nothing in a place that was great to do it.

Well, the best day to me was the parade: magical! One float was with local firemen, another float was with Jimmy James, who looked more like Marilyn Monroe than any man ever did. That day we'd have a big lobster cookout, often at Dennis's.

The best thing, though not to John, was that there was no telephone. It would take a few days to get used to it. But for John it was, "Jees, I've got to walk up to Bryant's!" He'd walk there five times a day, to that phone booth, and try to get his shows together.

When *Homicide* was born, I stopped going to P'town. I haven't been there in the last four years. But if I could figure out how to be in P'town from May to October and Baltimore from October through March, that would be happiness.

It's almost as if P'town isn't part of America. It's not harsh: It's a place where John, a nonathletic person and a sports bigot, rides a bicycle.

Hollywood Shuffle

BY ISABEL WILKERSON

A willowy actress the color of earth is making her way through the golden dream set of a Hollywood premiere. She has just had her big break, starring in a docudrama about starlets trying to make it in the big time. And this is the celebration, the glorious bath of hugs and backslaps and half-jealous exclamations of "Dahling, you were fabulous!" The woman in question has the cheekbones of an African sculpture and the full goddess lips that some blondes in Hollywood pay a whole lot of money for. She is trying to get her bearings when a white agent pulls her aside to give her some advice. "Listen," he says, convinced it's for her own good. "You're obviously the most talented girl up there. But you're not going to work in this town. You're a nigger black, and in this town, we like the Vanessa Williams type."

This is what actually happened to Tyra Ferrell, who, after that unwanted advice thirteen years ago, went on to a solid acting career, playing the single mother who loses her son in *Boyz N the Hood,* the

FROM *ESSENCE*

proper love interest of a white storekeeper in *Jungle Fever,* the glamorous owner of the beauty shop in *Poetic Justice,* and the wife opposite Wesley Snipes in *White Men Can't Jump,* among other roles. If the world were a different place, today she would probably be a black Susan Sarandon to Angela Bassett's, say, Meryl Streep. But the world—and Hollywood, according to more than a dozen black actresses and directors interviewed about their experiences—has yet to figure out what to make of black women and how to present full and accurate portrayals on-screen. And it has less to do with the Tyra-versus-Vanessa, dark-versus-light craziness the small-minded agent alluded to than with what Hollywood will do with either one of them.

Hollywood is a complicated machine that sends the rest of America an image of itself through the eyes of the white men who run the place. And for black women, that historically has meant being cast at the margins as either caretaker to the white characters or as a sassy bit of exotica. It is a measure of Hollywood's narrow vision of black women's roles that the Academy of Motion Picture Arts and Sciences has nominated only fourteen black women out of nearly seven hundred nominations for best actress and best supporting actress in the seventy years since the first Oscar was awarded for the 1927–28 film season. Only two black women have actually won and never as leading ladies—Hattie McDaniel for her role as Mammy in *Gone with the Wind* and Whoopi Goldberg as the screwball psychic in *Ghost.* Ultimately, both were rewarded for playing caretakers tending to the needs of the white lead characters.

Just as race relations are more muddled and contradictory in the 1990s, with blacks present in virtually every aspect of American life but few in control of very much—and most still struggling to survive—so is the big Hollywood mirror. Clearly we've come a long way from the days when black characters were summarily edited out of movies in southern theaters or when the best role a black woman could get was being maid to Miss Scarlett. On its face, the past year or so was a time to celebrate: *Waiting to Exhale* opened number one at the box office and made more than $65 million, thanks in part to the legions of black women who went two and three times to make sure it did well. It was a black woman (Whoopi Goldberg again) who presided over last year's Oscars. And a whole new class of young black actresses seemed to be everywhere in major roles, from Theresa Randle in *Girl 6* to Vanessa Williams in *Eraser* to Halle Berry in *The Rich Man's Wife* to Queen Latifah, Vivica Fox, and Jada Pinkett in *Set It Off.*

"Black women historically have been presented as either subhuman or superhuman," says Dianne Houston, the first black woman nominated for an Oscar in directing for her short film *Tuesday Morning Ride.* "Now we are starting to emerge as simply human, and that's a wonderful thing."

At the same time, there's another bittersweet reality. Last year no black actors or actresses were nominated for an Oscar during a time with perhaps more major roles for African-Americans than in recent memory. The post-*Exhale* explosion of sista movies many black actresses hoped for hasn't materialized. Some say the Hollywood powers-that-be still dismiss the success of *Exhale* as a fluke. But, more disturbing, some of the most talented black actresses say that no matter how strong a part they get, one thing does not seem to lead to another like it does for talented white actresses. Because, old-timers say, the world according to Hollywood starts with the white hero (Schwarzenegger, Cruise, Harrison Ford, take your pick) and adds everybody else like interchangeable Lego pieces.

"Hollywood has perfected the formula of the white male hero with the white girlfriend and the black male mentor or sidekick with no visible love life," says veteran TV actress Ellen Holly, author of the recent memoir *One Life.* "You see Brad Pitt and Morgan Freeman in *Seven,* or Harrison Ford and James Earl Jones in *Clear and Present Danger.* You see the white hero making millions, positioned against a young white female nobody they can hire for spit and a black celibate sidekick. Where is the black woman in this? Scrambling."

THE *EXHALE* ALUMNAE CLUB

There is hardly a black actress on the planet who in some corner of her mind did not imagine herself as either Savannah, Bernadine, Robin, or Gloria. The movie was the black actress's equivalent of the Hollywood Lotto. It was going to be big. It could make a career. No matter what anybody wanted, Whitney and Angela claimed the main characters, and the only roles left for the entire black female acting population were Robin and Gloria. Lela Rochon and Loretta Devine wore their too-tight dresses for that "Yeah, I'm desperate" look and got the parts. And the rest was a fairy tale. Or was it?

Loretta Devine is mulling this over in front of a plate of chicken and dumplings at an L.A. restaurant. "For us, we always have to start over," she says. Just the day before she had auditioned for a role she did not think she would get. She has a master's in fine arts from Brandeis, and after twenty years in the business, after Broadway, and even after *Exhale*, she still has to go out for casting calls and wonder if "she'll get it." She is taller and thinner than you expect, and not easily recognizable at first because of the braids hanging down her shoulders and because, in her eminent practicality, she is driving a Ford Contour, which it's hard to imagine somebody recently in a major motion picture driving. In her baby-powder voice, she explains the reality: "You may have been a star in the show, and the next month you're auditioning with the people who were extras. And it can be embarrassing if you're not ready for it."

It's a basic supply-and-demand problem: There's such a huge well of talent and so few places to put it that if there's a buzz about any role calling for a black actress, just about everybody in town shows up. There are other problems. Black leading men, the oldest barely forty (Denzel, Wesley, and Laurence Fishburne, mainly), are usually paired with women much younger than they, if they are paired with black women at all (remember Julia Roberts closing the hotel-room door on Denzel in *The Pelican Brief*, if you can believe it). Either way, a whole generation of actresses in their thirties and forties lose out.

On top of that, trained actresses who paid their dues in theater doing their Ophelias and Lady Macbeths must make peace with Hollywood's taste for stars imported from the music industry, where it has been easier for blacks to make a name for themselves. Whitney Houston came ready-made to Hollywood with an international fan club who wanted to see her on-screen. Toni Braxton is the latest singer to pursue a film career, as Diana Ross, Vanessa Williams, and Queen Latifah did.

Anyone in Hollywood will tell you that it takes more than acting ability to make it, anyway, and all the more for black actresses. Cicely Tyson did not get the big film roles after *Sounder*, despite her Oscar nomination. Even Angela Bassett, the reigning black screen diva, is not out there as much as blacks in Hollywood think someone with her talent should be, especially after *Exhale.* "As great as she is, she doesn't work enough," says John Singleton, the director who brought her to the masses when he cast her in *Boyz N the Hood.*

The biggest paradox is that while most black thespians try to squeeze through this giant bottleneck, perhaps the busiest person in Hollywood is a black woman with dreadlocks and no eyebrows: Whoopi Goldberg. Her career—playing mostly versions of her own wacky film self—seems out of the orbit of anyone black or white, male or female. She is a brilliant comedian whose talents fit easily into the white American perception of a black performer.

But just as Tiger Woods's millions do little to ease the way of blacks who like golf, Whoopi's singular screen persona does not lend itself to imitation from other black actresses. There's one Roseanne, one Phyllis Diller, one Lucille Ball. And there's one Whoopi Goldberg. And while she is able to do dramatic roles, it is also clear that white America seems to reward her most when she stays within the comfortable world of kitschy comedy.

THE OSCAR NOMINEE

Margaret Avery could do Katharine Hepburn or Bette Davis if ever they wrote parts like that for black women. She grew up watching old black-and-white film classics and "all those wonderful actresses with their cigarettes" and vaguely British accents. She studied acting in Los Angeles and took what she could get—regional theater and girlfriend parts during the blaxploitation era. Her lines in one movie required her to call the hero boyfriend "cheeky baby," and she worked it as if it were Shakespeare, to get it just right. "I never looked at it as fun," she says. "It was always, what might I have done to make it better?"

Eventually even those roles dried up. "Vonetta McGee, Lonette McKee, none of us could buy a job," she says. When those campy plots moved to television, so did Avery. If you look close enough at old reruns like *Kojak* or *The Streets of San Francisco,* you might see her doing the sophisticated prostitute–informer gig or playing the mother crying over the son who went to jail. She did a guest spot on *The Jeffersons* and was Lamont's girlfriend on *Sanford and Son* a couple of times.

Then came the part of a lifetime, a wonderful actress-with-the-cigarette role, Shug, the blues singer who is one third of a love triangle in *The Color Purple*. "I just said, 'Thank you, Jesus,' " says Avery, who was nominated for a best-supporting-actress Oscar for her role. "It was my first decent film.

"I knew this was going to be a really big movie," she continues. "I said to myself, *Make the most of this, Margaret*." She went to top Hollywood agencies to help build on the momentum. "They all turned me down. They said it was too difficult to manage a black actress. It wasn't worth their commission for what they would have to endure.

"After *The Color Purple*, I really got a jolt. I didn't work for a year and a half. The parts that followed were never pivotal in taking me to another level. They just kept me working. You just save and invest and prepare for when it ends. I went up for one role and the casting directors said, 'This role calls for someone to speak excellent English. Can Margaret do that? We need her to speak without a dialect.' They don't say that to Meryl Streep just because she does a Polish accent in a movie. If I speak in a southern dialect, they think that's me. I can't be acting."

In her perfect Queen's English, she says she relied on the college lecture circuit and television to sustain her after the Oscars were over. "I said, 'I can't wait 'til another black film comes,' " she recalls. "I did eight films since *The Color Purple* that went straight to video or the foreign market." She was last seen as Harry Belafonte's wife in a John Travolta vehicle, *White Man's Burden*.

In the meantime, she has tried to grow in other ways. "I have things in my life so I don't fall apart," she says. "So I don't give the business power over me." Avery has earned a master's degree in psychology and is working toward a Ph.D. She is also a single parent with a college-age daughter. "Right now I'm not young enough and I'm not old enough. I can't compete with Della Reese and Maya Angelou and the beautiful Ruby Dee. My time will come. I owe it to myself to be aware of the trends so I don't beat up on myself."

THE GOOD SOLDIERS

"I was up for a very big film," a poised and radiant black actress is saying. The woman speaking happens to be Sheryl Lee Ralph, who played in *Mistress* with Robert De Niro and *To Sleep with Anger* with

Danny Glover. She is in her dressing room on the set of *Moesha,* where she plays the stepmother. It's between rehearsals. "I screen-tested for this film. The director looked at me, straight in my eye. The man said to me, 'You're an incredibly talented actress. But you frighten me.' Amazing what comes out of their mouths. As an actress, you don't have to like it. But you have no choice but to get used to it." So she told herself this director just couldn't deal with strong women and left it at that.

Obstacles can come in all directions. In a world still run by men, black actors have increasing say in whom they are paired with, and some fall as easily into the White standards of beauty as the studio heads or, as some actresses say, look for leading ladies they can check out off the set. Vanessa Bell Calloway, another thespian who moves between television and film (from Joe Morton's love interest in *Equal Justice* to Angela Bassett's best friend in *What's Love Got to Do with It*), was up for the role of a girlfriend in a major film. The director, producer, and studio had approved her for the part. The leading man in the movie, "a very big black star in our industry right now," Calloway says, vetoed her. "I finally saw him, and I was like, 'What's up? Why are you blocking me for this job?' And this brother who should be trying to help everybody told me, 'You could play my wife or my sister, but you could never play my lover. Nothing personal, Vanessa. I think you're a great actress, but I am not attracted to you.' "

During Sheryl Lee Ralph's time in the business, there were years when there were no black films made, and thus no roles. For several years, the Hollywood NAACP had to omit the category of best black actress. "So few of us had worked in film," she says. "It was one of the saddest periods on record. There was nothing. And it was only yesterday."

To get through it, many actresses—Ralph, Calloway, Tyra Ferrell, Alfre Woodard—have made sure to have a life: husbands, children, carpools, homes outside Hollywood for some of them, faith in a higher power. In the recent past, four gifted survivors—Rosalind Cash, Madge Sinclair, Roxie Roker, and Butterfly McQueen—died back-to-back. Ralph lost mentors in that group. "So many of them went to their graves," she says, "never ever being given the chance to do their best work. Can you imagine what it must be like to have all that love and talent build up inside of you with *no place* for it to go?"

THE ALMOST MOVIE STAR

Tyra Ferrell always saw herself on that big screen even when the plantation-minded children in her Houston neighborhood made fun of the full lips and espresso skin God gave her. "Someone would call me big lips or black blueberry," she says. "I would go into the house and look in the mirror and watch myself cry. Then I would go into my closet and sit among my shoes and toys and convince myself my lips were beautiful. I'd be washing dishes, which was my permanent job, and I would look out the window at the trees and visualize myself on the stage and on the screen. The window was the screen. I could see myself."

She made it to Hollywood all right, but at first not the way she wanted. "I was doing a recurring role on *The Bronx Zoo* as secretary to Ed Asner. I was the one who'd say, 'You have a call on line one.' I was getting paid a thousand dollars a line. But I wasn't feeling full like after a good meal. I felt as if I were in a fog on the set. When the camera was on someone else, I felt empty. I wanted the camera to follow us. I wrote down that I was surrounded by black actors, and we were telling our stories and the camera was following us. I went home and put the piece of paper in my Bible." Before long she found herself on a set surrounded by black actors with the camera following them. She was in *School Daze*, the Spike Lee movie. That piece of paper in the Bible seemed to have worked a miracle.

But success in film still did not ensure acceptance by everyone. At a party after *White Men Can't Jump*, a black man went up to her and asked, "Why *you* of all people?" Ferrell herself had worried that she wasn't "pretty enough," but has learned to deal with the hostility and resentment. "Some of them just don't get it," she says.

She has worked in enough serious roles now to get a lot of offers but not enough that meet her standards and few that match her dreams. "I turn down roles where I come in for one line," she says. "I turn down all half-hour comedies. You notice that black comedies aren't nominated at Emmy time. I'm holding out for something more meaningful for me and for our people. I can only take roles I can be proud of."

*　　*　　*

A STAR TOO SOON

On those days when Jasmine Guy shows up at an audition with twenty or thirty other actresses waiting for their names to be called, people in the room know something's wrong with this picture. "Once, this girl leaned over and said, 'What are *you* doing here?'"

It's true what they say about fame being fleeting and fifteen minutes and all that. Jasmine Guy became a household name playing Whitley on *A Different World* and did *Harlem Nights* with Eddie Murphy. Lately she has been on the guest-star recurring-role circuit on television shows like *Melrose Place* and *Touched by an Angel*. She also did a low-budget action movie set in Jamaica. "I've done four pilots—none of them picked up," she says.

Sitting with her in the cushy white-on-white office of her publicity agent, I realize why we should be seeing more of her. Her hair is short and auburn now. She's wearing a red sheath dress that she models delightedly when I compliment her on it. She admits for some reason she is nervous about being interviewed and moves about the room to demonstrate every anecdote. She has a theatrical persona that makes every sentence a performance—hands extended like a ballerina's, head arching back with laughter—but also an unexpected sad, serious quality. Her normal speaking voice has an accent that's hard to place, sort of Boston by way of Atlanta. But in conversation her voice jumps from white southern to black Jamaican to Brooklyn ghetto girl—all hints of the geography she can cover when given the chance.

Instead of memorizing the lines for the next black Scarlett O'Hara, she now recites the serenity prayer about changing the things she can and accepting the things she can't. "If I get mad about white people, about men, that my career hasn't done what I wanted it to do, it's going to eat me alive. It's going to kill what beauty is in there. I've felt it, and I understand why people lose it out here. You internalize it and feel like you ain't nothing. You feel like a failure. It's hard to look people in the eye. I get a daily reminder that I'm not doing what people expected my career to do: 'Child, where you been?' They don't mean to hurt me. But it sits there in my mind. And I go, 'I'm nothing. Look what happened to you.'

"But it's okay, and I'm still all right even though I don't have a constant barrage of projects going out. There's a price for that kind of work, anyway. I worked for ten years straight, never vacationing. And I really didn't know what to do with just Jasmine. I didn't want to be by myself. I hated myself. I had to be with other people who loved me. And eventually the man thing—I thought I needed a mate all the time. Standards plummeted, let me tell you. I made so many exceptions and dropped so many little rules it wasn't funny."

Like everybody else, she wants to break free from the assumptions about what black actresses can play. "I used to fight the battles with my agents," she says. " 'Why can't I go up for a part that Meg Ryan and Julia Roberts are going up for? That's what I am.' They're like, 'They won't make this an interracial couple, the pretty woman thing.' I'm like, 'Do you know how many black prostitutes there are out there, and how many white boys go out to buy it?' That wasn't realistic to them. But they didn't want to be realistic. They wanted white people."

She knows it's not easy for anybody in this town. "I have darker friends whom the casting directors ask, 'Can you do that head thing? Can you be more ghetto?' " she says.

Like a lot of actresses, Guy is working on projects of her own. She wants to develop some Octavia Butler stories, for instance. In the meantime, she hits the audition circuit where the choices can be painfully backward. "I'm up for a slave role this week," she says. "Another miniseries set during the Civil War. They love that time. Do they not love that time? It's the same movie over and over. That's why I'm tired. I'm bored."

THE GRANDE DAME

Ruby Dee entered the business during the early 1950s, when all you could get were maid roles. And you just gritted your polished, high-falutin teeth and did it. Her first television role was a maid she thinks was named Hattie. "It was part of the atmosphere," she says. She finally graduated to fuller characters and was Lutiebell in *Purlie Victorious,* Ruth in *Raisin in the Sun,* has done Shakespeare on stage, and played too many roles to mention. "I did all right for a colored girl," she says.

Dee's career has lasted several decades, and yet, incredibly, she says, "I keep waiting for my big break. I'd like to see the marvelous and challenging roles I dream about and read in novels." She says she'd like to see the work of Zora Neale Hurston adapted to the screen, for instance. She has written and adapted many stage productions herself between film roles. And still, she says, "No matter how successful something is, you wonder, *Will I ever work again?*"

She is not convinced that Hollywood has changed all that much. So she has learned not to expect too much from the industry. "You're not surprised when you're not included in the main event," she says. "It's a very frustrating life and career unless you keep fighting for the things you love and believe in. The sanity is to find ways to be a human being and an artist despite the racism. And if you're lucky, you'll be a success."

Now do you remember the agent who told Tyra Ferrell she'd never work in Hollywood because she was supposedly, you know, the *N* word? Well, Ferrell later heard he died. And although Margaret Avery did not win the Oscar for Shug, she still has the Tanzanian wood carving of black figures clinging to one another that she received at the Black Academy Awards, a small, sequined affair held at some fabulous L.A. hotel every year the night before the Oscars. It honors the black film actors who were nominated—or should have been—and odds are will not walk away with the gold statuette the next night. "That tribute meant everything to me," Avery says. "It's a way to validate ourselves, because you can't get validation from Hollywood." And even though she has not had an easy time getting work since Shug, she's ecstatic over the success of Whitney and Angela and whoever else gets a break. Because, she says, they'll be needing an aunt or a mother or a friend or a big sister. And that means there will be a role for her.

Relinquishing Oz: Every Girl's Anti-Adventure Story

BY BONNIE FRIEDMAN

I was always stricken, as a child, at the moment when the Wicked Witch in *The Wizard of Oz* cried, "I'm mellllting!" The shocked anguish on her face, the way she crumpled to the floor—guilt overcame me. As much as I'd hated her before (and I had: She was cruel and she was voracious. She wanted everything for herself), suddenly, to my surprise, remorse washed over me, and painful sympathy: She was my own mother, dissolving!

Quick, she mustn't be let die! Prop her up! A terrible mistake must have been made! And the moment I had expected to feel thrilled triumph (as we would have if this were a boy's story: We're glad the knight slays the dragon) turned out to be in fact spiked with a baffling sense of betrayal.

But wasn't the girl supposed to win? Wasn't the Wicked Witch evil? And how had my mother snuck into it all?

The boy's coming-of-age story is about leaving home to save the

FROM *MICHIGAN QUARTERLY REVIEW*

world. The girl's coming-of-age story is about relinquishing the world beyond home. It is about finding a way to sacrifice one's yearning for the big world, the world of experience, and to be happy about it. At its center is the image of the hungry woman, the desirous, commanding, grasping woman who shows herself with a blow to our heart—her ultimate weapon—to be the woman we love most.

Or is she?

As a child, I wasn't sure. Watching the witch suddenly dissolve, I knew I'd glimpsed something. I was snagged. Distracted. The story stopped for me right there. I was no longer immersed. Because maybe one wasn't meant to vanquish the dragon. Maybe one shouldn't have hated that witch so much. Maybe, maybe . . . and a sort of unraveling happened—one had misunderstood, one had got one's signals crossed, one was too impulsive, eager, girlish. Precisely because it never got looked at—in girls' stories, in my own life, the plot rushed on—this unease remained: a suspicion of one's flaring impulses. A tendency to go vague. The sort of dubiousness that makes a student shoot her hand up in class, but then, quite slowly, lower it, and afterward trail home unsettled, head bent.

At a certain point in my own life, everything partook of this same confusion. I had gotten something I craved—a writing contract, a broomstick of my own—only to find to my dismay it wasn't what I wanted at all. I was blocked, locked, grounded. How had I learned to be paralyzed? In the absence of my own particular memory, I found myself obsessed with the great cultural memory of Dorothy in Oz. Besides the moment the witch's face alters, I kept thinking about the scene in which Dorothy is locked in the witch's keep. "Auntie Em!" she cries, in Judy Garland's signature throbbing voice, while Em, in the crystal ball, calls "Dorothy! . . . Where are you? We're trying to find you!" turning and peering and vanishing into Kansas.

"Oh, don't go away," cries Dorothy. But it's too late. Em, never even suspecting the possibility of Oz, is gone. How far the daughter has traveled from her mother! Into realms unimaginable. Like a girl who leaves home for erotic love and can't come back. Or a daughter whose ambitions transport her far from her mother's values. "Oh, don't go away!" rang in my mind, and my eyes dripped. Locked in my own prison, blocked in my work, I identified without knowing why. Gradually, though, I began to see how Dorothy's story is the story of many women and men who find ourselves stuck.

The Wizard of Oz is so familiar it resembles a childhood ritual more than a concocted work of entertainment. Even though I hadn't seen the movie in twenty years, when I watched it again the other night I found myself murmuring key lines with the characters. The rhythms were in my body like the rhythms of Mother Goose, like the pulse of a song that's on the radio so low you don't notice it, yet your feet tap to its beat, and you are nodding your head.

Dorothy is racing up the road, all in a frazzle. "Auntie Em!" she cries. "Uncle Henry!" Her little charge, Toto, has gotten into some natural, even hormonal mischief chasing Miss Gulch's cat. Yet the punishment will be dreadfully severe. It just doesn't seem fair! But Dorothy, like a quintessential adolescent, comes off as all elbows and histrionic gasps. She's only in the way. "Dorothy, please! We're trying to count!" her aunt chastises. "Don't bother us now," says Uncle Henry. They're gathering up eggs, and Dorothy will make them lose track. Financial troubles threaten the farm; there's no time for Dorothy's breathless complaints.

The situation is the same with the rest of the people in this dusty, grim world; the farmhands are all busy, or give silly heedless advice. "You going to let that old Gulch heifer buffalo you? Next time she squawks, walk right up to her and spit in her eye. That's what *I'd* do," counsels Zeke.

"Aw, you just won't listen, that's all!" says Dorothy. Her sense of what's crucial is so different from the adults', and no one really regards what she says as important at all, although it's obvious they love her. Her aunt seems impatient for Dorothy to grow up and realize what really matters (counting eggs; perhaps she'd like Dorothy to start noticing the eggs inside her), to give up childish concerns and take responsibility for the womanliness her body suggests she already has. Dorothy wears a pinafore that crams her breasts against her and spills into a frothy white yoke of blouse; every other woman in the movies wears a dress. Dorothy seems to have outgrown her childish frock without noticing, or perhaps she's installed in a sort of transitional training dress, like the training wheels on a bicycle before a child knows how to maintain her balance, or like a "training bra," those concoctions of padding and lace meant to train—not one's breasts, certainly. Well, then, one's mind into an acceptance of one's breasts. Or the boys in one's class into an acceptance of one's acceptability.

How tired out Aunt Em looks! One of the characters describes her face as "careworn," as if she'll soon be erased, rubbed away. Perhaps Em would like Dorothy to fill in for her, but Dorothy won't take the bit. She frolics, she indulges in what others see as self-absorbed emotion. In her exuberance, she tries idly walking the balance beam of the fencetop between the animal pens, tomboyish, but tumbles right into the hogs' slovenly pen. The big loud beasts start to trample her. She shrieks. Finally a man rescues her and the other farmhands rush up. Their circle of warm laughter is descended upon by the irate Aunt Em.

Dorothy's first fall is due to her carelessness, her carefreeness, her animal high spirits (she is like Toto, wandering after "trouble." If she were a witch, as the munchkins instantly recognize her to be, we'd call Toto her familiar). Dorothy can't keep her balance. It's as if, with those recent breasts of hers, she no longer knows how to hold herself; she is not used to the weight to being a woman yet. And, in this good middle-American tale, her burgeoning, fence-flouting femaleness lands her flat in the mire of—what? Degradation, being overrun by beasts, and, if unrescued by a good man, even death. Perhaps Dorothy falls *so that* a man will rescue her. The farmhands all come running. She gets them to show concern when Aunt Em won't. Unrescued, though, she would become a "Miss Gulch."

Who exactly is this Gulch? The word *gulch* comes from the Middle English word meaning to gulp, and refers to "a deep or precipitous cleft or ravine, especially one occupied by a torrent" and "containing a deposit of gold." The word *gulch* also meant "to swallow or devour greedily," the way a glutton or drunkard might, and the act of "taking a heavy fall."

A woman who is a gulch is a devouring, appetitive, carnal woman, a torrential woman who will swallow you up into her vacuumous cleft; she is a fallen woman who gulches others and makes them fall too, and she inhabits the sunken places. (I think of Shakespeare's witches on the "blasted heath," that obscure, gashed, watery wasteland. Those hags also draw their power from arousing taboo cravings.) The gulch is aligned with the Devil, with his clefts and his knack for snaring men by using their earthly wants against them. And, in the case of Kansas's particular Elvira Gulch, she is an aging spinster, which in the era of the movie meant she occupied a certain realm of death—undesired, undesiring of men, her sexuality considered a waste, her reproductivity a redundancy, sterile and thwarted. And yet, unlike Aunt Em, she pays a *lot* of attention to Dorothy.

We know from the start that Miss Gulch is a wanting woman—it is *her* demands that set the world of the movie in motion, that set Dorothy rushing up that road of dust in Kansas. The very first words of the picture are "She isn't coming yet, Toto. Did she hurt you, Toto? She tried to, didn't she?" with Judy Garland's frightened face staring straight into the camera toward the impending, wrathful She. In fact, the real, scarcely noticed precipitating event is Dorothy's choosing to go past Miss Gulch's house on the way home. She might have predicted Toto would again invade Miss Gulch's garden. When a farmhand suggests she choose a different way home, Dorothy exclaims, "You just don't understand."

When we see this acquisitive woman, she is anything but fat, as we might expect a ravenous "gulch" might be. She flies into the movie on her bicycle (historically the symbol of a liberated woman: The first bikes were made in retooled corset shops and gave middle-class women freedom of movement; bike makers, in turn, built the first airplanes. Stays to spokes to wings). Miss Gulch is a gnarled skinny vixen stoked with a purposeful fury. She almost trembles with energy. She *will* be satisfied.

Many of the scenes I focus on come from the black-and-white section, by the way. These scenes are like a person's own early history, crucial to understanding the color parts in the same way childhood explains an adult's demeanor, or Rosebud explains Citizen Kane.

"Ga-yle!" trumpets Miss Gulch, saluting Uncle Henry with his last name in a sort of perfunctory military way. "I want to see you and your wife right away. It's about Dorothy."

Uncle Henry stages a few jokes at Miss Gulch's expense. She says she's here because of Dorothy, but she keeps talking about her dog. She's conflated the two. "Dorothy bit you?" he asks. "She bit her *dog?*"

He blinks, holding a whitewashing brush. Apparently he's whitewashing the fence (walls and gates and doors of all sorts figure enormously here). Miss Gulch claims she's almost lame from where Toto bit her on the leg, but she's obviously lying—she immediately glances down and her face takes on an almost guilty look. Besides, she's nowhere near lame; she's one of the most vigorous women imaginable. She announces that Toto is "a menace to the community," when, from the looks of him, he could hardly hurt a fly—he's a tiny, yappy, bright-eyed terrier who extends a paw when Dorothy feels blue, and who remains patiently beside her while her mind roams in daydreams. In fact, he is the only one who pays much loving attention to Dorothy at all—he *is* her all, her "toto," her soul. He is also her mutual-gazer, her adoring lover, her loyal friend.

"He's really gentle. With gentle people, that is," Aunt Em points out.

Bizarrely, Miss Gulch does seem to have an impulsive shrinking terror of the dog—at one point she drops way back in her chair when he is near. It is as if she fears he might recognize her when no one else does, that he might expose her the way he later exposes Oz (it is Toto who drags the curtain away from the man operating the smoke and thunder machine: He has an instinct for truth).

Dorothy would give up everything she has to save him (she proves this when she runs away). Yet Miss Gulch wants to "take him to the sheriff and see that he's destroyed." Why? Out of mere vindictiveness? A warped desire to make Dorothy as lonely as she?

"Their magic must be very powerful or she wouldn't want them so badly," the good witch later says about the Wicked Witch's desire for the red shoes. Aunt Em also identifies the issue as power. "Just because you own half the county doesn't mean you have power over the rest of us!" she exclaims.

But Miss Gulch does. She comes equipped with magic: a slip of paper from the sheriff. If they don't give her the dog, she rants, "I'll bring a suit that will take your whole farm. There's a law protecting people from dogs who bite." How fast the dog has turned into the farm! No one questions this logic.

She claps open her basket (it seems like a torture device), and Aunt Em nods to Uncle Henry to pry the dog from Dorothy, who stares from Henry to Aunt Em, then runs weeping from the room. Aunt Em seems about to lose her composure to the gloating Gulch as she bursts, "Elvira Gulch, for twenty-three years I've been dying to tell you what I think of you—" yet, in classic fashion she concludes, "but now, being a Christian woman, I can't say it!"

Being a "Christian woman," being a woman gagged by the strictures of decorum, Aunt Em is left with the sole response of acquiescing to tyranny and holding her tongue. This is what a "Christian woman" does, her example teaches: She sequesters herself away in her house with her good name (although of course her remark is a marvelous example of passive aggression), while the Miss Gulches of the world cycle off in bitter triumph, what they want secure, for the moment at least, in their woven box.

"Boxes, cases, cupboards, and ovens represent the uterus," Freud noted. Miss Gulch has Dorothy's genie, her wild pleasure, caged up for herself. But her lock can't keep Toto; her basket is not secure. Toto pushes free and gallops back to his rightful owner.

This is a story about who owns what, as any archetypal story about women must be. It is about kidnapping and rekidnapping and ultimate possession. Merged with our mothers, unsure of our boundaries, women's drama often enacts the story of the self in jeopardy, the self that has been absconded with—raped, ravished, invaded, and annexed—and the struggle to get that self back. Demeter and Persephone, Hera and Io, Cinderella, Snow White, Sleeping Beauty, all are about self-possession and the struggle with a rapacious, devouring outside force.

Toto leaps in Dorothy's window (the window is one image for the mind here) and she embraces him. Quick, she realizes, "they" will be back: Her own home is in league with "them" (Aunt Em doesn't even consider challenging the sheriff's order or explaining her viewpoint to this invisible, commanding man. As with Oz's diplomas, what's on paper holds supreme magic). Dorothy heaves her suitcase onto her bed. She will run away.

Frog or dragon figures often begin archetypal stories, according to Joseph Campbell, who writes: "The disgusting and rejected frog or dragon of the fairy tale . . . is the representative of that unconscious deep . . . wherein are hoarded all the rejected, unadmitted, unrecognized, unknown, or undeveloped factors, laws, and elements of existence. . . . Those are the nuggets in the gold hoard of the dragon."

What is Miss Gulch's gold? The powers locked inside Dorothy that are yet unknown. Miss Gulch reveals Dorothy's home's fragility, its inability to keep Dorothy content; it is so much cardboard and whitewash before Miss Gulch's roar. "Then I'll huff, and I'll puff. . . ." Miss Gulch sets Dorothy on her way.

At the end of a long dry road, when she is merely a lonely figure, vulnerable and fatigued, Dorothy comes upon a caravan. It announces the presence of the celebrated Professor Marvel. The man is camped under a bridge, like the proverbial gnome. Clad in a threadbare cutaway and frilled shirt, and roasting wieners like a hobo, this fancy gentleman is obviously a fraud. Yet before Dorothy utters hardly a word, he gazes at her and proclaims that she is running away because "They don't understand you at home. They don't appreciate you. You want to see other lands. Big cities, big mountains, big oceans."

"Why, it's like you could read what's inside me," she exclaims.

Ah, so her motive isn't just to save Toto! Or, perhaps her two aims are one: To save her animal spirit, she must go out into the world. She is like the midwestern farm boy who wants to come east to college or west to make his fortune; she wants to leave behind the consuming farm. Home is the gulch, really.

Discussing why women through history hardly ever wrote, and why, when they did, they rarely achieved the free flight of genius, Virginia Woolf invokes women's confined experience. Women were kept home. They were kept knowing little. "Anybody may blame me who likes," she quotes Charlotte Brontë. And then Woolf asks, Why does Charlotte Brontë's character feel she deserves to be blamed? Because this character—Jane Eyre—climbs up on the roof while the housekeeper makes jellies, and looks over the fields at the distant view.

Jane Eyre longs for "a power of vision which might overpass that limit; which might reach the busy world, town, regions full of life I had heard of but never seen . . . practical experience . . . it is narrow-minded in their more privileged fellow-creatures to say [women] ought to confine themselves to making puddings and embroidering bags." Suddenly, though, Jane Eyre recalls Grace Poole's laugh. It is like being interrupted, as Dorothy so often is at the height of her happiness, by the mocking glee of Elvira Gulch: the cackle of a woman who flew off over the horizon and paid the price. (Air, pool, gale, gulch: Women are nature, ephemeral or eerie. How interesting that Jane Eyre mounts a house much the way Dorothy does to fly over the rainbow.)

"Ah," remarks the professor when Dorothy is amazed by his grasp of her innermost wishes. "Professor Marvel doesn't guess. He *knows*."

Perhaps he recognizes something of himself in her. But he also knows the world is no place for a young girl, and, like a good gate-guardian, he contrives to send her home.

He will read his crystal ball, he announces. He dons a turban with a central jewel on it reminiscent of the circular mirror doctors used to wear over their eyes when they wanted to see inside you. He swipes from inside Dorothy's basket a photo and looks at it in secret. It shows her and her aunt side-by-side at their front gate, both wearing fancy ironed dresses. It is a formal, posed picture in which the two show a quite public face. It is a startling photo, and it takes a moment to realize why. In all the informal scenes until now, not once have we seen Mrs. Gale smiling.

The professor gazes into the cloudy ball. Again it's as if he were seeing into Dorothy's head. He does what his sign urged her to let him do. He reads her "Past, Present, and Future in His Crystal."

He sees an older woman in a polka dot dress, he says. She has a careworn face. She's crying, he says. "Someone has hurt her. Someone has just about broken her heart."

"Me?" Dorothy asks.

"Well, it's someone she loves very much. Someone she's been very kind to, taken care of in sickness."

"I had the measles once. She stayed right by me every minute."

"She's putting her hand on her heart. What's this?! She's dropping down on the bed. Oh, the crystal's gone down."

Dorothy leaps up. She must get home! Her independence, it seems, will kill the woman who sacrificed herself for Dorothy, who allowed her own face to be worn away—who effaced herself—so Dorothy could have her girlhood and perhaps her beauty, the woman who literally *runs* about the farm from chore to chore. Why, she *chose* to be Dorothy's mother when she didn't have to (she's Aunt Em—Aunt

Mother. The use of mother-surrogates in fairy tales, of course, allows the more frightening emotions to surface). Dorothy's going out into the world is such an abandonment of the mother it may kill her.

How weak Aunt Em suddenly seems! It's as if, in leaving, Dorothy stole *her* Toto, her soul. The daughter belongs to the mother at least as much as she belongs to her own self. If she will have the world for herself, she must steal herself from her mother: It feels like seizing the cornerstone of a house—the other person topples.

Maybe the mother really believes she will die without the daughter, and she might, heartbroken: The daughter is the well in which the mother glimpses her own face. The daughter may be the part of herself that her mother loves best. Dorothy has kidnapped herself. The leaping dog and the scarlet shoes are symbols for Dorothy's own soul. Yet when the daughter leaves the mother, she too loses part of herself. She feels alone in an alien place: Dorothy when Em vanishes from the witch's crystal ball.

When Rapunzel flees her mother's tower she becomes an exile. Her lover is her means of escape (she is also literally his way out; she braids her body into a ladder for him, and knots her sheets for her own freedom, using bed as an escape). For seven years she and her lover live in a Sahara. Devoid of mother, the world is punitive, desolate, as Hades must be for Persephone, who also chose between sex and daughterhood (casting the daughter's rapture as abduction spares the mother from having to be angry at her own offspring). Ice is the punishment for sex: For each pomegranate seed the daughter savored, the mother inflicts a frozen month.

Luke Skywalker, in comparison, is evicted. His family home is destroyed *so that* he'll be forced to assume his manhood duties. He must relinquish home to save the world, like Hamlet or Superman, all of whom experience the destruction of their childhood homes. They are thrust out to the world right. Men leave home to restore it. If they don't leave, sickness and decay result. Oedipus's ignorant enjoyment of his parents' bed, Hamlet's prolonged aggressive delayed departure—all plague the land. Even *Sunset Boulevard*, which depicts the story of a young man who lives in what is symbolically the narcissistic mother's mansion, selling his soul for a gold cigarette case, is about social and inner corruption. Men must leave home or they themselves will destroy it.

The professor reads the fears Dorothy cannot admit to herself, and he knows just when to stop—at the brink of the unthinkable. The crystal's gone down; the mind obscures itself. Guilt drives Dorothy back home.

"I thought you were coming with me!" the wandering man says, in mock surprise.

"I have to get to her right away," Dorothy cries as she flees.

And now a curious thing happens. A tornado gusts up, just when Dorothy is coming back. Nobody seems to have predicted this. Again the farm is in jeopardy. It's not from Miss Gulch this time or because Dorothy is running away, but because Dorothy is returning.

The storm expresses Dorothy's own tempestuousness, the cyclone within her that she cannot allow herself to admit. She must be furious at having to give up the world for Aunt Em! Yet how guilty she would feel if she allowed herself to know this! Now it's Dorothy's own projected fury that threatens to wipe out the farm. Doesn't she wish it were wiped out? Then she would be released. Em's spell would be broken. But no—she mustn't, can't, shall not think that.

Quite a squall is brewing. A twister is coming in which everything—all objects, all meanings—will get twisted. It whirls across the horizon, a dark ascending coil like the probing mouth of a vacuum cleaner. The horizon itself is inhaled. Aunt Em, Uncle Henry, and the farmhands vanish into the storm cellar. Dorothy finds a deserted house. She stamps on the door of the cellar; they do not open up. It is as if she has projected her own abandoning behavior on them as if they are punishing her for her anger by withholding their presence. They have walked down into the underworld, marched into a grave in the earth. In fact, this may be exactly what Dorothy unconsciously wishes: If they abandoned her, she would not have to feel guilty about abandoning them.

On the surface, though, her sudden solitude is terrifying. Trees are ripped up. The front screen door blows off in Dorothy's hand. "Aunt Em!" she cries. In a twist, her own life is now in peril. The house looks just like what Elvira Gulch revealed it to be: balsa and paint, weightless and frail, like the court in which Queens and Kings judged Alice in Wonderland only to watch Alice surge bigger and bigger until she declares, "Why, you're just a pack of cards!" while they whirl away.

But Dorothy's return home might literally cost her her life: The house attacks her. The frame of her window (her own crystal) knocks her on the head as it goes down. She swoons onto her bed, and a peaceful expression comes over her. Her face divides. Her face looks superimposed on itself. The twin faces permeate each other, rock through each other, brows, noses, smiles nodding up and down as if agreeing to something marvelous.

In Dorothy's delicious dream her house flies into the air. It spins high, looking like a doll's house, a toy house, but when it comes down to earth its landing is real enough: It kills someone. Dorothy's first act is to crush a faceless woman. "She's gone where the gardens grow. Below, below, below," just like Aunt Em. Of course, it's an accident. But, as the Wicked Witch of the West cries, understanding precisely the nature of "accidents": "I can cause accidents too, you know." (This, ironically, is just what does her in: She incites an accident that dissolves her. Dorothy is capable of violence only under the guise of an accident.) The murder implement of this first act? Why, it's death by house, as if domesticity itself could bear down like the medieval torture of pressing, or as if the incarnated burden of housework could be hurled like a thunderbolt. Riding her house like a broomstick, Dorothy had lethal power.

Yet, ring the bell! This is cause for celebration. The wicked old witch at last is dead! Who is the Wicked Witch? Well, we can't quite see yet; nothing is visible but her feet on which gleam the scarlet power shoes.

Shoes figure in other tales about young women: In *Cinderella* they unlock the secret of the heroine's identity and liberate her from servitude; at the end of *Snow White* the evil queen is forced to dance in fiery-hot metal shoes, a punishment for her burning passions. Cuplike as a brassiere, snug as a vagina, shoes are both confining and emblematic of freedom. They are a potent fetish. How significant that the totalitarian Mrs. Marcos should have assembled an empire of shoes, a vast treasure trove of them, and that Marla Maples, Donald Trump's faux-royal bride, would return to the tabloids over the theft of shoes.

When the ruby slippers are removed, the dead woman's feet curl like party favors. What look like eensy bound feet beneath peppermint-striped stockinged legs retract under the house—she is gone; the house subsumed her. Hidden within those shoes was a stunted root of a woman. But her sister remains, summoned, it seems, by the other's death, or summoned—could it be?—by Dorothy's joy!

Like the dour Em who descends on Dorothy and the farmhands the moment they are all laughing, an incarnation of guilt, the Wicked Witch always appears at the height of Dorothy's festivities. And what are the festivities? In this case it's that Dorothy is being celebrated as the national heroine of a land peopled by adults the size of children, adults who sing songs (in Kansas, Dorothy was the only one who sang), adults who hang on Dorothy's every word and then repeat them to one another as she recounts the story of the ride that made her a sort of Abraham Lincoln to this race of people who will henceforth regard the day she fell (How liberating it is to fall!) as "A day of independence for all the munchkins and their descendants."

In this dream all her wishes have been fulfilled. Here they understand her. Here they appreciate her (and how!). Here are her other lands, her big cities. In the background rise giant mountains. And in the foreground—oh, the colors! The fabulous pinks, the paintbox oranges, the plant leaves gleaming like lollipops, and a river the Dippity-Do blue of a millionaire's pool. Here is a place drenched in rainbow colors, where a woman in a billowing white gown like an ambulatory cloud and with a voice like a trilling flute floats down in a bubble with words of welcome.

Glinda, the only witch with a name, is the very opposite of the skinny Wicked Witch. She is a vision of celestial femininity, clean and blond as can be, and swathed all in gossamer layers of veil as if she were incorporeal, almost rarefied out of existence. She contains a voice that could make your teeth ache it's so thin and high and cloying, a soprano on helium, a woman whose throat is so constricted she seems to be strangling, exquisitely. When I was a child, Glinda seemed more of a fraud to me than any of the other characters. She frightened me. Could I ever be like her? Impossible as being Tinker Bell or Jo or Julie Andrews as a nun in *The Sound of Music*. These women were perfectly clean. "P.U.," I thought when Glinda spoke, my childhood response when threatened by ultrafemininity.

It is Glinda who sets Dorothy on her yearning, winding way to Oz even though she knows from the outset that Dorothy has the power to go home now, if she'll only click her heels. But wait. I'm wrong. For the shoes to work, Glinda claims, Dorothy must believe they will. She must acquire a certain transformative faith. In other words, there's no point in running home until she's learned her lesson.

From the outset, from the *outset,* she wants to go home. As a child this baffled me. What was the matter with that girl? Why was she so pathetically homesick? Couldn't she have any fun? Even now it seems sad. Oz is a place for *her.* It is sensually delicious; it is full of magic, play, and song. Dorothy never names the witch as a reason she wants home. As Dorothy weeps outside the shut gates to the Wizard (and these are the words that make the locked doors swing wide, this is her liberating "Open Sesame!"): "Auntie Em was so good to me and I never appreciated it. . . . She may be dying, and it's all my fault. I'll never forgive myself—never, never, never, never."

How you goin' to keep 'em down on the farm? The answer is near at hand. Just look in the nursery. See under: Oz. The word "Oz," in fact, stands for the second half of the alphabet. Frank Baum was wondering what to call the magical land when he saw his filing cabinet, divided A–N and O–Z. Dorothy gives up half of everything in giving up Oz.

The quest is about reversal. Dorothy must reverse herself. Instead of satisfying her own need for appreciation, she needs to appreciate Em. Em didn't really fall on the bed, clutching her heart. Dorothy fell; her frame of mind attacked her. Health will return when Dorothy relinquishes her fury at Em. She must get angry at her own selfish self. Aunt Em has run away: She vanished into the earth, flinging Dorothy into the sky. How to restore the balance? Through empathy with Em.

"I had an Aunt Em too, you know," says the weeping gate-guardian, swinging open the door to Oz.

Her heart's desire has become Em, not the big world. She can't have both. Perhaps this is the answer to why Dorothy wants home so fast. Oz is exile, without a mother's love. Guilt spoils beauty. Kansas blights Over-the-rainbow already. The solution is to choose A–N, the land of definite articles: an egg, an acre, an aunt, the land of factuality, not Ozymandias.

But not until Dorothy believes she deserves Em can she have her back. Em is the Toto now. She's what's locked away. To earn her, Dorothy must turn every ounce of anger to guilt. She must convert desire for the world to desire for home.

"The pure products of America go crazy," wrote William Carlos Williams.

"I'm afraid you've made rather an enemy out of the Wicked Witch," Glinda remarks, although it was Glinda herself who managed this. She put the glitter shoes on Dorothy's feet. Why does she ensure that Dorothy can't live peacefully with the Witch of the West?

A person becomes taboo "for the simple reason that he is in a condition which has the property of inciting the forbidden desires of others and awakening the ambivalent conflict in them," says Freud. There is something compelling about the woman who flies on her own stick, who is mistress of her own castle, who keeps in her thrall men whom she uses for her own devices and beasts like boys that flock at her command. All this female power might *attract* Dorothy, so better make that woman verboten—better yet, her nemesis—from the start.

"You must prove yourselves worthy," Oz roars to Dorothy and her friends.

How?

"Bring me the broomstick of the Wicked Witch of the West"—again *making* the witch an enemy.

"We'll have to kill her first!" cries the smart Scarecrow.

Oz sets a test like the type set for a knight. The reward, traditionally, is the hand of the king's daughter. Here the romantic object is Em. Oz is lodged at the end of a long, glistening red hallway, a passage of ribbed arches like a gallery of wishbones: scarlet, internal, echoey. Oz is aim and obstacle. Egglike, legless, with an ample cranium that presages Marvel's balloon, he hovers, a floating head, thronged with salvers of green smoke and flames like an incarnation of Kubla Khan's "ancestral voices prophesying war." Dorothy has ascended into the fomenting, highly defended throne of the Mind-king. He gives her reason to accomplish what she may have secretly wished to do all along (she rehearsed this death from the instant she arrived; in fact arriving was synonymous with killing). She will be worthy of home when she destroys the Wicked Witch.

The Witch of the West is a woman who wants. She provides all the obstacles to Dorothy's quest—the malicious trees, the soporific fields. In fact, the whole place sometimes seems to exist in her control: As

Dorothy and her new friends sing and stroll blithely along, the witch watches them in her ball. They inhabit a small globe owned by her; the world is her paperweight. What do we actually know about her? She is thin and green, as if painted with the brush of mortality, the taint of envy. Something in her is already rotting. She is friendless, all who serve her enslaved by a spell broken only at her death.

"It's so kind of you to visit me in my loneliness," she croons when Dorothy arrives, kidnapped, into the rocky, remote fortress—and despite the sarcasm, there's a poignance to the words. Surrounded by robotic men, attempting to warm herself with a million flickering fires (she is a nightmare image of who Aunt Em might become if Dorothy left), wouldn't she actually like a daughter for herself? "My pretty," she calls Dorothy, a term of droll cherishing. Wouldn't a daughter be a balm for those gaunt arms, that scraped raw voice? The woman's starved! With her face thin as a chisel, her raggedy black dress binding her bony waist, she looks broken apart, fragmented, all the parts of her jutting in the fractured angles of a stovepipe rather than flowing in ample round maternal shapes. She is a sort of vicious pauper lusting for the impossible.

This depiction of an autonomous woman is of course a nightmare vision of feminine power, a grotesque of female appetite—as if to say that to be a woman who wants is to be a woman who can only want, whose wants are by definition out of control, oceanic, threatening to swamp the world like nature gone awry, or liable to suck back spitefully into herself on a salty tide all that she has engendered, a birthing in reverse. The suppressed has surfaced, and, volcanic, might blot out the world. "What is it that woman wants?" How strongly Freud resisted knowing, although all day long women told him their secrets. The fear of what women would want if they could want runs through literature like an underground river.

But can one imagine the bejeweled slippers on the witch's frame, with her ascetic mourner's garb? Ludicrous! It would be like a crone in a tutu or a child in a negligee. No, the scarlet heels are not meant for the witch no matter how she stretches out her elongated green fingers, gesturing first toward her mouth then toward the shoes, then toward her mouth again as if thoughtfully beckoning. They are an emblem of youth and sexuality. They are all this female pariah lacks. The shoes are glamorous, they cast a delightful glamour over others, a web of enchantment.

If the witch had the shoes, Dorothy is warned, the witch's power would be absolute. Would men then fall in love with her? After all, Dorothy's power is her ability to inspire love. If the Wicked Witch could make others love her while she retained her own controlling will, wouldn't her power be complete?

Across the very sky, writ in giant charred letters, the witch spells "Surrender Dorothy." Not surrender the shoes but surrender yourself.

The drama of the daughter's journey is: Who will control her? Will she capitulate to the Wicked Witch or will she make it home? Will she celebrate her own stubborn, lonely will, or will she become a selfless woman, freed from isolation? Locked in the witch's keep, she calls out to Aunt Em like Jonah crying from the whale where, as he put it, "the earth with her bars closed upon me."

"I'm frightened, Aunt Em! I'm frightened!" She sounds as if she is making atonement or admitting something at long last.

In response, Em emerges in the crystal, calling, "Dorothy! It's me! It's Aunt Em. Where are you? We're trying to find you!"

"I'm here in Oz, Aunt Em," cries Dorothy. "I'm trying to get home to you. Oh, *don't* go away!" for already Em is clouding and darkening and twisting until she reveals herself to be—what a shock—the gloating Wicked Witch.

"I'll give you Auntie Em, my pretty!" she sneers.

And doesn't she? In the crystal of the mind, the two are merged. The deathly witch is the other face of the nurturant Em; *M* is *W* from another angle.

How does it clarify matters to see Em as the Witch of the West? When I thought about Em, I always remembered a kind, loving woman. Yet viewing the movie as an adult, I noticed how grim Em is, and how forcefully nasty she can be.

"What's all this jabberwocking about when there's work to be done?" Em demands, descending on Dorothy and the farmhands, implying that the sort of daydreaming Alice was partial to through the looking glass will not be countenanced here. 'Twas brillig and the slithy toves, indeed! And when there's work to be done!

"I know three shiftless farmhands who'll be out of a job before they know it," she continues.

One of the men explains. "Well, Dorothy was walking along—"

"I saw you tinkering with that contraption, Hickory," she practically spits. "Now get back to that wagon."

Contraptions and tinkering! Why, it's almost as bad as jabberwocking.

"All right, Mrs. G," he replies. He lifts a finger in the air. "But one day they're going to erect a statue for me in this town—"

"Well, don't start posing for it now!" she cuts.

Even when she offers the farmhands a tray of phallic crullers she holds at waist height, it's because "you can't work on an empty stomach."

"You got my finger!" Hank exclaims when the flatbed of a cart is lowered on his helping hand.

Rakes, fingers, and crullers: incubators and wagons—the farm is a suggestive place, and what it suggests to Em is work and more work.

In contrast, the principle of the Emerald City is idleness. "We get up at twelve and start to work by one. Take an hour for lunch and then by two we're done. Jolly good fun!" sing the urbanites. Dorothy, who loves freedom, liberates as she goes. She unhooks the Scarecrow from his nail, oils the Tin Man where he's rusted (Hickory wanted to have a statue. Well, fine. The witch has made him a statue), cajoles along the lion who was so tormented by fears.

The men of Oz are all missing one key organ (the lion wants "the nerve!"). One suspects that, in Dorothy's mind, the men on Aunt Em's farm all lack an organ, too. The farmhands are embodied in the galley slaves whose long-proboscised faces mirror that of the Wicked Witch (these people almost have an *extra* organ). They are cruel to Dorothy only because they are under a spell. In Dorothy's dream, the farmhands appear in both their defiant and their servile incarnations.

Far from being a doting mom, Mrs. Gale comes across as an iron-gray matron who knows quite well, thank you, how to lay down the law. She is a sort of strict schoolmistress who won't stand for a moment of spring fever, not when there's multiplication tables to recite. Which is why it comes as a shock when she appears so terribly fragile as soon as Dorothy attempts to leave.

From the start of the movie, Aunt Em is angry. She is *furious*.

Is she envious of Dorothy's ability to daydream and sing while she herself is shackled to the farm? Is she jealous of the girl's latent fecundity (why doesn't Em have children?)? Is she afraid of becoming old and lonely? Perhaps she is angry that she has so much to protect Dorothy from.

Dorothy's unbridled growth ruptures the old unity with Em. "Who killed my sister?" Em demands in her witch incarnation. The dead sister is the childhood Dorothy, the female who disappeared and whom the new Dorothy has the most vital part of. In Dorothy's nightmare vision, Em stretches long fingers toward her. She is an ugly starveling who wants to make Dorothy like her. She can pursue Dorothy anywhere. Why, she even appeared when Dorothy ran clear across the county and into the carnie man's tent.

Em imprisons Dorothy. The terrifying hourglass the witch over-turns resembles a voluptuous scarlet woman draining red dust. If only Em could remove Dorothy's womanliness, the old joy would be restored! If only Dorothy could give Em back some years and re-turn her femininity, she wouldn't need to feel so guilty! (The ashen menopausal farm can't sustain its eggs. "This old incubator's gone bad," Uncle Henry reports. Em's badness is threatening.) "Give them back to me!" cries the Wicked Witch when she sees the ruby shoes on Dorothy's feet. They were hers once, apparently. "Give them *back!*" she insists.

But they are time, sexiness, red-mouthed beauty (Dorothy's lush lips are the first thing one notices in color). "Keep tight inside them," Glinda cautions. "Never let them off your feet."

And yet of course one's body does loosen and slip. Time is the movie's villain, in fact. The film begins mythically, with a scroll of words which name Time as the enemy: "For nearly forty years this story has given faithful service to the Young in Heart; and Time has been pow-erless to put its kindly philosophy out of fashion."

By faithfully serving her mother, a girl can resist the pull of time, a force so like mitosis, when a cell's twin nuclei fling in polar directions. In seeing her mother, in fact, a girl sees herself plus time. Can't the daughter restore to the mother what she herself has apparently de-voured? Mother and daughter drain into each other like two halves of an "ourglass," two crystals merged, two minds fused. How can they separate?

"Why didn't you tell Dorothy earlier that she just needed to tap her heels?" the Scarecrow demands at the end.

"She wouldn't have believed me," says Glinda, neatly. "She had to learn something for herself first."

What has she learned?

"It's that . . . it wasn't enough just to want to see Uncle Henry and Aunt Em. It's that—if I ever go looking for my heart's desire again, I won't go any further than my own backyard. Because if it isn't there, I never lost it in the first place."

To return to her family, Dorothy must redefine her heart's desire. She must stay home and not feel anything has been lost. The daughter must not come home resentfully. That might destroy home, much as the caged woman in Rochester's attic and the chained woman in Roderick Usher's basement finally burn down their mansions. She must choose home happily.

The story is a mother-romance. The girl had thought it was her own self that was missing. But the cost of finding that self was mother.

"Think to yourself, 'There's no place like home,' " Glinda instructs.

Dorothy shakes her head from side to side as if to say no to Oz, no to Oz, and murmurs the words hypnotically, casting a spell over herself: "There's no place like home." Her whole family appears.

No place like home. For men, the situation is different. Home and world aren't either/or. Odysseus leaves to fight and find adventure knowing home waits. Men go and are loved. They are in fact loved more for going: That's brave. Penelope weaves and unweaves. Her calendar is filled and unfilled. But her marriage bed is rooted in the earth. It won't blow away.

Odysseus is valued for his rich experience. Experience in a girl means just one thing, and it's no good. Leave home and you lose it, girls learn. Leave home, and home leaves you. The photo in your basket will transform: The woman who had smiled will die. The world is an alien, forsaken place; go into it and you will be alien and forsaken. Leave home, and you murder it. Only if you stay, can it, and you, be safe.

"We thought for a moment she was going to leave us," Uncle Henry says.

"But I did leave—"

"Lie quiet now," Em interrupts. "You just had a bad dream."

"But it wasn't a dream. It was a place. . . ."

"Sometimes we dream lots of silly things when—"

"No, Aunt Em, it really existed. . . . Doesn't anyone believe me?"

"Of course we believe you, Dorothy."

Em does seem to believe for a moment, although it's not clear exactly what. That the experience was real for Dorothy? Em interrupts talk of departures; that's "a bad dream." Perhaps she's willing to concede an internal departure happened, and the fever is quenched at last. Or perhaps really, mysteriously, Em actually *does* believe in Oz. For one enchanted moment this seems true.

Dorothy, thrilled to be back and believed, smiles at Em's smiling face. Maybe Em wanted to trust all along in Dorothy's "jabberwocking," maybe she secretly values what she feels impelled to mock. Maybe dreaming will heal her too.

But Dorothy's not dreaming any more, she vows. "I'm not going away ever, ever again. Oh, Auntie Em," she cries in her final declaration of love to the woman she quested for so well and long: "There's no place like home."

Variety Photoplays

BY EDWARD FIELD

*F*or several years in the mid-fifties, during a period of uncertainty and depression in my life, I haunted a seedy movie house on Third Avenue off Fourteenth Street in Manhattan, left over from an earlier era, with its name, Variety Photoplays, in evocative twenties neon on the bulb-studded marquee.

Recently, before an off-Broadway theater company took it over and modernized it, it was threatened with demolition, a victim of rising real estate values and the AIDS scare, having been closed by the city because of "unsafe sex acts" between men taking place on the premises. But in the period when I used to go there, it was the usual smelly and ordinary Bowery theater, mostly patronized by bums—all male, I might add, for only rarely did a woman enter—and in my time, at least, rarely did an unsafe sex act happen, though that was not the whole story.

For VP, as my friend Alfred Chester and I called it, had a specialized clientele, too, for whom it was a jerkoff house, one of the safer, and

FROM *PARNASSUS*

therefore encouraged, forms of sexual contact nowadays, but then strictly illegal. Unlike later on, when it became an openly gay movie theater with porn films and complete freedom to wander around doing anything you wanted, in those days a black usher with the oiled, conked hair of the period patrolled the aisles with his flashlight, and if he caught sight of anyone fooling around with a neighbor, the offender was expelled.

This did not seriously inhibit such activity, nor was banishment much of a punishment in an era when the law exerted heavy penalties on any homosexual behaviour. It was remarkable that, in a time of regular raids on gay bars, the police rarely came in. Perhaps it was a case where more was permitted on the lowest level, among the dregs of society.

Besides an extraordinary art deco marquee outlined in neon, VP had an old-fashioned museum-piece of a box office—a free-standing booth, inhabited by an old, shabby man of uncertain nationality, but certainly foreign-born. It cost fifteen cents when I first went there, twelve cents in the morning before eleven—this was part of the Bowery scene, remember—and only went up to eighteen and then twenty-four cents later.

The films were a double bill of ancient B-features, one invariably a Western, rarely worth paying much attention to, unless you were a fan of the genre. Still echoing in my mind, though, is a song from one of the accompanying features, never heard since, that starts, "When you wish upon a star . . .," a bouncy tune of the early thirties, rather than the syrupy song in *Snow White.*

Besides the bums, VP catered to the kind of men, working-class on the whole, who generally did not identify themselves as gay or dig the gay scene in bars and public cruising grounds, but preferred to dart in for anonymous sex and afterwards melt back into the general populace. For instance, I had it off several times with a man who came in the few afternoons a year when he was let off early from work the day before major holidays. I learned when to expect him, before Christmas and New Year's, and he seemed to recognize me distantly, too, but this was not a place for friendly conversation. I tried to imagine what his "outside" life was like, the job and family that occupied him completely, except for those occasional forays that satisfied another side of his nature. It was a mystery, something like the Hasidic Jew with ear-locks who more recently cruised the gay scene on the West Side waterfront in his car.

At different times of the day or days of the week, VP catered to special classes of customers. Mornings at eight, when it opened, the time I liked it best, night workers, like cabbies, might drop in after the shift for a fling of quick sex and a snooze. Sunday, family men appeared, Italian mostly, in flight, I imagined, from the heavy domestic scene at home in crowded tenements after the heavy Sunday dinner. They had probably participated in such groping in the dark all their lives, like the parallel prole sex scene, traditional back then, in the steam rooms at Coney Island bathhouses, where the men were so packed in they rocked with one mass erotic release.

As I approached the box office of Variety Photoplays with my money ready so as not to linger too long in view of passersby, I was already sexually aroused, my eyes trying to spot through the glass doors who was walking through the lobby ahead between orchestra and balcony, or perhaps standing around to smoke a cigarette. Frequently, I suffered pangs of disappointment if a sturdy fellow was leaving just then, someone I would have liked to fool around with. Or, mysteriously, I might see another passing through the lobby whom, though covering the theater from top to bottom, I never found.

On entering, it was possible to walk up and down the aisles as if looking for a seat, actually checking the place out, without arousing too much suspicion from the usher, who of course knew the score. Furtiveness, I should explain to the younger, liberated members of the class, was part of sex in those years, and to this day I prefer sex to be secret, the sexual and gay revolutions having come too late for me, and years of therapy never having done a thing for me in that area.

The balcony, for smokers, had two upper sections on either side of the projection booth (according to architectural historian Christopher Gray, who wrote about it in *The New York Times,* "a small museum of antique apparatus"). Only on the right side of the balcony (if you were facing the screen) did hanky-panky go on. And behind this was a standing room with a wooden barrier, where it was easy to get together with someone, since, standing against the barrier, no one could see what you were doing below the shoulders, though weekdays, the usher with the conk waved us down, if seats were available. Sunday matinee, when the theater was full, standing room was allowed, and the usher couldn't control the action.

In the orchestra, the front half nearer the screen was the contact area, though you couldn't rule out anywhere in the theater. The men's room was straight ahead to the left of the screen itself (if there had ever been a stage, it had been removed), so, going in, you were in full view of the audience. But that was not a serious discouragement to repeated visits. I found myself sauntering in frequently, as if I had a urinary problem.

Plenty went on in the john, with its two porcelain stand-ups and one booth, despite it being a smelly hole. The whole theater had an extraordinarily funky smell, from age, the proximity of the lava, the bums and their bottles, stale bodies, and unlaundered clothes, especially in winter or wet weather. As I entered from the street, I breathed it in like an aphrodisiac, even a whiff of freedom. For this was the lowest period of my life. I had been in a form of therapy called Group Analysis that had so many meetings, it had the deleterious effect of wiping out my usual social life. More serious than that, as a gay man among a group of straights, in that benighted age when gay meant sick, I was expected to "change" when my "interpersonal relationship" problems had been solved. So the other group members, with the best will in the world and out of love for me, constantly attacked my neurotic substructure, which largely meant my interest in sex with men.

After a few years of this, it is no wonder that my main contact with the real world became Variety Photoplays. Instead of going to look for a job in the morning, as I intended to do when I left the house, I'd get off the subway at Union Square and, as if drawn by a magnet, veer off and head for VP. A few hours of action there would leave me suicidal, I'll admit, though I will never dismiss as worthless the experience of wanking innumerable men of all ages, nationalities, colors, and sizes. The responsible citizen the group was trying to make me into—someone with a job, an apartment, and a girlfriend—was simply not for me, and VP was a good place to slink off and lick my wounds, so to speak. It was an affirmation of my identity and the validity of my desires on the most elemental level.

I was pretty sure never to meet anyone I knew there, either. Most gays are pretty conventional and go where other gays go for sex, and at conventional times, and then not usually to piss-holes like VP. Though Beauford Delaney, the great black painter written about by Henry Miller, who left for Paris at the end of the fifties, never to return, was often in the orchestra section, where he connected with the Greek and Italian immigrants who were among the regulars. I used to see his wise face beaming at me as I came down the aisle almost any afternoon, and we acknowledged each other. Later, in the sixties, when I was in Paris, I would visit him at his studio in Montparnasse.

A few years later, after I had stopped going to VP, Alfred Chester started attending, though he said he preferred the Comet, another jack-off house just south on Third Avenue, that he described, under the name of the Rocket, in his well-known story "In Praise of Vespasian," the tale of a compulsive cruiser. But by then, as I could tell from the stories he told about them, both movie houses had already changed and become openly gay, even though officially, gay liberation was still some years off. But it was extraordinary that in his fiction, Alfred Chester wrote as though it had already arrived.

Outside of the regulars, most of whom I avoided, I liked the variety—off the screen, I mean. Even an occasional bum was worth a diddle sometimes. If there was a vacant seat next to someone who looked interesting, there was no harm in slipping into it and letting knees touch as if by accident. With coat or jacket on laps, it was easy to shift a hand to your neighbor's knee (his lifting his elbow off the armrest was a sign to move in under it), and from there, unbutton his fly, eyes innocently on the silver screen where cowboys were chasing Indians. Bums never minded coming in their pants, already stiff with dirt and cum, but those with higher standards brought Kleenex or had their handkerchief ready. Most of the patrons of VP had stains on the front of their pants, but since they were usually workingmen, it didn't seem to matter, except perhaps on Sunday when some of them had "gone out for a walk" in their good clothes.

The sounds of the movie, often hoofbeats and gunfire, masked most of the heavy breathing and sighs, though there is a great variety in response to touch, and a great variety of orgasms as well as organs. There was one delightful little round Italian man who appeared to be in his sixties—he whispered that he worked on a barge, when I asked him—who giggled uncontrollably at any contact. Once in a while, I couldn't help getting fond of one or another of the men, and looked forward to seeing them again, but the romance was more with the movie house itself. In repeated contacts with the same person, the glamour usually did not hold up. I remember a cab driver, only there mornings, whom I found terrifically sexy, and fooled around with several times behind the wooden barrier in the balcony, until one day the stink from his foreskin was so bad I couldn't take it and had to flee to the men's room and scrub my hand.

I did talk with people sometimes, usually in whispers in the seats, or standing on the stairs to the balcony, or briefly in the john. One man with an enormous cock that never quite got hard told me of his experience in prison, where he fooled around in the laundry room. Another man told me the story of a sex experience with his son staying in his room, and bed, when he was on leave, though this may have been a pornographic invention to make our dalliance more exciting for him. In the morning he told the son to go over and get the cigarettes from the table. The boy said, "But I'm hanker, Dad." "So what? I am, too," the good father said. And when he saw what his son had, they fucked when he got back into bed.

I even occasionally took someone home to my cold-water flat in Little Italy, but was never successful in making a single friend, for these men were part of a world where this kind of sexuality could be expressed only within certain limits. I was no freer than they were, and besides, would have had to fight my Group, whose psychotherapeutic principles I believed in, if I had set up a liaison with another man—though much like gay Catholics I knew, I could sin and sin again, if I repented afterwards. While I gave lip service to the goals of my Group, I would not forgo the blessings that were offered within the shabby walls of VP, which, unexpectedly but appropriately, were freshly painted one day a bright orange with jungle vines and flowers all over them.

When the theater was boarded up and threatened with demolition, the darkened, deteriorating marquee seemed to stand as a memorial to an aspect of male sexuality of another time, as well as to a part of my youth I value more and more, as with AIDS and age, my sex life becomes one of remembrance and nostalgia.

The Death of Camp: Gay Men and Hollywood Diva Worship, from Reverence to Ridicule

BY DANIEL HARRIS

*"If all the time the manager of the theater holds back the good roles
from us, may we not insist upon understudying the stars?"*
—ISAK DINESEN, "THE DELUGE AT NORDERNEY"

Sometime in my childhood and very early adolescence, I acquired,
while living in the very heart of Appalachia, a land of lazy Southern
drawls, a British accent. No one around me had a British accent; my
family was American, and my peers were budding good old boys
whose fathers drove tractors and pickup trucks and spoke in an un-

FROM *SALMAGUNDI*

musical twang that I, a pompous fop in my teens, found distinctly un-dignified. Given the hearty, blue-collar community in which I grew up, the origin of my stilted style of delivery remained a complete mystery to me until, as an adult, I began to watch old movies. Over and over again in the voices of film stars as different as Joan Crawford in *Mildred Pierce* and Katharine Hepburn in *Suddenly, Last Summer,* I heard the echoes of my own voice, the affected patrician accents of characters who conversed in a manufactured Hollywood idiom meant to suggest refinement and good breeding, the lilting tones of Grace Kelly in *Rear Window,* Bette Davis in *Mr. Skeffington,* Tallulah Bankhead in *Lifeboat,* or even Glinda the Good Witch in *The Wizard of Oz.* In that tour de force of bitchy camp, *The Women,* the all-female cast speaks in two distinct accents, the harsh American cockney of the kitchen help who squabble about the muddled affairs of their wealthy mistresses, and the high-society, charm-school intonations of the Park Avenue matrons who rip each other to shreds in the gracious accents of an Anglophilic argot concocted by the elocutionists at the major studios. Only Joan Crawford, the inimitable Crystal Allen, a vulgar, social-climbing shop girl who claws her way up to the top, can speak in both accents as the occasion requires, one for when she is at her most deceitful, hiding her common upbringing beneath the Queen's English of the New York aristocracy, and the other for when she is being her true self, a crass, money-grubbing tart who gossips viciously with her equally low-class cohorts at the perfume counter. To an insecure gay teenager stranded in the uncivilized hinterlands of North Carolina, the gracious ladies of Park Avenue and Sutton Place embodied a way of life more glamorous and less provincial than his own.

The influence of Hollywood films was so pervasive among young homosexuals like myself that it insinuated itself into our voices, weak-ening the grip of our regional accents, which were gradually over-ridden by the artificial language of an imaginary elite. Even today I have never succeeded in exorcizing Joan, Bette, Grace, and Kate from my vocal cords where they are still speaking, having left the indelible mark of Hollywood's spurious imitation of classiness, culture, and gen-tility branded into my personality. This strange act of ventriloquism represents the highest form of diva worship and is the direct outcome of my perception in my youth that, as a homosexual, I did not belong in the community in which I lived, that I was different, a castaway from somewhere else, somewhere better, more elegant, more refined, a little Lord Fauntleroy marooned in the wilderness. In my unconscious imitation of the voices of the great film stars, I was seeking to demonstrate my separateness, to show others how out of place I felt, and, moreover, to fight back against the hostility I sensed in the homophobic, redneck world around me by belittling its crudeness through unremitting displays of my own polish and sophistication. I was not attracted to Hollywood stars because of their femininity, nor did my admiration of them reflect a burning desire to be a woman, as the homosexual's fascination with actresses is usually explained, as if diva worship were simply a ridiculous waste product of gender conflicts. Instead, it was their world, not their femininity, that appealed to me, the irrepressibly madcap in-crowd of *Auntie Mame,* of high spirits and unconventional "characters," of nudists and Freudians, symphony conductors and Broadway prima donnas, who lived in a protective enclave that promised immunity from shame, beckoning me with its broad-mindedness and indulgence of sexual eccentricities.

For me and countless other gay men growing up in the intolerant world of small-town America, film provided a vehicle for expressing alienation from our surroundings and linking up with the utopic homosexual community of our dreams, a sophisticated "artistic" society inhabited by Norma Desmonds and Holly Golightlies who, while breakfasting at Tiffany's, spoke a type of English heard only in the back lots of MGM and Twentieth Century-Fox. The homosexual's involvement with Hollywood movies was not only more intense but fundamentally different from the involvement of the rest of the American public. Film served a deeply psychological and political function, that of asserting our superiority to the parochial societies of our childhood and formulating the stereotypic homosexual persona of the upper-class aesthete who was as cultured and sensitive as his straight peers were brutish and uncouth. At the very heart of gay diva worship, in other words, is not the diva but the almost universal homosexual experience of ostracism and insecurity which led to what might be called the aestheticism of maladjustment, the gay man's exploitation of cinematic visions of Hollywood grandeur to elevate himself above his antagonistic surroundings and simultaneously express membership in a hedonistic demimonde.

If the pre-Stonewall homosexual's worship of Hollywood served psychological functions that had nothing whatsoever to do with the actresses themselves, the hard-bitten personalities of such Machiavellian careerists as Joan Crawford and Marlene Dietrich were certainly not irrelevant to gay men's fascination with them. In fact, we related so intensely to the steeliness of characters like the murderous Bette Davis in *Little Foxes,* who, with chilling equanimity, stands by as her choking husband writhes in convulsions before her, clutching his heart and helplessly groping for his missing blood-pressure medication, that we used them as substitutes for ourselves, refashioning them in our own images. In the homosexual's imagination, Hollywood divas actually became gay men, undergoing a strange sort of sex change operation from which they emerged, not as women, but as drag queens, as men in women's clothing, honorary butch homosexuals, such as Joan Crawford in *Johnny Guitar* playing Vienna, a hard-boiled saloonkeeper who guns down her rival, Mercedes McCambridge, or Tallulah Bankhead in *Lifeboat* playing a shipwrecked reporter, adrift in the Atlantic, who uses her diamond Cartier bracelet as bait to catch fish. Drag queen imagery pervades gay men's discussion of the legendary Hollywood actresses, of Gloria Swanson, whose "acting has more than a whiff of the drag queen about it . . ."; of Vivien Leigh, whom gay author Paul Roen identifies with "for the simple reason that I know she's really not a woman"; or of Mae West, who was "Mount Rushmore in drag," as well as "the first woman to function as a leading man," and who, for decades, was even suspected of literally being a biological male until her postmortem finally convinced her skeptical gay fans that her curvaceous hips and imposing bosom were the real thing and not prosthetic, foam-rubber devices. Because of our fiercely fetishistic involvement with diva worship, the star was masculinized. She even in a sense traded places with her gay audience, who used her as a naked projection of their frustrated romantic desires, of their inability to express their sexual impulses openly in a homophobic society, and to seduce and manipulate the elusive heterosexual men for whom many homosexuals once nursed bitterly unrequited passions. In the process of this transference, she was voided of both her gender and her femininity and transformed into the homosexual's proxy, a transvestite figure, a vampish surrogate through which gay men lived out unattainable longings to ensnare such dashing heartthrobs as Clark Gable, Humphrey Bogart, and Gene Kelly.

Although at first sight gay diva worship seems to have been an aspect of traditional gay culture that was as giddy as an adolescent girl's moonstruck infatuation with her teen idols, the homosexual's love of Hollywood was not an expression of flamboyant effeminacy but, in a very literal sense, of swaggering machismo. For all of the lush sensuality of Greta Garbo melting limply into the arms of John Barrymore in *Grand Hotel* or Elizabeth Taylor batting her eyes at the impotent Paul Newman in *Cat on a Hot Tin Roof,* diva worship provided effeminate men with a paradoxical way of getting in touch with their masculinity, much as football provides a vicarious way for sedentary straight men to get in touch with their masculinity. Despite appearances to the contrary, diva worship is in every respect as unfeminine as football. It is a bone-crushing spectator sport in which one watches the triumph of feminine wiles over masculine wills, of a voluptuous and presumably helpless damsel in distress single-handedly mowing down a lineup of hulking quarterbacks who fall dead at her feet, as in *Double Indemnity,* where Barbara Stanwyck plays a scheming femme fatale who brutally murders her husband and then dumps his lifeless body from a moving train in order to collect his insurance policy, or in *Dead Ringer,* where Bette Davis watches calmly as her dog lunges for the throat of her gigolo boyfriend. As one gay writer wrote about his attraction to the classic cinematic vamp, "as any drag queen can tell you: Beneath all those layers of cosmetic beauty lies the kind of true grit John Wayne never knew." Strip away all of the star's glamour and one finds, not the diva, but a glorified self-portrait of the gay man himself, the demoralized queen who used the celebrity's strength as a therapeutic corrective of his own highly compromised masculinity. Before Stonewall, homosexuals exploited these cold-blooded, manipulative figures to overcome the pervasive sense of powerlessness they experienced as a vilified minority. To counteract their own sense of degradation, they modeled themselves on the appealing image of the thick-skinned androgyne-cum-drag-queen, a distinctly militaristic figure who, with a suggestive leer and a deflating wisecrack, triumphed over the daily indignities of being gay. Even today, gay men still allude to the star's usefulness in enabling them to "cope," in offering them a tough-as-nails persona that they can assume like a mask during emotionally trying experiences in which they imagine themselves to be Joan Crawford in *Mildred Pierce* building her restaurant empire or Bette Davis in

Dark Victory nobly ascending the stairs to die alone in her bedroom, struck down in the prime of her life by a mysterious brain tumor. In an article on Ruby Rims, a female impersonator so immersed in celebrity culture that he has even named his cats "Eve" and "Channing," the *New York Native* describes how, in the gay imagination, diva worship becomes a source of power that enables homosexuals to fight back through imitation, through the often unconscious reenactment of Hollywood scenarios in the course of real-life experiences:

> [Rims] finds that if he is angered or frustrated by something or someone, he can usually give vent to his feelings by becoming Bette Davis . . . "She's a release for me," he said, his face brightening. "I can walk right up to someone and say"— gasp—" 'You're an asshole,' and blow cigarette smoke in their face."

Quite by accident, by pure serendipity, the diva provided the psychological models for gay militancy. In a paradoxical way, celebrity culture helped radicalize the subculture. The homosexual's inveterate habit of projecting himself into the invincible personas of Scarlett O'Hara in *Gone with the Wind* or Alexandra Del Lago in *Sweet Bird of Youth* prepared the ground psychologically for the political resistance that was to come in the 1960s and 1970s when the gay man's internal diva was at last released from the subjective prison of his fantasy world to take the streets by storm. When drag queens fought back at Stonewall, chances are that what they had on their minds was the shameless chutzpah of their film icons, whose bravura displays of gutsiness they were reenacting, much as Rims pretends to be Bette Davis to buck up his courage, to retaliate against assaults to his dignity. Homosexuals consumed, assimilated, and recycled Hollywood images in such vast quantities and with such intense passion that it is interesting to speculate whether gay liberation would have been delayed had gay men not found inspiration in these militant paradigms. Shit-kicking amazons in sequins, ermine, and lamé became so integral to homosexuals' self-images that they helped them to tap hidden reservoirs of masculinity and to look at themselves as something more than just perpetual victims, as despicable pansies too weak to defend themselves from the brutality of the police. In this way, something as retrograde and conformist as popular culture, with its uncritical advocacy of materialism, success, and blissfully domestic heterosexual relationships, was actually used for radical purposes, enabling a despised subculture to defend itself from the very America Hollywood celebrated. In the absence of the gay-positive propaganda in which contemporary gay culture is saturated, film became a form of "found" propaganda which the homosexual ransacked for inspiring messages, with his imagination recycling the refuse of popular culture, reconstituting it into an energizing force.

As Rims's comments reveal, one aspect in particular of the Hollywood actress's persona that appealed to gay men was her bitchiness, her limitless satiric powers, as in *The Women*, where the characters taunt each other with such venomous comments as "Where I spit no grass grows," "Your skin makes the Rocky Mountains look like chiffon velvet," and "Chin up—that's right, both of them," or in *All About Eve*, in which Bette Davis toasts the slanderous critic who raises his wineglass to her across a restaurant by taking a ferocious bite out of a stalk of celery. Homosexuals were drawn to the image of the bitch in part because of her wicked tongue, her ability to achieve through conversation, through her verbal acuity, her snappy comebacks, the control over others that gay men were often unable to achieve in their own lives. The fantasy of the vicious, backstabbing vagina dentata always quick on her feet, always ready to demolish her opponent with a stunning rejoinder, is the fantasy of a powerless minority that expresses aggression through language, not physical violence. Straight men express aggression through fistfights and sports; gay men through quick-witted repartee and caustic remarks. Straight men punch; gay men quip. Straight men are barroom brawlers; gay men—bitches. By providing the models for the beautiful shrew who, in film after film, attained a kind of conversational omnipotence, Hollywood fueled the homosexual's love of archness, of withering irony, which became the deadliest weapon of all in the arsenal of popular culture, providing the pre-Stonewall homosexual with a way of expressing contempt for the society that had placed him in such an untenable position. If the Hollywood diva inadvertently helped each gay man nurture, like his own inner child, his own inner diva, and thus strengthened his will to resist his degradation at the hands of a homophobic society, wittiness was the primary element of his revenge, the method by which he gained the upper hand over his enemies, remaining in possession of the battlefield long after the victims of the winged barbs he hurled had beat a hasty retreat. Given the centrality to the subculture of the image of the arch queen, it is not an exaggeration to say that gay politics grew out of gay wittiness whose acerbic muse was the mordant Hollywood goddess, Mae West, who takes on a whole town of sanctimonious churchgoers in *My Little Chickadee,* or Rosalind Russell in *Auntie Mame,* who rids herself of her nephew's despicable girlfriend by throwing a dinner party at which she serves rattlesnake canapés. Wittiness was the first very tentative step toward gay liberation, a vitriolic expression of discontent, of our disdain for American prudery, which we reviled through an ineffectual verbal protest, a compulsion to denigrate, to engage in cutthroat bickering, which eventually reached critical mass and led to concrete political action. Bitching, in other words, was a form of protopolitics. It channeled the bitter frustrations of homosexuals' lives into a pronounced conversational mannerism that marked an important symbolic stage in the gay man's effort to translate his otherwise impotent rage into practical measures for social reform.

Hollywood suffused the gay sensibility, not only because of its usefulness as "found" propaganda, but also because of the power of the new medium to build group solidarity. Because homosexuals are an invisible minority whose members are not united by physical characteristics and who are indeed often unrecognizable even to each other, they must invent some method of identifying themselves as a group or risk falling into the politically crippling state of fragmentation that for decades kept homosexuals from organizing themselves to protect their basic civil rights. Blacks are united by their skin color, Chicanos by their language and place of origin, and the handicapped by their infirmities. Homosexuals, however, are united by something altogether less tangible: by their tastes, their sensibility, by the books they read, the clothes they wear, and the movies they watch. Before the gay sensibility developed, homosexuals constituted an alienated diaspora of scattered individuals who lived a splintered existence in localized pockets where they strove to efface every identifying mark that might compromise them in the eyes of outsiders, breaking their cover and thus leading to their professional downfall and personal humiliation. For a minority trying so vigorously to erase itself, political unity was a contradiction in terms. With the codification of the gay sensibility and the liberation of men trapped in the solipsistic isolation of intense shame, the homosexual suddenly recognized that he belonged to a group, an elaborate network of fellow solipsists who began busily to establish connections with each other, partly through shared tastes in popular culture whose cinematic heroes lent an unprecedented centrality to the previously disjointed and atomized nature of gay life. Hollywood divas were drafted, often without their knowledge, into the role of quasi-gay-liberation leaders whose charismatic presence unified a body of followers who flocked together, not necessarily because of their idol's peculiar talents as an actress, but simply because she provided a kind of magnet that assembled large numbers of gay men who established a new type of esprit de corps as the votaries of a particular pantheon of goddesses. Film divas have been so important to gay culture because of the role they played in consolidating it, in bringing together legions of gay men, whom such women as Mae West and Tallulah Bankhead, like pied pipers, led out of the closets to commune together as fans, as a semipublic coalition of admirers who sealed their bonds through the religious worship of Hollywood stars. Fandom, in other words, was an emphatic political assertion of ethnic camaraderie, as was the gay sensibility itself, which did not emanate from some sort of deeply embedded homosexual "soul" but arose as a way of achieving a collective subcultural identity.

Up until the 1960s, the performer served as a bellwether, a prophet without a religion, a platform, a cause, a messiah whose disciples were more in love with themselves than they were with their star. The priority of audience over artist becomes particularly clear in the case of the ultimate bellwether of the docile gay masses, Judy Garland. Her concerts during the 1950s and 1960s were so popular among homosexuals that, in each city in which she appeared, her performances emptied local gay bars, whose patrons came out en masse to hear a dazed and disoriented performer, slumped over the microphone, croak out the broken lyrics of songs that, in her final days, she had difficulty remembering. Garland's force as a lodestone, an excuse for a public gathering of homosexuals, emerges in the existing accounts of her concerts, which gay men describe as orgiastic rites of blind idolatry in which screaming multitudes of homosexuals, whipped up into a frenzy by such plaintive songs as "Over the Rainbow" and "The Man That Got Away," wept out loud, laying on the stage at their divinity's feet altars of flowers. "It was as if the fact that we had gathered to see

Garland gave us permission to be gay in public for once," one older gay man wrote of a 1960 concert, while another described a performance he attended as "more a love-in than a concert":

> When Judy came onto the stage, we were the loudest and most exuberant part of that audience. We not only listened, we felt all the lyrics of all the songs. Judy Garland was all ours; she belonged to every gay guy and girl in the theater. I like to think that we were the greatest part of that audience; the part that Judy liked the best.

Although Garland was in many ways a brilliant performer, homosexuals describe the raucous, gay-pride "love-ins" that erupted spontaneously during her concerts as if she were simply the catalyst for a social occasion. Her uncritical mass appeal helped overcome our fragmentation to create for only a few hours, within the safe confines of an auditorium, an ephemeral, transitory "community" which lured us out of the closets in order to experience the unforgettable thrill of a public celebration of homosexuality. Those commentators who insist on trying to explain gay diva worship exclusively on the basis of the intrinsic appeal of the particular star, as a result of her pathos, suffering, vulnerability, glamour, or sexiness, to give only a few of the reasons that have been offered, have in many ways chosen as their starting point a mistaken premise. The answer to the proverbial question "Why did gay men like Judy Garland so much?" is that they liked not her so much as her audience, the hordes of other gay men who gathered in her name to hear her poignant renditions of old torch songs which reduced sniffling queens to floods of self-pitying tears. The hysterical ovations her audiences gave her were in some sense applause for themselves. Garland was simply the hostess, a performer who good-naturedly rented out her immense reputation as an occasion for a huge gay party, a dry run for Stonewall, a dress rehearsal for the birthday bash of the burgeoning gay rights movement, which her last and most important concert, her funeral, was to inspire only a few years later. Gay diva worship, in short, can be seen as a sublimated form of self-worship.

The shared knowledge of popular film created the very foundations of camp. Homosexuals quickly incorporated into their conversations and style of humor a body of subcultural allusions, including such things as Carmen Miranda in *The Gang's All Here,* singing "The Lady in the Tutti Frutti Hat" in eight-inch platform heels on a runway framed by giant strawberries; Marlene Dietrich, wearing a blond Afro crooning "Hot Voodoo" in *Blond Venus* while chorus lines of cavorting Negresses wearing war paint do the cakewalk behind her; or Maria Montez in *The Cobra Woman,* dancing a kootch dance in a slinky, sequin snake dress as she selects terrified subjects for blood sacrifices, who are borne off shrieking to their unhappy fate. Through constant reenactments of the scripts of Hollywood movies in our private conversations, we created a collage of famous lines and quips, which, after frequent repetition, achieved the status of passwords to an illicit world of the initiated, who communicated through innuendo, through quoted dialogue pregnant with an unspoken subtext. A miscellaneous body of canonic lines were lifted straight out of the masterpieces of popular culture and exploited as a way of declaring our membership in the forbidden ranks of a secret society:

Toto, I don't think we're in Kansas anymore.

But you are, Blanche, you are in that chair.

I've always depended on the kindness of strangers.

Buckle your seatbelts, it's going to be a bumpy night.

What is the scene? Where am I?

What a dump!

Jungle red!

When gay people engaged in camp before Stonewall, they were often laughing at the misuse of popular culture as a means for accomplishing something it was never intended to do, that of identifying themselves to other homosexuals and triggering in their audience instantaneous recognition of stock expressions, gestures, and double entendres which strengthened the bonds that held them together. Even today, a performer as gifted as Lypsinka, whose acts consist entirely of an intricate series of quotations from films, succeeds as a brilliant comic by virtue of her uncanny ability to play upon her audience's gleeful sense of unity as a minority, an ethnic group that relives, long after we have securely established other channels of communication, the power of allusion to increase solidarity. Lypsinka simply mouths the words "no wire hangers" or "Barbara, pleeeeeease!" and her audience disintegrates into laughter caused, not by the intrinsic hilariousness of the lines, but by the delight we take in the unanimity of our response, in our virtually reflexive recognition of the source of the allusions, an esoteric knowledge that contributes to the elitist pleasure of a coterie sealed off from the rest of the uninitiated American public.

Camp and diva worship also served a more narrowly personal function than just providing us with a repository of subcultural narratives that became our own private language. Before Stonewall, allusions to such films as *The Women, Mildred Pierce, Now, Voyager, A Streetcar Named Desire,* or *Gilda* were ingeniously incorporated into the extremely delicate business of cruising for friends and sex partners, many of whom would undoubtedly have been far too timid to state their preferences openly. How much simpler it was to encode one's sexual orientation into something as elusive and uncompromising as a taste for a particular actress whose name could be dropped casually in the course of a conversation in hopes that one's partner would pick up the gambit and agree that he did indeed like Judy Garland, that Mae West was outrageously funny, and that Tallulah Bankhead was, as she herself once said, "as pure as the driven slush." As exemplified by that time-honored expression "a friend of Dorothy," the association of one's sexual orientation with a particular taste in film provided a useful come-on for cautious gay men, who could reveal themselves to others without risking exposure, since only a fellow insider would pick up on the allusion, thus allowing the homosexual to circumvent the potential embarrassment of a dismayed or even hostile reaction to a flat declaration. Over the decades gay men became so adept at encoding their forbidden desires into camp allusions that a sort of collective amnesia has descended over the whole process and we have lost sight of the fact that our love for performers like Judy Garland was actually a learned behavior, part of our socialization as homosexuals. Many gay men still mistake their cultish admiration for the likes of Tippi Hedren, Kim Novak, or Barbara Stanwyck as an expression of an innate gay predisposition, as if the love of actresses was the result of a physiological imbalance in our enlarged hypothalamuses, of a diva chromosome in our DNA which produced a camp sensibility that somehow preceded our awareness of our homosexuality.

Very early on in the history of the homosexual's obsession with Hollywood, the nature of camp began to change. Irony was always present in the subculture's involvement with celebrities, partly because of the homosexual's sly awareness that he was misusing something as naive and wholesome as popular culture, with its golly-gee-whiz, Kansas-bred Dorothys and its Norman Rockwell happy endings, to reinforce something as illicit and underground as his solidarity with other homosexual pariahs. As time went on, however, the note of facetiousness implicit in many gay men's treatment of Hollywood became louder and louder, until the wry smile of camp became the cackling shriek of the man who could no longer take seriously the divas he once adored. By the early 1960s, some gay men had begun to express an element of revulsion from our obsequious fawning over celebrities. Patrick Dennis's 1961 camp masterpiece *Little Me* provides a clear instance of the increasing skepticism homosexuals were bringing to their involvement with Hollywood. The novel purports to be the memoir of Belle Schlumpfert, a.k.a. Belle Poitrine, a great film actress, but in fact this imaginary autobiography, complete with hilarious photographs documenting Belle's meteoric rise to fame from her humble beginnings as the daughter of a scarlet woman, is an irresistibly scathing satire of a megalomaniac piece of trailer trash who uses the casting couch as a trampoline to catapult herself into stardom. By the 1980s and 1990s, the pantheon of immortals, while still treated reverently by many gay men, had become fair game for ridicule, as when New York drag queens commemorated the 1981 release of *Mommie Dearest* by dressing up as Joan Crawford and kicking life-size effigies of her daughter Christina up and down Christopher Street. Similarly, in 1987, *New York Native* columnist Dee Sushi imagined a hypothetical Broadway musical based on *Whatever Happened to Baby Jane?* in which a chorus line of spinning wheelchairs would whirl across the stage like dervishes to the accompaniment of a song entitled "But Cha Are!"

One of the reasons for the change from reverence to ridicule, from Joan Crawford as the bewitching siren to Joan Crawford as the ax-wielding, child-beating, lesbian drunk, is that, in the minds of younger homosexuals, the diva is perceived as the emotional crutch of the pathetic old queen, the geriatric spinster who, surrounded by his antiques and registered crockery, compensates for the loneliness of his thwarted life by projecting himself into the tantalizing hourglass figures and haute couture ball gowns of his favorite actresses. For gay men under the age of forty, the classic film star has become the symbolic icon of an oppressed early stage in gay culture in which homosexuals sat glued to their television sets feasting their eyes on reruns, achieving through their imaginations the sense of self-worth that gay men now achieve by consuming the propaganda that our political leaders disseminate in such alarming quantities. For the contemporary homosexual, who prides himself on his emotional maturity and healthiness, the use of the diva to achieve romantic fulfillment through displacement is the degrading and politically repugnant fantasy of the self-loathing pansy whose dependence on the escapism of cinema must be ritually purged from our systems. We accomplish this catharsis by creating through conversations, theater, and even cabaret acts images of the vulgarity and psychological desperation of glamorous actresses, of Joan Crawford clobbering Christina with a can of bathroom cleanser or chopping off the head of her faithless husband in *Strait-Jacket*.

John Weir's novel about AIDS, *The Irreversible Decline of Eddie Socket*, revolves around this act of purgation. Like Rims, its dying protagonist attempts to face his bleak future by staging what he calls "Barbara Stanwyck moment[s]." With his inspired sense of melodrama, he appears to be a typical example of a gay man with a relentlessly active internal diva but, far from finding her "empowering," she becomes a vampire that feeds on his vitality, an incubus that saps his life of its reality and makes him feel that "the whole fucking world was in quotes. Was death going to be in quotes, too?" Lying in his excrement in his hospital bed, abandoned by the nurses and orderlies who are too afraid to touch him, he wonders out loud to a friend:

> Who's the main character in my life? . . . Who is starring in my life? It can't be me . . . I'm just a walk-on . . . Not even a supporting player. Not even a cameo appearance by a long-forgotten star. I'm just an extra. No one else is starring in my life. That's why they're halting production. It's a bad investment for the studio.

Returning from the hospital, his friend has an hallucination that can be interpreted as a diatribe against the gay escapist whose obsession with actresses diminishes the reality of his life, starving it of its meaning, and providing a safe emotional haven where the gay man anesthetizes himself to the difficulties of being a homosexual. As he sits on a crosstown bus, Elizabeth Taylor appears out of the blue and proceeds, before his very eyes, to pull herself apart like Lego blocks in order to disabuse him of his slavish adoration, first removing her contact lenses, then her chin, cheeks, breasts, left buttock, and right knee-cap, until he realizes that, despite all of her glamour, "she's a walking prosthesis," "a pile of rubber parts on the floor between us . . . all diminished." Stuffing herself into a shopping bag, she hobbles off the bus, no longer the tantalizing emblem of the life the homosexual cannot live, but a Mr. Potato Head. This apocalyptic image of Taylor's self-destruction is pivotal to a book that is, in many ways, an anticamp requiem, an expression of the young homosexual's mounting impatience with the retrograde use of Hollywood as a security blanket, the method by which the pre-Stonewall gay man once avoided his life, barricading himself in his closet.

The untouchable image of the Hollywood deity was also tarnished by the fact that, in the late 1960s and 1970s, gay men began holding their proto-gay-liberation leaders to a higher political standard. Because of the role actresses played in bringing gay men together as fans and instilling in them a sense of national identity that transcended the fragmented world of lonely solipsists that existed before Stonewall, homosexuals were at first unswervingly loyal to their patron saints and remained largely blind to their glaring deficiencies as the subculture's unofficial envoys to mainstream society. As we became more politically aware, however, and more conscious of our own clout as a unified minority, we became more and more impatient with the patronizing maternalism of early gay politics, which had produced the great matriarchy of mother hens who hovered protectively over their broods of gay fans. After Stonewall, we were no longer satisfied with the crumbs of celebrities' halfhearted comfort and support, with the meager consolation they offered for the humiliation of our social ostracism, which rarely amounted to more than such ambiguous statements as "you poor little darlings" or "leave them alone, you bullies, they're so harmless."

In a 1971 issue of *The Advocate*, an interesting flurry of letters was published that shows how uncomfortable gay men were beginning to feel with the tepid politics of maternalism. An outraged fan of Mae West wrote in to express his amazement at a passage he discovered in her autobiography which read:

> In many ways homosexuality is a danger to the entire social system of western civilization. Certainly a nation should be made aware of its . . . effects on children recruited to it in their innocence . . . As a private pressure group it could, and has, infected whole nations. The old Arab world rotted away from it.

In the weeks that followed, hard-core gay fans, unshaken in their devotion to their idol, leaped to her defense, bending over backwards to exculpate her from such damning evidence and blasting her accuser as a unpardonable turncoat ("some fan!" one die-hard admirer complained). Even West's personal secretary, Robert Duran, no doubt a homosexual himself, wrote in to offer the feeble excuse that the quotation had been taken out of context and that, far from being homophobic, "Miss West has always glorified gay people."

One of the reasons that our attitudes toward divas changed so dramatically throughout the 1960s is that we outgrew our idols, who could not keep pace with our own political development but remained stagnant symbols of gay oppression, content to scratch our ears like celebrity lapdogs. Just as homosexuals found the fantasy of achieving romantic fulfillment through their vicarious projection into the persona of the film star incompatible with their new sense of dignity after Stonewall, so they defected from the once swollen ranks of their proto-gay-liberation leaders, who were retired as obsolete political vehicles and consigned to a vast museum of gay kitsch. Homosexuals picked up the discarded costumes and exaggerated mannerisms of these fading reputations and turned them into a communal grab bag for Halloween pranks, using the graven images of the old religion as satiric playthings for quaint camp pastimes. The temple of celebrity worship was pillaged and defiled, and the sacred vestments became dresses for drag shows, with gay men wearing the girlish ponytails and clown-white makeup of the ravaged Bette Davis in *Whatever Happened to Baby Jane?* or wrapping themselves in the Mama Cass muumuus of Shelley Winters, who, according to female impersonator Charles Pierce, was so fat that she ate cereal out of satellite dishes and had been granted her own zip code.

The homosexual's rebound from popular culture was also inspired by the ambivalence toward lowbrow entertainment that lies at the very heart of the gay sensibility itself. In the years before Stonewall, Hollywood enabled the homosexual to express his alienation from the uneducated American public by cultivating the aestheticism of maladjustment, the use of conspicuous displays of tastefulness to rebel against philistinism, to distinguish himself from the boorishness of the society that despised him. And yet aestheticism was an extremely problematic solution to the often harrowing challenges facing the effeminate homosexual. Most gay men had neither the means nor the education to avenge themselves against the contempt of their oppressors by cultivating the invulnerable persona of the aristocratic dandy, who filled his rooms with Oriental objets d'art and decadent Aubrey Beardsley prints. The ideal of the aesthete, of the impeccably tasteful devotee of the religion of beauty, is an aristocratic ideal, one that requires considerable leisure, as well as financial means, and which posed a particularly punitive economic burden on men who were themselves as ignorant of high culture as the plebeians whose tastelessness they sought to denigrate by exhibiting their own savoir faire. The movies therefore provided a poor man's aestheticism, a cheap means of satisfying the frustrated aesthetic sensibility of florists, hair stylists, waiters, and bank clerks who would otherwise not have been able to erect protective divisions of elegance between themselves and disapproving heterosexuals. One of the primary elements of camp, the obsession with popular cinema, became an integral part of gay life as a result of its psychological utility to a group of men pathetically striving to step out of their class entirely and take refuge in the sumptuous lives of the well-to-do. Using the only materials they could afford, the images of extravagant wealth available in film—the fabulous gowns, palatial estates, penthouse love nests, mink stoles, and Rolls-Royces—they devised a clever method of shielding themselves from bigotry through the vicarious experience of unattainable affluence.

As Susan Sontag makes clear in "Notes on Camp," however, the sensibility of the overbred dandy, with *Les Fleurs du Mal* in one hand and *Au Rebours* in the other, is a "snob" sensibility, one that reviles the very medium that fueled the lower-middle-class homosexual's fiction of superiority. The gay sensibility is thus at war with itself, on the one hand feeding on the accessible glamour of Hollywood and, on the other, afraid of debasing itself through its obsessive contact with Tinsel Town's cheapness. The same cinematic images that sustain the homosexual's aestheticism are tainted with the chintziness and mediocrity he is seeking to escape. Because of the dilemma facing the would-be dandy, reverence and ridicule go hand in hand. Implicit in the homosexual's adoration of the star is his revulsion from her. This contradiction erupts in such iconoclastic acts of celebrity desecration as the San Francisco Yuletide performance of "Christmas at the Crawfords," an annual burlesque of the famous 1949 radio broadcast in which Joan Crawford, rather than cooing graciously into the microphone in an effort to convey the impression to her listeners of being the perfect, selfless mother, whips out a coat hanger and, bellowing homicidal threats, thrashes her negligent daughter right on the spot. Similarly, in the New York drag festival Wigstock, celebrity desecration figures so prominently that the whole spectacle often degenerates into a funeral in honor of the dead diva who is paraded around by ghoulish drag-queen pallbearers, by men dressed up as Agnes Moorehead after she breaks her neck in *Hush, Hush, Sweet Charlotte* or *Psycho*'s Janet Leigh mauled by "Mother."

The new fascination with the diva as kitsch, a laughingstock, a reptile in a dress who cussed like a trooper and threw drunken tantrums in public places, was the result, not only of a contradiction intrinsic to the gay sensibility, but a contradiction intrinsic to the very nature of glamour and the medium of film itself. A key aspect of homosexual camp stems from two central factors that, while having nothing to do with the gay sensibility, have nonetheless given it its distinctive shape. They provided the impetus for a common form of gay mockery which originated in our disillusionment with our once "empowering" role models who, as they became older and lost their position of preeminence in American society, could not sustain their prestige in the eyes of their gay fans. Changes that occurred in the careers of the women behind the legends also occurred in the gay man's attitude toward himself and in the uses he was able to make of Hollywood glamour. What happened to the real diva also happened to the imaginary one, so that the fate of these two mythical beings was closely linked. They had become part of us; we had incorporated their style into our own. When they declined, we declined; when they were discredited, we were discredited.

Given how integral the star's aura was to the homosexual's sense of power and masculinity, the humiliation the celebrity experienced in public was something the gay man, as her idolator, experienced in private, on the level of his self-conception. In addition to old age, a second factor led to the actress's devastating loss of credibility. If glamour is a hoax just waiting to be exposed, the very camera that exalted these women was also the agent of their downfall, the instrument of their torture, the divinely sanctioned method of punishment for their pride. A capacity intrinsic to the medium of film, its ability to record for all posterity the effects of age on the divas' bodies, created an essential element of modern homosexual camp: its obsession with decay, decomposition, and decrepitude, with a seventy-year-old Joan Crawford in black fishnet tights playing a circus ring mistress in *Berserk* or an unsteady Dietrich clinging for support to the stage curtain, her wig askew, her lipstick smeared, her voice no more than a hoarse whisper as she wailed out a drunken rendition of "Where Have All the Flowers Gone?" By the 1950s, the careers of Dietrich, Crawford, Davis, and Hayworth were essentially over. But—and herein lies the secret ingredient of gay men's recipe for camp—long after their idols' reputations had begun to decline, the cameras kept rolling even as these sex goddesses turned into withered hags before our very eyes, shriveling up into mummies as they fought tooth and nail to revive their waning careers, finally sinking into the unfathomable depths of B-grade horror flicks, playing ax murderesses and psychotic forgotten stars. And then, with the advent of television, the nightly broadcast of reruns drove the final nails into their coffins: For the first time in history, gay men were allowed to see, virtually side by side, what these women once were and what they had become, watching one night a glamorous Bette Davis in *The Letter* at the height of her career and the next a battered old crone starring in *Whatever Happened to Baby Jane?*, glaring bewildered at her gruesome reflection in the mirror where she stood in pigtails and pinafores, her ancient face caked with the makeup she troweled on for her part at her own insistence. Without reruns, there is no camp, for camp is about the death of glamour, about the shattering of the sacrosanct illusion of the actress's inimitable aura of youth and invulnerability, about knocking the idol off her pedestal, and dragging her through the mud, subjecting her decrepitude to the same minute scrutiny to which the medium of film once subjected her beauty. Camp is rooted in the gay man's profound disillusionment with celebrity culture. It expresses betrayal. It is the gleeful sadism of the fan who has been tricked, who discovers that he has been complicit in an elaborate swindle, a monstrous lie, who realizes that his youthful cinematic fantasies are false, that his role models are marionettes, crude trompe l'oeil puppets whose talent and glamour were all smoke and mirrors. At the core of gay hero worship is its own negation; at the heart of glamour—the grotesque. Beneath the diva's loveliness were the seeds of the ridicule that was to come. Out of this loss of innocence, homosexuals have created a macabre form of ethnic humor in which they dance on their former role models' graves, reliving again and again the hilarious realization that the diva was not a goddess, that she was flesh and blood, that she got fat just like they did, that she got wrinkled just like they did, that she had miserable lives and horrid children and crippling diseases and financial crises and even died just like they did, but with one major difference: In the case of the diva, the press was there to get it all down, to record every pratfall and black eye and lesbian affair and drug overdose and nose job and trip to the fat farm and convalescence in the Betty Ford Center.

If camp is fueled by the ability of film to record the ravages of time, to document the process of aging as homosexuals had never seen it before, it has also been shaped by another seemingly unrelated factor, the rise of investigative journalism and the invasiveness in modern life of the media, which suddenly brought gay men in closer proximity, not only to the divas' deteriorating bodies, but to their chaotic private lives. Within the last twenty-five years, a rash of tell-all biographies has catered to the public's insatiable desire for information, including three poison-pen memoirs of Crawford, Davis, and Dietrich by their ungrateful daughters, who, to the delight of millions, committed immensely entertaining acts of literary matricide. In the course of this unprecedented media barrage, the gay man's internal diva suffered a significant blow to her dignity. The press changed the entire psychology of diva worship, altering it so radically that celebrities could no longer serve the same invigorating function of inspiring us with pride and determination. As a result, homosexuals were left with an unburied corpse festering in their imaginations, the lifeless remains of a public figure who did not carry the same weight of authority and who was therefore subject to the necrophiliac depredations of camp. The homosexual's mockery of his heroines is something he is also doing to himself, using the humor of celebrity desecration as an anesthetic for the amputation of an obsolete part of the gay psyche.

The change from reverence to ridicule can be explained by a simple fact: Devotion always ends up consuming its object, demanding ever greater intimacy with the source of its obsession. And yet intimacy is the very thing that destroys reverence, that turns reverence into ridicule, for idolatry can be maintained only through distance, through aloofness, through the celebrity's ability to keep her gay public at bay, always wondering, always guessing at what lies behind her magisterial facade, at the mysterious goings-on in the heart of the inner sanctum behind the electric fences and the bodyguards. While remoteness and ignorance are the primary requirements of the primitive folk religion of homosexual celebrity worship, everything in modern secular society conspires to eliminate this distance, to close in on the immediate cause of the gay man's fascination, to hunt it down like game and force it out into the open. Driven wild by our need to know more about the people we fetishize, we sic the press like dogs to get the scoop, to open the can of worms, to snap the shot of the illicit rendezvous at the secret hideaway, to record every gaffe, every candid moment of the frazzled star without her makeup, looking hideous in a T-shirt and sweatpants as she slips out the back door of the drug rehabilitation clinic. The hunger of the crazed gay fan for ever more detailed information about his role models sets in motion the very investigative machine that ultimately erodes the foundation of his blind, selfless devotion. In a secular society based on an untrammeled free press and accustomed to the high standards of truth that a free press instills in us, it is impossible to maintain the conditions of mystery and remoteness that make something as superstitious and old-fashioned as Hollywood idolatry possible in the first place. Gay diva worship is a cult that requires the blind faith of credulous fans who are content to kowtow and genuflect and never to even think of peeking behind the curtain. Camp is what happens when the curtain is lifted. The irreverent humor of the drag queen dressed up as a trembling Katharine Hepburn, a dazed Peggy Lee in a scarf and black shades, or a haggard Tippi Hedren in *The Birds,* her teased-up wig a nest of carnivorous sparrows and seagulls, represents the last gasp of idol worship in a secular age, the passing of a mode of religious experience, whose funeral gay men celebrate with delightfully deranged fervor. Camp is the final rite of the religion that failed, the satirical requiem of the heathen fetishist who has lost faith in his god, who has watched too many reruns and seen too many incriminating photographs and read too many kiss-and-tell biographies to believe in the myth of glamour. Gay men have created a school of ethnic humor out of what amounts to the fundamental religious crisis of twentieth-century popular culture.

But camp has always been something more than just the death throes of pagan idolatry in a secular age. It has also served, as we have seen, to consolidate group identity through the mastery of a body of cinematic allusions to such pivotal gay films as *The Women, Sunset Boulevard, All About Eve, A Star Is Born, Whatever Happened to Baby Jane?*, and, more recently, that belated camp masterpiece, *Mommie Dearest*. Because gay culture is becoming less closeted, however, the need to seal our furtive communal bond through the secret handshake of Hollywood trivia is disappearing, and with this disappearance, a crucial element of the gay sensibility has been thrown into jeopardy. Liberation is destroying the need for celebrity culture as a group marker, as a way of expressing tribal inclusion in a private membership club of the cognoscenti who have other less circuitous ways of meeting and socializing now that the whole purpose of communicating in code has disappeared after the explosion of mega dance clubs, gay men's choruses, computer bulletin boards, phone chat lines, bowling leagues, Gay and Lesbian Sierra Clubs, and self-help Bible study groups for gay Mormons in recovery. Many homosexuals under the age of thirty have never even seen a single film starring Joan Crawford, let alone relished the magnificent biographical ironies of *Mildred Pierce* or savored the equally astonishing biographical ironies of *A Star is Born* or seen Bette Davis's hair fall out in *Mr. Skeffington* or Rita Hayworth dance in *Gilda* or Marlene Dietrich play a melancholy and infinitely wise courtesan in *Shanghai Express* who turns sadly to an old suitor and laments, "It took more than one man to change my name to Shanghai Lily." While gay culture is still obsessed with celebrities (although primarily as a political force, a PR tool for promoting "visibility"), young gay men no longer have the same involvement with popular culture that they had when the movies served almost as a social intermediary, a matchmaker, a badge to identify oneself to other members of the clan, other "friends of Dorothy." As the forces of social stigma and oppression dissipate and the factors that contributed to the making of the gay sensibility disappear, homosexuals' most significant contribution to American culture, camp, begins to lose its shape. The grain of sand, our oppression, that irritated the gay imagination to produce the pearl of camp has been rinsed away, and with it, there has been a profound dilution of the once concentrated gay sensibility. Camp cannot survive our ultimate and inevitable release from the social burden of our homosexuality. Oppression and camp are inextricably linked, and the waning of the one necessitates the death of the other.

Playing Oscar

BY STEPHEN FRY

A few years ago, I sat for the British artist Maggi Hambling as she painted a series of portraits of me. Not long afterward, she embarked on a series of drawings and sculptures of Oscar Wilde, and, as it happened, I was asked to play Wilde in a film of his life. Hambling, who has the true artist's ability to be simultaneously earthy and mystical, played with the coincidence by doing a series of drawings in which I "morphed" into Wilde. She has a very high and real sense of Wilde's importance to artists everywhere and was delighted at my good fortune, just as I was delighted when, a year later, she won a competition to create the first statue of Wilde to be erected in central London. I couldn't help feeling a tinge of envy, however. While I am not suggesting that to make a statue or a painting of Wilde is easy—far from it—the materials an artist uses allow a kind of displacement, a passionate, engaged objectivity, that is denied an actor. I was going to

FROM *THE NEW YORKER*

have to use my voice, my face, and my body. No wax, bronze, oils, or acrylics for me—just my own befuddled self.

"Playing Oscar" could be the title for as hellishly postmodern and self-reflexive a game as was ever devised. To pose as Oscar Wilde, the author of "The Truth of Masks," a man perceived by many (himself often included) to be posing as one who posed at being a poseur—how many Chinese boxes in a hall of how many mirrors does that make?

The first rule, I have discovered, when embarking on such a project is to block your ears and lock up all mailboxes, real or electronic. Letters arrive. Oh, how letters arrive.

Dear Mr. Fry, I hope you will not be forgetting that the key, the only key, to Oscar is that he was and is, first and foremost, *Irish*. . . .

Dear Mr. Fry, Wilde's works whinny and shiver with Victorian gay underground codes. Do not shirk the force of his sexual identity. . . .

Dear Mr. Fry, Wilde's love of his wife and family is consistently overlooked by biographers. I trust you will not fall into the same error. . . .

Dear Mr. Fry, Wilde's lifetime yearnings toward Roman Catholicism are central to any understanding of . . .

Dear Mr. Fry, I draw your attention toward Wilde's "Soul of Man Under Socialism." Oscar's unique brand of libertarianism is scandalously overlooked by contemporary . . .

Dear Mr. Fry, Oscar Wilde was in reality a woman. This secret was passed on to me by my grandfather, who had a lesbian affair with her in Bad Ischl, June, 1897. . . .

Dear Mr. Fry, It is a little-known fact that Oscar Wilde did not die in 1900 but in 1962, after pursuing a successful career in theatre and the electric cinema under the name Charles Laughton. . . .

Dear Mr. Fry, Oscar Wilde's soul entered my body on August 9, 1963. . . .

Dear Mr. Fry, Oscar Wilde and the Marquess of Queensberry were in reality one and the same man. . . .

I have spared you the weird ones.

If I were to say that all my life had been a preparation for playing Oscar Wilde, I would (aside from sounding ridiculous) be laying my tender rear horribly on the line. Yet I had been made to feel for years that this might be true. I have had archly nudged into me the winsome phrase "born to be Wilde" more times than I care to remember. "The chubbier you get the more you look like him," I have been told. "If you can't, no one can." And "Let's be honest. With a face like yours, it's the only lead you'll ever get. Otherwise, it's a life of Gestapo interrogators, emotionally constipated cuckolds, and Bond villains."

It is certainly true that even if I had never been an actor I should have always felt drawn to Oscar Wilde. However, knowing that I was to play him; reading and rereading his works and the endless catalogue of Wildeana that surrounds him and his circle; listening to so many voices inside and outside my head telling me who he was, what he was, and why he was; and entering debates on hair, gait, accent, laugh, favored cigarette, average daily alcohol intake, and sexual position of choice—all this turned the six months that preceded Day One Principal Photography into a period of slightly trippy, disengaged fever.

Disengaged because our project, *Wilde,* was a British film, which meant that I could never be certain it was going to happen. British production has no continuity. Each project has its own financial structure, its own checkbook, whatever the past credits of the filmmakers. The producers, Marc and Peter Samuelson, and the director, Brian Gilbert, had made *Tom and Viv,* a film that was well received and profitable, but *Wilde* had to be put together from scratch. The perceived disappointment (financial disappointment, that is) of the film of Christopher Hampton's play *Total Eclipse,* with Leonardo di Caprio as Rimbaud and David Thewlis as Verlaine, led me to believe, doomily, that the equation "literary faggots = box-office poison" was being chalked up on all Hollywood blackboards.

Without American money or promises of American distribution, our film would founder, and this was not the kind of film into which an American star could be even halfway convincingly sandwiched. I remember saying to Jeremy Irons at some industry wingding last year that I would believe I was truly cast, and not about to be replaced by a big name, only when a production car arrived to pick me up at my home and take me to the set for the first day's shooting. "No," Irons said. "When the car *returns you home* from the first day. That's when you know." When the cameras finally did roll, then, it came as something more than a relief to wave farewell to the wretched world of preparation and to the imprisonment of endless choice. Filming is, at bottom, blessedly technical. It's about hitting marks, staying in frame, fighting light, and learning lines.

What is preparation, after all? Preparation and research are hot buttons hit by all interviewers when talking to film actors. "What research did you do?" "How did you prepare?" So far as I can tell, they don't ask concert pianists the same questions, but then concert pianists can't offer good copy along the lines of "I put on forty pounds in two weeks," or "I became a voluntary inmate in an asylum for the criminally insane," or "I lived among Kurdish rebels for ten years," or "I cut my head off and learned to talk by pulsing my navel in Morse code."

How did I prepare to play Oscar? The answer is that I really do not know. Acting, especially film acting, is simultaneously mysterious and banal. This is neither to raise it above nor to lower it beneath any other form of endeavor, for the same qualities, I suspect, hold true in tailoring, dentistry, and claims adjusting. Unfortunately, an emphasis on the mystery of acting sounds like hideously unacceptable pretension, and an emphasis on its banality sounds like disingenuous philistinism. The mediahedin's appetite for film information grows on what it feeds on. No one outside the worlds of engineering, carpentry, or insurance wants to understand their processes, but everyone, it seems, wants to be able to talk about magic hour, aspect ratios, Foley edits, jibbing, crabbing, panning, and actors' choices—whatever the hell they are.

Furthermore, any film of a more than minuscule budget these days comes with its own Electronic Press Kit, or EPK—one of those featurettes about the making of the making of a movie. Before a film is out, we've all seen the storyboard, read the screenplay, marveled at the SFX computer arrays in Seattle, and lived through the production crises with the producer, the director, and the actors. The unkind have suggested that some EPKs, such as "The Making of 'Independence Day,'" offer a much more stimulating and coherent narrative than their parent movies. The real advantage for all, however, is that the interviews and the shootings of shootings which the EPK contains can be controlled and efficiently channeled through to the numberless *Entertainment Tonight*-style programs that now litter the floor of global TV like used lottery scratch cards, which allows the big names to do a great deal of their interviewing in one hit, freeing them up to spend more time with their ranch managers and divorce attorneys. Most of them have no choice in the matter. It's all there in the contract, next to the moral-turpitude rider and the agreement to undergo spot urine tests for Class A drugs, but when explanation crashes through the front door, mystery creeps blushing out the back.

The irony—or the joke, perhaps—about making a film on Wilde is that the process described above is a refinement on Wilde's own celebrity of a hundred years ago: a created thing that might be offered as a boilerplate for all the celebrity mania that was to follow. Wilde was nationally famous before he had written a single memorable work—famous as an undergraduate, famous for being famous, and pilloried in the cartoons and comic cuts for his exotic dress sense and his too-utterly-utter aesthetic sensibilities. He was paid to tour the United States to publicize *Patience,* a Gilbert and Sullivan operetta that guyed him and his circle. Certainly he earned his fame later, with the huge success and notoriety of his literary and dramatic works. But up until his trial, in 1893, the public view of Wilde was that the most famous thing about him was his fame—a logic loop all too familiar to contemporary celebrities.

I can remember the first time I heard of Beatrix Potter. I can remember the first time I heard of Harriet Beecher Stowe. I can recall with piercing clarity the moment when the name Fyodor Dostoyevsky first came to my ears. (It was in a Norwich café bearing the improbable name Just John's Delicatique.) No matter how hard I try, however, I am unable to think of a time before I had heard of Oscar Wilde. It is as if he had been with me always, like Christ and the Queen.

Not just with me, either. I have tried this out with godchildren and nephews of the tenderest years and the most Disneyfied sensibilities.

Just as offering "Scooby what?" will result in an immediate "Doo," so asking "Oscar what?" will produce an instant "Wilde." In our vulgar world, the name Oscar Wilde has become a logo. And the name has an existence quite independent of the life of Oscar Fingal O'Flahertie Wills Wilde, born 1854, died 1900—a man none of us have ever met. The name has a meaning wholly distinct, too, from the works of Oscar Wilde: plays, poems, criticism, articles, essays, short stories, children's tales, and a novel.

And what of Wilde the man? He stood for Art. He stood for nothing less all his life. His doctrine of Art was so high that most people thought he was joking. The English, who to this day believe themselves quite mistakenly to be possessed of a higher sense of humor than any other nation on earth, have never understood that a thing expressed with wit is more, not less, likely to be true than a thing intoned gravely as solemn fact. We British, who pride ourselves on our superior sense of irony, have never fully grasped the idea of fiction—of *ironism*. Plain old sarcasm is about our mark. When Wilde made an epigram, it was, at best, "clever." Clever, like funny, is an English insult of the deepest kind. That minority of English men and women who rejoiced in Wilde's downfall because they were truly sickened by the idea of one man's carnal association with another are almost to be admired, for there was at least a kind of honesty in their hysteria. Most of the hands that were rubbed in glee when Wilde fell were rubbed because all that he stood for fell with him. Damn Wilde for the dull and uninteresting crime of putting his organ of generation in certain places and there was no need to contemplate his real crime, which was not sexual inversion but moral, political, spiritual, and artistic inversion. His imprisonment allowed late-Victorian England to roll up into a sack the work he had done and hurl it like a poxed odalisque into the Bosphorus. In that sense, the public exposure of his homosexuality was a great intellectual disaster: It contaminated the greatness of his work in the eyes of the world, most especially his work in discursive prose.

A hundred years later, it is Victorian life that is disgraced in our eyes, and Wilde stands now as the Crown Prince of Bohemia: an almost messianic figure to those who want to show their allegiance to Art and Beauty; a saint to those whose recently legitimated sexuality needs its heroes and martyrs; a role model to those who in adolescence have glimpsed the possibilities of self-realization and now tremble terrified on the brink of bourgeoisification. To call Wilde messianic sounds overblown and risks nasty letters from the religious, but there are obvious parallels with the life of Christ. Wilde was despised and rejected; he made fools of the pharisaical elements of society; he had disciples; he was betrayed by one he loved; he sat in his red plush Chelsea Gethsemane knocking back the hock and seltzer while all those around him told him to flee before the entrance of the soldiers, a scene that was neatly retold by John Betjeman:

> "Mr. Woilde we 'ave come for tew take yew
> Where felons and criminals dwell
> We must ask yew tew leave with us quoietly
> For this *is* the Cadogan Hotel."

Then he rose again to become within a short time after his death the most widely read and translated English-language author in Europe after Shakespeare, and he lives with us now in boxer shorts, playing cards, coffee mugs, coasters, and pencil sharpeners.

In our age—which mistakes, as did Wilde's, style for culture and culture for art—is Oscar now just a symbol, however potent? Besides, how dare one assume that the case for Wilde is proved? Despite his hyperbolic image, there are millions out there who have only the dimmest sense of him.

A gentleman approached me one day when we were shooting *Wilde* in Hyde Park. "What's all this, then?" he wanted to know.

"We're making a film about the life of Oscar Wilde," I replied.

"Ah, the great man himself," the gentleman said, nodding wisely. "I have a record of him singing live, you know."

"Excuse me?"

"Yes, live at the Desert Inn, Las Vegas. The best version of 'Mad Dogs and Englishmen' you'll ever hear."

I have said that there was never a time I could remember when I had not heard of Wilde. I had great need of him. Without trampling once more over the well-trodden ground of English public-school education, I must ask you to picture me at the age of thirteen, on a rugby field deep in the heart of the English countryside, shivering, scared, and miserable. Waterloo may have been won on the playing fields, but it was not the only battle to be fought there. I drew up lines between the athletic and the aesthetic, the barbaric and the beautiful, the prose and the passion, the inner and outer lives of *Howards End.* "Only connect" was not my text, however. This was war. Early knowledge of my homosexuality only served to define the issue more clearly. There was a world of brutish shouts, mud, tribal intolerance, boasting about girls, and contempt for ideas, and there was another world, whose doorway stood in the school library.

God knows how many books I found there to endorse my tiresomely traditional solipsistic achings—biography, autobiography, and slim volume after slim volume cataloguing the pansy path to freedom. From Norman Douglas to Robin Maugham, by way of Gide and Peyrefitte, I read—jasper cigarette holder in hand and tasseled smoking cap on head—how the dark clouds of post-Victorian philistinism could give way to the Mediterranean sunlight in Florence, Capri, or North Africa. Beckford and Byron had traveled the same route a century earlier, but it was Wilde whose spirit reigned at these feasts of light and color and silks and poetry and carnal freedom.

That last point sticks, of course. Are we talking sexual tourism here? Is this what all that high talk comes down to—a greasy intellectual and pseudoaesthetic justification for following the pervert's pilgrim trail to Tangier? Well, hypocrisy is never good, and I cannot deny that, as a flushed adolescent in a dusty library, much of the thrill I got from reading of the world of the aesthete came from the notion of a place where one could swan about in costly raiment with houseboys and ephebes in tow—and not a rugby player in sight.

Thank the Lord I was born too late for all that, for the sun has set on that world, and I can utter a pretty convinced good riddance to it. There was never anything greatly ennobling in the theory of it, and, frankly, the practice, for all its camp refinements, never endowed the practitioner with any more artistic glamour or literary credibility than calling a rent boy up to a hotel room does today.

Yet, even in my relatively recent adolescence, Wilde—except for *The Importance of Being Earnest,* which through the genius of its perfection was separated from the personality of its author and granted a kind of amnesty—stood only for the unspeakable vice, for secrecy, shame, and exposure. John Lehmann, who was a contemporary of Harold Acton, Cyril Connolly, and Brian Howard at Eton, in the twenties, recalled in his autobiography the day when the headmaster, Cyril Alington, "a man who delighted in intellectual surprises and paradox," took as the text for his chapel sermon Wilde's *The Happy Prince*:

> When the name of the prisoner of Reading Gaol boomed forth in those hallowed surroundings one could immediately sense the change in the atmosphere. Scarcely any boy dared to look at the opposite pews except in a glazed, rigid way; jaws were clenched and blushes mounted involuntarily to innumerable cheeks. It was a moment of horror and panic: no one knew what was coming next, and everyone was thinking exactly the same thing.

Any gay man will recall the adolescent experience of watching television with his parents and flushing fiercely when a word like "homosexual" was used or when a gay-pride march was featured on the news. The name Wilde, even fifty years after Lehmann's schooldays, still sent fire to my cheeks when it was publicly spoken, for all the fire he may have lent my spirit when privately contemplated.

I admire, therefore—I truly admire—those heterosexual insiders who set a high value on Wilde. There is a purity in their motive. It was easy enough for a Jewish nancy boy like me to draw solace from Wilde the outcast, Wilde the sexual renegade, Wilde the Irishman, Wilde the mocker and baiter of the imperial values that still hung in the air above the parade ground like Crimean cannon smoke. Had I, by the tiniest genetic alteration, been good at rugby and stirred by girls, would I then have been able to see the real point of Wilde? Or would I, like so many of my countrymen, have thought of him (if at all) as not much more than a brittle, queeny wag with crimped hair, a possible source of inspiration when trawling the dictionary of quotations for a best man's speech, but of no more meaning and no more importance? Well, we have to start somewhere, and if nothing else will lead us toward truth the loins may as well. Just as long as the heart and the mind follow and finally overtake, then maybe nothing has been lost. Perhaps there is nothing so very bad after all in finding reality by following an illusion:

There is at least gold at the end of Wilde's rainbow. To chase Judy Garland as a gay alternative to beastly real life may be warm and sweet and cozy, but there is nothing over her rainbow but the black-and-white reality of the familial backyard. The Munchkins don't exist; it was all a dream.

I was about seventeen when I emerged from my Firbank, Douglas, Acton, and Howard phases. I don't regret my teenage posturings and the fantasy years of collecting limp leather editions of decadent, consumptive poets and penning violet-inked diary entries, but these days I must confess that, if pushed, I would rather lose every Oriental silk dressing gown I own than a single pair of sensible corduroy trousers. *Autres temps, autres pantalons.*

I still retain affection for that luxuriantly poisonous style, but it is, I suppose, not much more than literary drag, and, like so many drag acts, it can become tiresome. At any rate, it has nothing whatever to do with Oscar Wilde or his works. Indeed, such images are only part of what the current jargon labels the "self-oppression" to which we are all prey. Wilde's courage lay not in his "alternative sexuality" but in the freedom of his mind. To picture him primarily as a gay martyr *avant la lettre* is, I think, to play into the very hands of those who brought him down a hundred years ago.

Yet I know that it is the sexuality and, most especially, the sex that will excite the interest of the press—above all the British press—when *Wilde* is released. I have had advance notice. A few months ago, the Sunday edition of the *Daily Mail* published a piece on Jude Law, the astonishingly talented young actor in *Wilde* who plays Lord Alfred Douglas, Wilde's lover, the beautiful, petulant, and tempestuous youth known as Bosie. (It was Wilde's relationship with Bosie, the son of the Marquess of Queensberry, that brought him to trial and subsequent imprisonment.) The *Mail* decided that there was a story in the fact that I am gay and Jude is straight, and so it reported that during our "love scenes" together I had to have my penis taped to my stomach to spare my own blushes, not to mention those of Jude Law and the crew. I stared at this story (apparently given to the *Mail* by an insider on the set) amused and amazed, quite undecided as to whether to be flattered or insulted. The fact is that I never actually had to take all my clothes off during the shooting of the film. Wilde, it is generally agreed, did not like to have Bosie Douglas see him naked, for Bosie was not much aroused by Oscar's generous helpings of flesh. So the story was entirely, wholly untrue. For the *Mail,* however, it was a story too good to check. The newspaper wanted it to be true: It had to be true, for it reduced Wilde and his nature (and me and mine, not that that matters much) to the level of sexual beast. Fry is a whoopsy. He had to lie next to an attractive young man, therefore he must have sustained an ungovernable erection. It stands, as it were, to reason. "The penis mightier than the word" has long been the slogan of the British newspaper editor.

"In the old days men had the rack. Now they have the Press." So Wilde wrote in "The Soul of Man Under Socialism." "In France they manage these things better. . . . They limit the journalist, and allow the artist almost perfect freedom. Here we allow absolute freedom to the journalist and entirely limit the artist. English public opinion, that is to say, tries to constrain and impede and warp the man who makes things that are beautiful in effect, and compels the journalist to retail things that are ugly, or disgusting, or revolting in fact, so that we have the most serious journalists in the world and the most indecent newspapers." Wilde was very forgiving, however, and he went on to say of journalists that it was not their fault that they were obliged "to supply the public with what the public wants. . . . It is a very degrading position for any body of educated men to be placed in, and I have no doubt that most of them feel it acutely."

Wilde's forgiveness makes me ashamed of my own intolerance of and anger toward the ghastliness of tabloid journalism. I would like to hope that playing Wilde taught me the humility to be arrogant enough to empathize. It certainly confronted me with endless examples of that primary paradox of his greatness. Wilde's life was one of supreme individualism, but its effect was one of supreme generosity. To fulfill his real self—the eternal Socratic goal—he followed through in life the artistic technique of the imaginative penetration of the lives of others.

When his friend Oswald Sickert died, Wilde went to Sickert's home to comfort his bereaved wife, but was told that she was inconsolable and seeing no one. He persisted till the widow finally agreed to see him, and talked to her hour after hour about her husband, conjuring him back to life with memories and anecdote. Her wailing turned to laughter. Remarkably enough, Wilde even charmed the Marquess of

Queensberry on their first meeting. Bosie and Wilde had been lunching *à deux* at the Café Royal when Queensberry came into the room. Bosie approached his father and invited him to Wilde's table. Queensberry reluctantly consented. After twenty minutes, Bosie left them together, deep in conversation, where they remained for the rest of the afternoon.

Oddly, therefore, the chief memory I have of playing Oscar is not one of spouting epigrams and setting the table in a roar but one of listening and reacting. W. B. Yeats remarked what a great listener Wilde was, and Sir Arthur Conan Doyle is said to have once left a dinner party raving about the man's gift as a conversationalist. "But you did all the talking," his companion pointed out. "Exactly!" Conan Doyle said. To follow Wilde's life on film—often to be actually saying the very things he said in the very places he said them, in the Café Royal in Piccadilly, or walking along the same path he and Bosie Douglas walked along when they first got to know each other, in the gardens of Magdalen College, Oxford—is a disorienting experience. I couldn't possibly be Wilde, but, at further risk of pretension, I certainly feel that playing him has somehow allowed me to be more myself.

I am often asked what I think Wilde would make of our film. All I can be certain of is that he would be kind about it. When Wilde hit upon the idea of Dorian Gray, the beautiful youth who stays young while his portrait ages and takes on the scars of his dissipation, he kept quiet about it. He had once revealed another story idea at the dinner table only to find it written up in a magazine a month later. He wrote to the plagiarist to say that stealing the story was the act of a gentleman, but neglecting to tell Wilde that he had stolen it was not. Such affable chiding was as bitchy as Wilde got. Most people remember the story of Wilde's saying, in response to a witticism, "I wish I had said that," and Whistler's famous reply, "You will, Oscar, you will." That exchange tells us everything we need to know about the difference between Whistler and Wilde.

"De Profundis," the letter that Wilde wrote to Bosie Douglas from prison, is, so far as I know, the greatest and most honest letter ever written. Its title means "from the depths," and it sets out in painfully beautiful language the history of Wilde's relationship with Bosie, his sense of how his life went wrong, and his interpretation of what prison and suffering had taught him. "The supreme vice is shallowness. Whatever is realised is right" was Wilde's last great chime, and he struck it again and again in "De Profundis." To discover the self and develop it to its full realization, that is our duty, Wilde wrote. He knew perfectly well that his downfall would be perceived as the downfall of this philosophy:

> People point to Reading Gaol, and say, "That is where the artistic life leads a man." Well, it might lead to worse places. The more mechanical people . . . always know where they are going, and go there. . . . A man whose desire is to be something separate from himself, to be a Member of Parliament, or a successful grocer, or a prominent solicitor, or a judge, or something equally tedious, invariably succeeds in being what he wants to be.
>
> That is his punishment. Those who want a mask have to wear it. But with the dynamic forces of life . . . it is different. People whose desire is solely for self-realisation never know where they are going. They can't know.

This is the sticking point for many. To hear what they think of as their reward in life being described as a punishment infuriates them, and it could infuriate them only because they suspect it to be true. This is why Wilde is still the Crown Prince of Bohemia. We stand at a threshold in our lives where we look into our futures and see the permanent attachment of a mask, the final adoption of a set of values and "core beliefs" which will see us through to the end, and then we turn and look back at the gigantic, Promethean figure of Wilde—whether we picture him, cigarette in hand, at a table in the Café Royal, generous in wit and high on fame, or bowed over a deal table in a prison cell and cramped with dysentery—and ask ourselves if we have the courage to be like him, by which we mean the courage to be like ourselves.

Whether *Wilde* the movie will "take" or not I cannot possibly guess. Some may be furious over sins of omission or commission; others may balk at its candor or necessary compression of detail. I know there will be letters telling me, "When Wilde was arrested, Reggie Turner was in the room, yet you have him alone with Robbie Ross," or "You have him facing the jury in court, but in fact the jury was behind him," and so on.

We come down to this: Wilde was a great writer and a great man. Great in his kindness, great in his sympathy, and great in his courage. He is still enormously underestimated as an artist and a thinker, especially in his adopted land of England. The subject of *Wilde* the film is not Oscar Wilde's work but his life, yet if it turns any one person to his writings, and most especially to the essays, to the stories for children, and to "De Profundis," then it will have been of some service. For my part, I should be able to return to playing stock English foils, corrupt lawyers, Persian-cat-stroking villains, and epicene fools with a lighter heart.

The Men Who Knew Too Much

BY MARTIN SCORSESE

*T*wo actors loom so large in our collective consciousness that it seems almost redundant to state their importance. But I'll state it anyway: James Stewart and Robert Mitchum were two of the greatest actors in movie history. On the surface, they seem to make a nice contrast: Stewart, the gawky, boyish idealist, and Mitchum, the laconic, disenchanted loner. But each of them had a much more complex persona than this contrast suggests. And these two supposedly disparate actors shared something essential. The malaise of postwar America made a star out of Mitchum, and it remade Stewart's already established star image from the inside out.

I'm not sure that Robert Mitchum would have become a star had he been born at an earlier time. His world-weary reserve and sad-eyed nonchalance were so much a product of his era, they would have made little sense in the twenties or thirties. Even Humphrey Bogart, who originated the depiction of disenchantment in American movies, had

FROM *PREMIERE*

hope. For Mitchum, hope was never even a possibility. The first time his character appears in Jacques Tourneur's *Out of the Past* (1947), fishing by a lake with the girl he loves, you know his happiness is only temporary. And when a deaf mute (Dickie Moore) arrives to tell him he has a visitor, Mitchum knows his fate has caught up with him. There's a kind of Eastern calm and resignation in the early Mitchum (*Out of the Past, Pursued*—a personal favorite of mine, and an example of that unusual subgenre the *noir* western—and Nicholas Ray's wonderful *The Lusty Men*).

The tributes to James Stewart rarely mention the radical change in his screen persona that took place after he returned home from the war. They focus instead on his Frank Capra movies from the thirties, and on *Harvey*. But the fact is that after World War II, an obsessiveness crept into Stewart's work: a solitude, a deep anger at the world. If the prewar Stewart stood for something essentially American, the postwar Stewart stood for something truly universal. It's difficult to think of another American star who remade his own image so thoroughly, so bravely. The only comparable examples are Dick Powell (a thirties crooner and a forties hardcase) and the lesser known John Payne and Dennis O'Keefe (who began as male ingenues and ended up as tough guys). But these actors worked throughout their careers in B pictures, which gave them greater mobility than Stewart had.

The new phase in James Stewart's career began with *It's a Wonderful Life* (1946), in which he pours all the physical energy he can muster into his portrayal of a man at the end of his tether; and with the strange little film *No Highway in the Sky* (1951), in which he plays a scientist driven to extremes by an obsessive scientific fear no one shares. It was in the eight films that he made with Anthony Mann (from *Winchester '73*, in 1950, to *The Man from Laramie*, in 1955) that Stewart's new depth—with its mixture of deep compassion, profound anger, and extreme physicality—was allowed to flourish. The characters he played for Mann were self-centered, driven by greed, and almost suicidally fixated on a single-minded pursuit—they were quite often just plain mean. Stewart and Mann were supposed to do *Night Passage* together, but they quarreled, and the movie was made by another director. It's a shame that such a creative partnership had to end, but it was inevitable, given their tense exploration of such dangerous territory. Unfortunately, their parting seemed to affect Stewart so adversely that he seldom publicly mentioned his Mann films.

James Stewart's work reached unparalleled emotional frankness in Alfred Hitchcock's *Vertigo* (1958). The close-up of Stewart waiting for Kim Novak to emerge from the bathroom, remade as the woman of his dreams, is unlike anything else in his career, in Hitchcock's career, or in movie history. And the last shot of the film is the greatest example I know of a director and an actor merging to create an epiphany. *Vertigo* is the last of the four films Stewart made with Hitchcock—it's difficult to imagine what they could have done as a follow-up.

Stewart did some interesting work after *Vertigo*, particularly in two films for John Ford in the early sixties (*The Man Who Shot Liberty Valance* and *Two Rode Together*), and also in *Anatomy of a Murder* (1959) and *The Flight of the Phoenix* (1966). But a lot of his later performances are in a mellow key, as if he'd shocked himself with his fifties work. Mitchum, on the other hand, continued to experiment. He may have publicly presented himself as a nonchalant professional just showing up to collect a paycheck, but it's obvious that he was drawn to unusual and ambitious screen projects—most notably *Track of the Cat, Home from the Hill, The Wonderful Country,* and *El Dorado*. And, of course, Mitchum achieved something quite remarkable in *The Night of the Hunter* (1955): a stylized, hallucinatory embodiment of the charisma of evil. In the 1970s his acting took on a simple tragic authority, particularly in *The Friends of Eddie Coyle*.

I had the great pleasure of working with Robert Mitchum in 1991, on *Cape Fear*. When I greeted him warmly on the set, his response to "How are you?" was something along the lines of a gruffly mumbled "Still alive." It was only later that he told the following story: Lex Barker was walking down the street one day when he ran into someone he knew. The acquaintance asked how he was and the actor replied, "Very well. The doctor has given me a clean bill of health!" Then he dropped dead onto the sidewalk. After that, Mitchum never elaborated on his own well-being. I only met James Stewart twice, at what were official and formal occasions. He was appropriately polite, but curt. It seems characteristic that these two giants so underplayed their private selves, for their professional selves will forever occupy a place of honor in our artistic pantheon.

What Do Movie Producers Do?

BY BARBARA MALTBY

*M*y early attraction to the movies began in the usual way—faithful attendance at Saturday-afternoon matinees. But the venue was most unusual—a small-town, suburban theater whose manager, Mr. Emma, wearing white gloves, greeted every patron, young and old, by name and shook each person's hand. Mr. Emma's style and manner were my first and last experience in anything akin to graciousness in the movie business, a business characterized by wildly egocentric, if not downright sociopathic, behavior.

Actually, the movie business suffers from an institutional form of bipolar mood disorder. On any given day it can raise you to the heavens or cast you into the depths at least two or three times. The money is there; no it's not. The star has committed; no she hasn't. The meeting is tomorrow; no, it's been canceled . . . indefinitely. As an example, I got a phone call a few months ago telling me that a project I had started in 1984 was finally about to begin production. The script, after numer-

FROM *THE AMERICAN SCHOLAR*

ous revisions, was in good enough shape for Robert Redford to commit to play the lead role, that of a fictional president. In 1993, however, the project was sold to Rob Reiner's company, Castle Rock, and they bought out my contract with Redford and Universal. I received my fee and associate producer credit, but I have had no further involvement in the movie beyond feeling grateful that it was finally being made.

The immensely long and tortuous journey that the script had taken to reach this point is a saga that reflects what I have come to know and think about the movie business. So given the nature of that business, I wasn't surprised when, a few weeks after the first call, I got another call. Redford had changed his mind and had dropped out of the project, but maybe, just maybe, they would be able to get Michael Douglas to play the part and salvage everything. Inured to the ups and downs of this project over the last decade, I barely registered either piece of news. Life in Hollywood is a delicate balance between protecting one's sanity and avoiding a slip into full-blown cynicism. This was a project, after all, that had been six weeks from production once before. In fact, the story behind it may be just as good as the movie.

The project, which began life as a script called *The President Elopes,* is now known by the unimaginative title of *The American President.* Its lurching journey toward the Bethlehem of an actual starting date has intrigue, surprise, despair, and possibly redemption. But most of all, recounting the story of *The President Elopes* answers the question I am most frequently asked: "What exactly do producers do?"

Before taking up *The President Elopes,* I need to explain certain fundamental facts about the movie business in order to show how difficult it is to get a movie made. First of all, very few movies of any kind are made relative to the number of stories and scripts that are written and submitted and even paid for. Most submissions never get optioned. (An option is a contract that gives the exclusive, though time-limited, right to develop the material for film.) Of those stories that are optioned, I suspect that less than one out of every three hundred ever makes it into production and into the theaters. In my early years working with Robert Redford, when it was my job to screen all the projects submitted to him, I was reading up to five hundred scripts and books a year, and I never recommended more than twenty-five to him. Good screenwriting is immensely difficult to find, precisely because it is so very difficult to do.

The most important fact about the movies to keep in mind is also the most obvious—money is at the heart of all moviemaking. In this business, movies are usually referred to as "product," as in "Columbia doesn't have enough product in the pipeline." This so-called product exists for one purpose alone—to make a profit, preferably an enormous profit. Only independently financed, non-Hollywood movies intended for smaller audiences have the luxury of freely exercising artistic intentions. In the minds of most Hollywood executives, art, at best, equates with a European breakthrough hit such as *Enchanted April.* At worst, art means a movie with a dismal two-week run at a fine-arts theater; then, with luck, its video rights are sold so that some of the costs can be regained.

In Hollywood, a "bad" movie means one that is noncommercial, that has no appeal for a mass audience. Such a movie might be too intellectual or too soft (which is another way of saying it's just a woman's film), or it might be too offbeat or even too serious.

The kind of "good" story that Hollywood is looking for is the blockbuster hit that appeals to a huge audience—*Jurassic Park* or *Lethal Weapon,* for example. This all-or-nothing approach has a potential for disaster. An expensive movie that fails to find an audience can nearly wreck a studio. Some movies cost as much as $70 to $80 million to produce. In fact, *Waterworld* cost an astonishing $150 million. That seems like an absurd amount to spend on a movie. But consider this— the *average* cost to make a movie in 1995 is $50 million, more than double what it was five years ago.

Then, too, a studio doesn't start to see profit just because a movie earns back its production costs. A general rule of thumb for considering profitability used to be that a movie had to earn two and a half times its initial cost before it broke even. Now that movies can cost anywhere from five to one hundred and fifty million dollars, there is no such simple yardstick. What hasn't changed is the number and kind of added costs that can extend the point of profitability from several times the cost of production to a point someplace north of infinity—"the rolling break" it's actually called. For example, additional expenses come from advertising, making film prints, overhead charges of 15 to 25 percent that the studio imposes for use of its facilities and personnel, and, not least, interest payments on the money the studio borrowed from the bank in order to make the movie in the first place. What this means is that there is no clear definition for predicting when a film will break even, particularly for a very expensive movie, and most particularly when the stars of that movie have a gross participation in the profits and start taking a percentage of box-office returns from the very first dollar. This situation explains why a movie like *Forrest Gump* can theoretically still be in the red after grossing more than $300 million. With expenses so high and profits so tenuous, one can understand why Hollywood is so averse to taking risks and why it usually goes for the lowest common denominator and thus the largest audience appeal.

The need to pay back all those costs above the initial investment also explains why good small movies are often yanked from theaters after the first week. A studio doesn't want to spend any money on advertising unless it is guaranteed that the advertising will build enough of an audience to make it worthwhile. It would rather write off the loss. This is exactly what happened to *King of the Hill*—a movie I produced in 1993—despite its surprisingly good reviews.

In the movie business, money is power. Money defines the culture of Hollywood, a culture that is narcissistic, amoral, insular, and insulated—and I believe I'm being charitable in this description. Robert Altman's movie *The Player* is an accurate view of this world. Paul Attanasio, the writer of *Quiz Show,* who happens to live in New York, remarked that "people in Hollywood seem so ingenuously nice but it masks a deep cynicism and a killer instinct. New Yorkers, on the other hand, have a surface cynicism that hides a surprising naïveté." I think it's an apt description of the Hollywood mentality—even some women have had to adopt it, though, until recently, women haven't been a real part of the system.

Hollywood has traditionally been run by men—now mostly young men. The reason for this is simple: action-adventure movies that aspire to be blockbusters must appeal to the young men who will see the movie four or five times; so who better to understand the viewers' taste than other young men?

Fortunately, there are other criteria for assessing what might make a good movie. Of course, this is always subjective, but since I was working for just one person, I had to satisfy only two people's standards—mine and, of course, Robert Redford's. *Ordinary People,* a novel that we were sent before it was published and became popular, is a good example. I realized, with surprise, that it was set in Lake

Forest, Illinois, the town where I grew up. But my response to it was based on something more than a personal shock of recognition. It contained three compelling main characters and a powerful and evocative story line with which most people could identify. However, it was the interplay between the controlled outer behavior of the characters and the anguish and turmoil just beneath that polite surface that was most significant. It is the tension between those two planes that is the stuff of real drama. It didn't take a genius to see any of this. But it did take some ability to see beyond the book's potential soap-opera quality and episodic structure to the movie it could become. I quickly sent it on to Redford with a five-star recommendation.

As a result of *Ordinary People*'s success, I began to work on the development of Redford's in-house projects—that is, projects we developed within Wildwood, his film division, for Redford to star in or direct. Developing movies, which takes up as much as 90 percent of a producer's time, comes in stages. First, you need to find a good piece of material. It could be a book, a treatment, or an already existing screenplay. The second stage usually involves finding the option money necessary to get things under way. Fortunately, I didn't have to expend much energy on this stage, because Redford's interest in a project tended to guarantee the financing, and Michael Ovitz, renowned Hollywood power broker, was there to make things work.

The next stage is the heart of what is known in the trade as "development hell." It begins with trying to find the right screenwriter for the project—an ordeal that can take months. The writer you want might not be available or might want too much money. Perhaps a writer can't be found because no one seems to have the right skills for that particular project.

Once you do have the writer, work begins on the script itself. This is the time when, to borrow from Mr. Eliot, the shadow truly falls between the conception and the reality. Creativity cannot be programmed; good work cannot be extracted by contractual obligation; and writers are, by definition, vulnerable. Screenwriters are particularly vulnerable because, unlike playwrights, they do not control the project they are writing. They are hired, which means that they can be fired at any time. The only advantage they enjoy is that they are paid whether or not their work is acceptable. Thus screenwriting can be financially rewarding while still subjecting the writer to a considerable amount of pain and rejection.

Under the best of circumstances, it takes about three years to develop, produce, and release a movie. That leaves a lot of room for things to go wrong. People in Hollywood are always waiting—for a writer to finish, for a phone call to be returned, for a meeting to be scheduled, for an actor or director to decide if he or she wants to be involved.

I have been on both ends of that particular problem. For four years after *Ordinary People* was released, Robert Redford didn't make another movie; he had kept a lot of people waiting for a commitment that he couldn't seem to make. One of the problems with being a star is that you have too many choices, and this can lead to paralysis in decision making. Redford's impasse was finally broken when he agreed to star in *The Natural* for Barry Levinson's company. At the same time, I got a job offer from ABC Motion Pictures to be an independent producer, essentially doing what I was doing already—but doing it not for an individual but for a company. After spending ten years with Redford and after a four-year dry spell, I decided that it was time for me to move on.

Going to work for ABC Motion Pictures seemed to solve a number of problems while also creating new ones. First, it meant functioning without Redford's protection and clout. In the movie business it is very useful to be aligned with a powerful person. I had been in an ivory tower at Redford's company, working with a man of intelligence and taste who had the rare power to make any movie he wanted. I had been sent every good (and not so good) script and book without having to scrounge, woo, or con anyone—necessary activities for almost all producers. Michael Ovitz used to call me at least three times a day. He was desperate to get Bob to work. At ABC, Ovitz would *return* my phone calls, but without my Redford connection, he certainly had no need to call me.

Most difficult to deal with, however, was the loss of a kind of seamless communication and shorthand that I had had with Bob Redford, whose taste I shared and who loved to talk about interesting movie ideas. The head of production for ABC was a different animal altogether. He was in Los Angeles, which meant I had to communicate with him by phone. And although he was smart, he had a very short attention span, which is not uncommon in Hollywood. He wanted every potential project to be reduced to a single sentence. "*Terminator Two* meets *Pretty Woman*," he might say. This is what is known as a "high-concept" idea—easily understood, easily sold.

I wasn't good at high-concept delivery or ideas, and he wasn't interested in listening to complexity or nuance. "Stu, Stu," I'd say, "hear me out. This is a great idea!"

"Don't have time, babe, gotta go, people in my office . . ."

Sometimes I'd just get the single word, "Boorriinng."

Then one day Stu came to New York, and, as they say, we did lunch. I had just read *The President Elopes* and fallen in love with it. It was more a thirties romantic comedy than something high-concept, but I had nothing to lose. Anyway, I figured that Stu couldn't hang up on me while we were sitting at the same table.

"So," I began, "I think I found this terrific story. It has two great roles for stars." (It's important to lead with that.)

"Like who?" he interrupted.

"Well, Redford. Meryl Streep. It's about a fictional president, a bachelor, who left behind the girl he loved when he became obsessed with politics. She has never forgiven him and, it turns out, has bought his family's old farm, which, coincidentally, is on the site of a proposed federal project that is politically crucial to him. The catch is, she won't move. He decides he'll go talk to her. She's a young Katharine Hepburn type and consequently isn't impressed by his power or charm. She turns him down. He, of course, falls madly in love with her again. . . ."

At that point, Stu interrupted me. "I love it. I see the whole thing—let's get it." He quickly pays the bill and we go back to the office, where he calls L.A. and tells the ABC lawyer to start negotiating with the writer. I began to see a few advantages to this new job. Stu may not have been able to listen, but he had no trouble making decisions.

Within a few days, I had flown to L.A. for meetings with Stu and the writer, whose name is Bill Richert—an auspicious beginning for *The President Elopes*, or so I thought at the time.

In that initial meeting the story began to change. The president was now a widower with a small child (more sympathetic, you see), who was very unhappy as well as lonely in the White House. The reelection campaign was about to begin, but the president seems strangely removed from it all. And then he falls in love, but with the wrong woman—a woman who is politically dangerous because she won't play the Washington game. She has seen what too much power does to the male ego. She resists his advances, though she must leave Washington to do so. He has to find a way to go after her, in disguise of course. By spending time incognito as an ordinary man, he finds again the core values that made him want to be president in the first place, and he wins her heart.

Bill, the screenwriter, and I had six weeks to produce the new draft. It seemed like plenty of time, but then I wasn't familiar with Bill's work habits. I gave Bill three days to start, and then we were to go over his new pages together. Three days later, he told me he needed another three days. Three weeks later he had done about ten of the requisite one hundred twenty pages that make a full screenplay.

At that point my life became devoted to getting Bill to work. I'd call and wake him up at ten A.M. I'd call at eleven to announce I was arriving with coffee and donuts, which was when he actually got out of bed. About two in the afternoon, he'd finally be at the typewriter, while I sat in the other room waiting for him to produce the pages we would go over together. Usually they were strange and quite wonderful, but they were rarely on the point of the story since Bill refused to outline or plot scenes ahead. Planning would destroy his creative juices, he claimed. Thus, my job was to provide the narrative coherence to his gifted imagination. He was a screamer, in a sort of caffeine-fed, nonviolent, ex-alcoholic, black Irish sort of way—just excitable, he would say—so we worked at high pitch for four weeks, every day and every night until we had a script.

Then we did a second draft based on Stu's reactions. We knew that there would be a third draft once we started sending it to directors, and then a fourth and fifth and so on, because, after all, that's what always happens. Usually, too, the original writer is replaced by someone deemed better at structure or dialogue or romance or whatever it is that, right or wrong, the story seems to lack.

But this was not to be Bill's fate—at least not yet. Instead, there was an unexpected move out of left field that threatened the project. Cap Cities bought ABC in 1985 and decided to shut down its motion picture division. Because I had brought *The President Elopes* to ABC, the project came back to me in turnaround when ABC was disbanded.

Now that I wasn't affiliated with any company for the first time in my career, I began to understand the unsettling implications of being an independent producer. My first step was to find a new home for *The President Elopes* with a studio or company that would be willing both to pick up the costs already charged against it, which now amounted to half a million dollars, and to put up new money. I might mention another disadvantage to being an independent producer: We get very little money unless a project actually goes into production. So only a tiny amount of that half million came to me—about eight thousand dollars, actually—for my time and effort during the development period.

I sent the script to about fifty different studios, production companies, and stars, including the person at Redford's company who had taken my place. Although it seemed ironic at the time, I shouldn't have been surprised that Redford ended up optioning the script. There are only a few stars who can play a president, after all.

So three years after I left, I was back at Wildwood as the executive producer of *The President Elopes*. Executive producer, by the way, is a title that is usually given to the person responsible for the project existing in the first place, either because he or she owns it or has gotten the financing. The producer, on the other hand, has the daily responsibility for managing the physical as well as the creative parts of producing the movie.

There is an even more arcane hierarchy having to do with such credits as coexecutive producer, coproducer, and associate producer—all of which, in descending order, refer to a variety of responsibilities. Whatever the title, the duties and functions are rarely the same from movie to movie.

Back at Wildwood, the development nightmare began all over again. I tried to shepherd Bill again, but unsuccessfully. The day of his deadline, having assured me that everything was completely under control, he turned in a draft with a tacked-on ending that was only two-thirds finished.

The writer who replaced Bill—for that was of course what had to happen—was his polar opposite. He worked from three A.M. until four-thirty P.M. At first this seemed like a blessing, but such compulsiveness doesn't necessarily breed a light and romantic heart. He turned a witty and charming tale of seduction and resistance into a story about two people who spend their time together talking about their feelings. Very New Age but hardly a recipe for emotional tension or humor.

Now the secret in all great love stories is that some kind of barrier must exist between the two lovers. If two people meet, fall in love, and then nothing gets in their way, there's nowhere for the story to go. The problem with the late twentieth century is that traditional barriers such as feuding families, class, color, sexual taboos, or marriage rarely apply.

The tension and surprise of *The President Elopes*, therefore, lay in the ironic twist of watching a woman say no to a man with the charm of Redford and the power of a president. Her very resistance is why the story works. Even though the next writer was chosen exactly because he seemed to have a feeling for this kind of Tracy-Hepburn relationship, for some unfathomable reason, he was only interested in the president's relationship with his dead wife, a character who had intentionally never been in any version of the story. Three months later, this stubborn writer was also off the project.

We had now spent four years and more than $2 million on this movie, and we were back at square one. You must surely be wondering why we continued to bother. The answer is easy. Bill's initial version had enormous charm and great emotional gratification, which were derived from its themes of personal *and* national transformation and redemption. It also had something more unusual—real flair.

And so we continued. The "we" at this point, some five years after I had first started working on the story, consisted of the people who had replaced the people who had replaced me at running Redford's company. At this point, I was also a salaried producer on other Wildwood projects (which was very lucky considering that eight thousand dollars).

To condense things: Since 1989 and before its sale to Castle Rock, another $2 to $3 million has been spent on the development of *The President Elopes*, bringing the total to more than four million dollars. Five additional writers have worked on the script, none successfully. It seemed that every story solution only created a new story problem. Several directors preceded Reiner. With one of these directors, we came within six weeks of production. The crew was hired and sets were being built—but we still didn't have a good script. The latest version, written by Lowell Ganz and Babaloo Mandel, the writers of films such as *City Slickers,* was funny in a macho, political sort of way, but much of its romance and charm was sacrificed. Since these problems could not be resolved before the projected start of *A River Runs Through It,* production had to be halted.

A similar halt threatened after Redford pulled out of the movie last year. His decision did not surprise me, however. He had always been drawn to the story for its intense romantic appeal as much as for its skewering of power and politics. Reiner, on the other hand, wanted to make a more realistic version of the story, perhaps because of the success of *Dave,* a film that bore a close resemblance to *The President Elopes* in tone and feeling. But when Michael Douglas quickly agreed to take Redford's place and Annette Bening signed on, production was finally assured.

The movie opened in November 1995. It has garnered much publicity and many good reviews. But a small sidebar drama is actually taking place, a subplot introduced at the last minute. Aaron Sorkin, the current writer, has gotten the Writers Guild to award him sole screenplay credit, not because he so substantially reworked earlier versions of *The President Elopes,* but because he claims that *The American President* is an *original* script of his that Reiner hired him to do a year before *The President Elopes* was acquired. At the Writers Guild hearing, Sorkin's lawyer also claimed that Sorkin had "no access to prior writers' materials until the time of arbitration"—that is, until just two months ago.

This contention certainly challenges my credulity. Without directly impugning Sorkin's account, I can only say that I never heard about this "original" screenplay of Sorkin's until now. My own notes from 1993, when Reiner was negotiating with Redford and Universal, mention that Reiner would, "with Aaron Sorkin as writer, do a completely new script, less comical, more real than the Ganz/Mandel version, which is what he, Reiner, saw." In several 1994 interviews in *Variety,* Reiner denies having read the screenplay, but he does confirm talking with Redford and the people at Wildwood. This fact alone is enough to establish a chain of story transmission under the rules of the Writers Guild. Sorkin himself, after the Writers Guild ruled in his favor, has now admitted that he heard about *The President Elopes* directly from Redford and actually read "several" pages of the Ganz/Mandel version. The important thing to note is that a "new version" is not an "original" one. And for one familiar with the many different versions of *The President Elopes,* the draft of Sorkin's screenplay that I read is still clearly derived from Bill's, despite its many changes. Sadly, the result of the Writers Guild's acceptance of Sorkin's initial claim is that Bill Richert, whose original idea it was, will receive no credit or remuneration at all. This sudden announcement of Sorkin's also provides an interesting postmodern flavor to this article. Maybe *The President Elopes* was never made after all, and *The American President* is some sort of surprise stepchild come to claim all the inheritance.

Now the story behind the production of *The President Elopes* isn't exactly the norm in moviemaking, but it's not all that abnormal either. In fact, I have another project, which was started in 1980, that still has a very faint possibility of being made by Robert De Niro. What is typical of *The President Elopes,* however, is the almost daily roller-coaster ride of good news followed by bad news followed by a ray of hope followed by a sinking feeling followed by relief followed by unreturned phone calls.

The difficulties and frustration I went through with *The President Elopes,* and with the movie business in general, do not negate the great satisfaction and real luck that have also been mine. I have worked with people of great vision and skill. And I have seen patience rewarded. More important, I haven't lost the sense of magical power—the power to electrify an audience—that a good movie has. I believe that *Ordinary People, A River Runs Through It,* and *King of the Hill,* the three movies I have had a hand in making, are examples of movies that both entertain and illuminate. All three share certain characteristics, though with no conscious intent. That all were originally books is not surprising. Books comprise a major source for movie projects, because you don't have to start from scratch to develop a story and characters. All three movies are about families and the difficulty that family members have in understanding and communicating their feelings to one another. All three feature two brothers, one of whom is killed or in serious danger and whose trials necessarily provoke change in the family, even when change is strongly opposed. In each case, much of the emphasis in the story is on the father-son relationship—a particular concern of Robert Redford's. Witness that same relationship in *Quiz Show,* for instance.

As I've said, these similarities were not intentional. Each had quite a different genesis. *Ordinary People* was sent to me in manuscript. *A River Runs Through It* was an underground classic that had been much sought after by many people in the movie business. Norman Maclean refused all offers and then decided that he would, with help, attempt to write his own screenplay. That screenplay was brought to the Sundance Institute, and Redford was asked to direct it. However, even Norman Maclean thought his own script wasn't very good, and eventually he assigned the rights to Redford, and I was charged with finding a new writer for it.

King of the Hill, A. E. Hotchner's memoir about growing up in St. Louis during the Depression, was unknown to me, but I was interested in working with Steven Soderbergh after seeing his movie *sex, lies, and videotape.* Hotchner's, it turned out, was a book Soderbergh had always loved.

I am immensely proud of these three movies and of the way they touched their audiences, but I have one regret—I fear that all three failed in making the mothers fully three-dimensional characters. I can't ascribe this to some male plot, and it was not for a lack of trying. In *Ordinary People* I thought the mother was the most indelible person in the story. She was a person so overcome with pain at the loss of her son that she would not allow herself to feel anything at all. That avoidance made her appear cold, even cruel, to her remaining son; but it masked a heartbreaking vulnerability and an unconscious terror at being overwhelmed by feeling. She could not see that true survival for herself and her family lay in exposing the pain she worked so hard to control. Her failure was far more tragic than it was villainous.

Mary Tyler Moore had been Redford's first choice to play the mother since he had seen her walking on the beach one day. He had been struck by the difference in persona between her public vitality and the vulnerability he saw in her as she walked alone in the rain. It was exactly the quality that the mother should have—relentlessly "up" and in control in front of others but hiding a profound fragility. This fragility made her sympathetic, despite her coldness to her son.

On screen, however, Mary Tyler Moore somehow came across tougher than we had imagined. The film editor thought this was great. He wanted the mother to be something of a villain, to make the movie more dramatic. He reassured Redford that she would still manage to be sympathetic. As a result, Redford did not shoot a new scene that had been written. It showed the mother talking to her gynecologist, which in itself would have been something of a first, since this most fundamental of relationships to women is rarely if ever shown on screen. In it, the mother refuses to recognize the signs of stress the doctor sees in her. The more sympathetic he is, the more she denies her state of mind and the tears that begin to fall from her eyes. It was a great scene.

When we saw the first rough cut of the movie after the shooting was finished, it was clear that it had been a real mistake not to shoot that scene or some smaller moments that could have shown the terrible price the mother was paying for her rigidity. Redford decided to shoot several of them despite the added expense. Unfortunately, fate intervened in the form of an actors' strike, and the scenes were never shot, leaving some people in the audience unable to understand the mother's complexity. This is a perfect example of the ways in which movies are both collaborative and sometimes accidental in their outcome.

In *A River Runs Through It,* the mother barely exists in the original novella. The challenge in the movie was to invest her with some dignity and dimension, even though she seemed to play such a small role in the actual story. I don't think we were successful in giving her that dimension, but there was a moment when her own awareness of her peripheral role could have been given more emotional effect. It occurred in the voice-over that accompanied the scene in which the Norman Maclean character tells his parents about his brother's death. In it, Norman and his father remain seated while the camera shows the mother moving slowly and painfully up the stairs under the tremendous weight of that terrible news she has just heard. Over the scene you can hear Norman's voice, as read by Redford, say: "My mother turned and went to her bedroom where, in a houseful of men and rods and rifles, she had faced most of her great problems alone." It is a line that gives the woman's life a dignity and meaning that one might otherwise miss. Unfortunately, that line was cut from the final version because it theoretically interrupted the flow of the scene. Perhaps it did, but in my opinion something very important was lost. "God is in the details" in the way movies are edited, as in all other things.

As for *King of the Hill,* the poor mother in that movie suffered not only from poverty and an unsympathetic husband but also from tuberculosis. She was potentially the archetypal victim, a characterization I wanted to avoid. Since her son possessed enormous imagination and humor, which were instrumental in his own survival, and since these traits clearly did not come from his taciturn father, his mother was the likely source of them. If she had been funny and inventive even in the face of trauma, it would have made her a less passive character. Unfortunately, my concern was not shared by the director, and victim, I believe, she was, though it did not seem to hurt the film.

Having said this, I also say that, for me, these films connect to all that is best about making movies. In a darkened theater, in the company of others, it is possible to enter completely into another world and there be shaken to our roots, transported, and even transformed. And to sit in an audience while watching a movie you've been part of—hoping that the audience will feel what you feel—is also a terrifying and thrilling experience. With great good luck, if all goes well, the movie takes over, even though you've seen it a hundred times before, and you become one with the audience. That's when you know it has all been worth it.

Highbrow and Hard-core

BY JOHN POWERS

*I*n David Cronenberg's new movie, *Crash,* there's a sexual encounter that is, well, creepy. The hero, James Ballard, played by James Spader, has become fascinated by the liberating eroticism of automobile accidents. Pursuing his obsession, he's in the backseat of a car, about to have sex with a crash victim (Rosanna Arquette) who's wearing heavy braces on both legs. Ballard is just lifting her ankle over his shoulder when he spies a gaping scar on the back of her thigh. He tears open her fishnet stockings, undoes his trousers, and enters the scar.

These are the days of Perversion Chic. After a decade in which America often seemed to be gripped by a new Victorianism, kinkiness has abandoned the margins and begun conquering the mainstream, which is increasingly filled with tales of cross-dressing and sodomy, incest and child rape, bondage, bestiality, and necrophilia. The line between art and pornography keeps growing fainter. Flip on the tube

FROM *VOGUE*

and a woman named Annabel Chong is boasting about being filmed while having sex with 251 men at one go. Walk into a bookstore and you'll find *The End of Alice*, A. M. Homes's lip-smacking novel about pedophilia and child murder. Pick up a newspaper and the headlines trumpet the tragedy of JonBenet Ramsey, the six-year-old winner of beauty pageants (themselves a kind of kiddie porn) found violated and murdered in her mutimillionaire parents' home. Go to the movies and they're screening Lynne Stopkewich's eerily gripping *Kissed,* whose freckle-faced young heroine makes love to corpses, exclusively male: "*That* way," she says, "I'm straight."

Of course, there's nothing new about sexual extremism, as Caligula or de Sade could have told you. But Eros, too, has its history, its eruptions and dormancies, and as we approach the millennium—itself a trigger for all sorts of freakishness—the familiar categories are breaking down. No one seems quite sure what a perversion is anymore, let alone a pervert. Yesterday's sleazeball is today's cultural hero: Hollywood now treats Larry Flynt as an adorably crass defender of cherished constitutional values—the Thomas Paine of pornography.

"We live at a time," writes Camille Paglia, "when the chaos of sex has broken into the open."

ARISTOS AND RABBLE

For centuries, the liberty to violate sexual taboos was a privilege enjoyed by the upper classes: Roman emperors, French marquises, priapic Victorian gentlemen, and SS officers in squeaky black leather. Eventually, such freedom was passed on to the new aristocrats of modernism—cutting-edge artists and intellectuals conversant with *The Story of O,* the pornography of Georges Bataille, the lambent lewdness of Robert Mapplethorpe. For the avant-garde, sexual transgression wasn't simply a pleasure, it was a duty: *Épater le bourgeois!*

It's only in the past forty years that such aristocratic decadence started trickling down to the mainstream via European art films like *Belle de Jour,* the Helmut Newton portfolio, Anne Rice's vampire novels, and Madonna's book, *Sex,* with its earnest S&M scenarios, teasing glimpses of celebrity lesbianism, and chirpy remarks on the pleasures of being sodomized.

Even as middle-class sexual notions were being altered from

above, they were being transformed just as radically from below, by the ongoing explosion of trash culture. *Hustler* magazine. Supermarket tabloids. *Pink Flamingos.* Lurid daytime talkfests ("I slept with my mother's boyfriend!"). *Debbie Does Dallas* in the local video store. Unintentionally hilarious tell-all books like *You'll Never Make Love in This Town Again,* in which "innocent" young hookers talk about fellating George Harrison as he played the ukulele or ecstatically drinking Jack Nicholson's urine. ("In many ways," says a hooker of Nicholson, "he's quite a gentleman. Although he never offered to pay me, one time he offered to pay my cab ride home.")

In fact, it's precisely the mixture of aristocratic decadence and white-trash fiesta that gives Perversion Chic its savoriness—at once chilly and lurid, stylish and crass, wised-up and unreflective.

UP THE ANTE

What used to be daring has become banal, routine. A glimpse of nudity was once a titillating perk of going to the movies. Now, thanks to hapless soft-core programs like *Red Shoe Diaries,* naked bodies are beamed right into our homes. And the movie sex scene has become a dreary cliché. Is there anything more tiresome than the obligatory lovemaking montage with its soft-focus humping, silhouettes of erect nipples, and rippling male buttocks glazed with peach light?

To get noticed these days, you must push the envelope. Just as *Playboy* was forced to start showing pubic hair because *Penthouse* did, today's Perversion Chic artist needs to keep stretching the limits of mainstream acceptance. Mere sex is out, transgression is in. Naively horny teen comedies like *Porky's,* in which guys ogle bare breasts, have given way to *Kids,* whose director, Larry Clark, casts an unsavory eye at his jailbait cast. Harold Robbins was once renowned for writing raunchy sex scenes, but today they seem almost quaint (the missionary position!) compared with the hot action in, say, Laura Reese's novel *Topping from Below,* with its nipple clamps and bondage leathers, water sports and sexual murder.

Despite highfalutin palaver about artistic "transgression" (a concept that grows more stale each day), the pressure to raise the sexual stakes is primarily commercial. This is most obvious in advertising, which must constantly produce racy new imagery with the power to grab us and shake us up—like last year's notorious (and withdrawn) Calvin Klein ad in which a clammy older man tells prepubescent children to undress, then comments on their bodies. This ad was about nothing more than creating a frisson and staking out the company's claim to be the cutting edge of the sexual zeitgeist.

THE EMPIRE STRIKES BACK

For the past fifteen years, puritanism has kept threatening to regain its hammerlock on the national psyche. Everywhere you looked there was a new antisex crusade—and a new justification for it. Incest went from being a hush-hush aberration to a staple of talk shows and celebrity bios. The Salem Witch Trials returned in the form of the child-molestation scare. Most chillingly, AIDS brought the ashen taste of mortality to the very act of making love.

But every cultural movement produces a counterreaction. Book chains like Borders now boast huge erotica sections, and our movie theaters will soon be filled with even more libidinous fare—*Boogie Nights* (about a porn star), *Bliss* (about sex therapy), and *One Night Stand* (about you guessed it). Many people are now saying to hell with safe sex and PC shibboleths. Child abuse is no longer simply the stuff of earnest sermonizing: Whether it's *Kids* or Calvin Klein ads, the murderous pedophile in *The End of Alice* or Adrian Lyne's decision to make a new, more explicit film of *Lolita,* people are making fashionable entertainment of turning children into sex toys. In *Crime and Punishment,* the murderer Raskolnikov has a wrenching dream in which an innocent little girl's face suddenly takes on the lewd, lipsticked look of a whore. What was the ultimate nightmare to Dostoyevsky—the corruption of innocence—is now called the Little Miss Colorado beauty pageant.

And while HIV is still very much with us, heterosexual sodomy is becoming a familiar entrée on the erotic menu: Last year at Cannes, at least five films spotlighted male-female anal sex (including *Crash* and André Téchiné's *Thieves*), and it's even more routine in novels. Halfway through Susanna Moore's vaunted thriller, *In the Cut,* the heroine, Frannie, is in the police station with her lover, a cop who may or may not be a serial killer. Whipping out his handcuffs, he suddenly bends her over a desk, pulls down her panties, and sodomizes her. A true citizen of Perversion Chic, Frannie doesn't worry about whether the guy's wearing a condom or even think "ouch." She merely tells him she liked it, then masturbates to climax.

LAST TANGO IN GUYVILLE

Until recently, the power to define eroticism has belonged to men. We've all been bombarded by male visions of sex, be it *Playboy*'s so-called philosophy, Henry Miller's happy-cocked boasting, Brando's buttery meditations in *Last Tango in Paris,* or the byzantine love scenes of the late Harold Brodkey, who described cunnilingus with the exhaustively enthusiastic precision of Bobby Fischer dissecting a classic chess game.

While this traditional male power has hardly disappeared, its cachet has melted. These days, *nothing is more boring than the sexual fantasies of heterosexual white men.* At worst, they seem oppressive and pathetic—masturbatory. At best, they're old hat—the same old huffing and puffing we've been watching our whole lives. Nowadays, sex books by straight white guys are greeted with enthusiasm only when, as in Michael Ryan's touching sex-addiction memoir *Secret Life,* they resound with breast-beating remorse.

This helps explain the mockery that greeted Richard Rhodes's sexual memoir, *Making Love: An Erotic Odyssey,* in 1992—nobody wanted to read about some guy literally measuring his penis (six and a half inches, if you're interested). It explains the cavernous yawn that greeted Robert O. Butler's erotic novel *They Whisper*—just another middle-aged white guy writing about the women he's bonked. And it explains why David Lynch's new movie, *Lost Highway,* seems so flaccid, despite the story's sexualized murder and peep-show nudity. Although it contains the most incandescent sex scene in years, we've been down this particular highway too many times before.

THE FEMINIZATION OF PORNOGRAPHY

Movie sex is still dominated by male directors (Susan Streitfeld's *Female Perversions* is a notable exception), but the same isn't true of fiction. For the first time, serious women writers are publishing lascivious novels under their own names; in fact, today's wildest erotic writing comes from "bad girl" writers who revel in conjuring up behavior that good girls aren't supposed to enjoy.

In earlier days, the patron saints of female erotica were Anaïs Nin and Erica Jong. Now they're the almost talent-free Josephine Hart— whose 1992 blockbuster *Damage* demonstrated the huge market for chichi, sex-drenched erotica—and the very talented Mary Gaitskill, whose 1989 short-story collection *Bad Behavior* brought a professional matter-of-factness and tough-minded sensibility to the precise description of what women do in bed with men. Her stories use sex to tackle questions of power, desire, and control, a theme underscored by the very title of her fine new book: *Because They Wanted To.*

Whereas the early women's liberationists often seemed moralistic about sex, today's feminism-influenced writers care less about judging particular acts (spanking, for instance) than about teasing out their psychological underpinnings. The important thing is not what kind of sex you perform but who's calling the shots and who's receiving the pleasure.

This perfectly valid idea achieves its reductio ad absurdum in the delirious *Topping from Below,* whose heroine, Nora, gets involved with Michael M., the man she believes responsible for the S&M murder of her sister Frances. In what can only be considered a wild implausibility, Nora is soon letting the "powerful, riveting, dangerous" Michael make her do the same things her sister did. At one point, he tells her that he'd ordered Frances to have sex with his dog. He then calls the Great Dane into the room to have sex with Nora, who not only complies but rockets to an orgasm. The moral is obvious: Having sex with a Great Dane is great as long as the woman enjoys it, but if she's been bullied into doing so, it's wrong. If a man wrote a book like this, he'd be hanging from a lamppost.

THE JOYLESSNESS OF SEX

The great sexual revolution of the sixties was all about achieving pleasure, even ecstasy. The point of Erica Jong's "zipless fuck" was to feel good.

In contrast, the favored style of Perversion Chic is cool, distant— like the pretty, blank faces in perfume ads that draw you in with a promise of sex but also make it seem like it wouldn't be any fun.

Of course, sometimes the cool style has genuine power, as in the new movie *Kissed,* whose most shockingly successful moment comes when, in an act of exaltation, its heroine, Sandra, strips off her clothes and makes love to a dead young man's body. By deliberately playing down what's outrageous in Sandra's sexual bent, filmmaker Stopkewich manages to take us deeper inside a strange world in which the dead have more sexual allure than the living (a theme echoed in Peter Greenaway's forthcoming *The Pillow Book,* an exquisite, extremely sexy film about calligraphy, death, and desire).

More often, however, this distant approach suggests profound emotional anorexia. As they shuttle between bloody car crashes and bouts of weird sex, the characters in *Crash* seem zombified, incapable of entertaining a normal human emotion. The same is true of *In the Cut,* whose narrator, Frannie, talks to us in a fussy, clinical prose that sounds exactly the same whether she's discussing her writing class, witnessing a blow job, or being cornered by a serial killer. As she lies bleeding after having had her nipple cut off, she's thinking about the correct grammatical form to describe her experience (she chooses third person). Frannie can't get it together to feel anything—even about her own murder.

RELIGION?

Such joylessness bespeaks longing, the yearning to escape. For all their emphasis on transgressing social norms or making naughtiness hip, today's sexual stories exude the poignant sense that ordinary life is flat, frustrating, deprived of spiritual resonance. Faced with such a life, even weird sex takes on Eros's traditional function: It becomes a way of making oneself whole or achieving transcendence, however brief or tentative. It puts us in the presence of sacred mysteries.

Nowhere is this clearer than in *Crash,* the purest expression to date of Perversion Chic. Its style is chilly and clinical, its characters affectless, its sense of eroticism utterly outrageous—sick. There are at least as many sex scenes as in the average porn flick, but the film is deliberately unarousing. All the lovemaking, whether gay or straight, twisted or "normal," is joyless and obsessional; it's rooted in the characters' rapt fascination with the apocalyptic violence of car crashes.

Yet for all its emphasis on the raw physicality of naked flesh and crumpled metal, *Crash* is not about sex or cars. It's the story of people who, living in a mechanized world inimical to deep feeling, are struggling to soar beyond the world of bodies to a different, more meaningful existence. Ballard and his wife, Catherine, are turned on by car crashes not because they are inherently kinky but because they are seeking a new way of feeling, a new form of communion, a new approach to keeping their marriage alive. Like nearly everyone in today's sex-drenched but dissatisfied culture, they are looking for Something More. As Ballard tells Catherine in the closing scene, "Maybe next time, darling, maybe next time."

SHOCKED, SHOCKED!

By now, our culture has become so flagrantly sexualized that you don't have to choose to consume sexual messages—they're already consuming you. But it's one measure of the contradictions in the American psyche that, even as media culture adopts a blasé attitude toward the most brazen sexual behavior, most of us don't really want to look at it head-on. *The People vs. Larry Flynt* has a good time making fun of the bluenoses who try to ban *Hustler*, but the movie itself didn't dare confront the audience with what that magazine contains, all the galloping misogyny, gynecological photos, and mirthless jokes about child molesting. If director Miloš Forman had spent five minutes filling the screen with actual pages of *Hustler*, the rest of the movie would have seemed fatuous. Rather than snickering at the squares who disapproved of Flynt, the audience would have been shocked by just how much dirt there still is in sex.

The Ghost at the Feast

BY GEOFFREY O'BRIEN

1.

To unravel my first associations with Shakespeare is like trying to clamber back into the core of childhood. My parents worked in the theater—my mother as actress, my father as director and theater owner—and stages figured early on as places of magical transformation. Seeing the process from the wings did not make it any less magical: quite the contrary. The stage was a place where people became other than what they were, in a fully real alternate world. The most highly developed aspect of that other world was called Shakespeare, conceived not as an individual but as an inventory of places, costumes, roles, phrases, songs.

Countless artifacts served as windows into it: a book of cutout figures for a toy theater, based on stills from Olivier's *Hamlet; Classic Comics* versions of *Hamlet, Macbeth,* and *A Midsummer Night's Dream*; recordings of John Barrymore as Hamlet and Olivier as Henry V and

FROM *THE NEW YORK REVIEW OF BOOKS*

(most memorably) and Old Vic *Macbeth* whose bubbling-cauldron sound effects and echo-chambered witches' voices haunted me for years; splendidly melodramatic nineteenth-century engravings of Hamlet in pursuit of his father's ghost, Romeo running Tybalt through, Caliban and the drunken sailors carousing on the beach; prints of Sarah Siddons and Edmund Kean in their most famous roles; a whole world of Victorian bric-a-brac and accretions out of Charles and Mary Lamb; Victor Mature as Doc Holliday in John Ford's *My Darling Clementine,* reciting "To be or not to be" in a Dodge City saloon. There were productions, too, of which I remember none better than John Gielgud standing alone in modern dress on the stage of a school auditorium on Long Island enacting the abdication of Richard II; and there were Olivier's three Shakespeare movies, the most recent of which, *Richard III,* had its American premiere on television in 1956.

It was a world that came into focus very gradually, little pieces clinging to memory out of a whole at first immense and vague. Probably the first details absorbed were of props and clothing—a crown, a dagger, a robe—augmented gradually by gestures, phrases, half-understood speeches. I can just about recall the uncanniness, on first encounter, of the exclamation "Angels and ministers of grace defend us!" Even more peculiar in their fascination were those words not understood at all: aroint, incarnadine, oxlips, roundel, palpable, promontory. No subsequent encounter with lyrical poetry ever exercised the initial hypnotic power of such a phrase as "Those are pearls that were his eyes."

This Shakespeare existed outside of history, like Halloween or the circus. He was the supreme embodiment of the Other Time before cars or toasters, the time of thrones and spells and madrigals, imagined not as a dead past but as an ongoing parallel domain. So it was that I came to participate in a sort of religion of secular imagination: a charmed world whose key was to be found in the plays themselves, in all those passages where Shakespeare, through the mouth of Puck or Jaques or Hamlet or Prospero, appeared to give away the secret of a mystical theatricality, a show illusory even where it was most palpable.

The plays were just there, a species of climate: a net of interrelations extending into the world and generating an unforeseeable number of further interrelations. Why this should be so did not seem particularly important. Having managed to bypass the didactic initiation into Shakespeare favored in most schoolrooms—where every aesthetic pleasure must be justified in the name of some more or less hollow generality about will, or fate, or human relations—I didn't need to look for reasons for the endless fascination. Certainly the sociology of the sixteenth century, or the development of the English theater, or the mechanisms of religious and political thought in early modern Europe seemed to have little to do with it. Any piece of writing, after all, came with such local meanings attached; every Elizabethan and Jacobean play was loaded to the brim with comparable social revelation. Something else had motivated a culture to adopt this vocabulary of situations, roles, and locations as the materials for its collective dreaming: something less susceptible to quantitative analysis than scope or invention. What but some mysterious generosity in the author could make possible such an infinitely flexible repertory for the theater of the mind?

If any era could call that flexibility into question it is a post-postmodern moment skeptical by now even about its own skepticism, and unable to refrain from an anxious cataloguing of inherited knowledge it can neither quite forget nor celebrate altogether without qualms. Shakespeare is the past, and the past is something we don't know quite what to do with; we toy uncertainly with a millennial sense of impending drastic rupture, as if preparing to say good-bye to everything, even Shakespeare. With or without regrets: On one side there is the conviction (to quote from a notice posted recently at the MLA*) that "the current explosion of the uses of Shakespeare often consolidate elite and dominant culture" (the notice goes on to speak disparagingly of "Shakespeare's status as high cultural capital"), on another the gloomy suggestion that in our present debased condition we are barely worthy of Shakespeare at all.

Nonetheless a sort of boom has been announced, and by virtue of being announced has gained official media recognition as a phenomenon; the Globe is at last reconstructed in South London (the culmi-

---

*The notice requested submissions for an anthology to be titled *Shakespeare Without Class: Dissidence, Intervention, Countertradition*, edited by Bryan Reynolds and Don Hedrick.

nation of a long and loving process which has involved among other things a rediscovery of Elizabethan construction techniques); new editions and CD-ROMs proliferate; a humorous compilation entitled *Shakespeare's Insults* becomes a best-seller, with accompanying magnetic Wit Kit; and in the wake of last year's films of *Othello* and *Richard III* we have been given in short order a *Hamlet*, a *Twelfth Night*, a sort-of *Romeo and Juliet*, some large chunks of *Richard III* interspersed in Al Pacino's immensely entertaining filmic essay *Looking for Richard*, and a *Midsummer Night's Dream* (directed by Adrian Noble) still to come. It isn't exactly the Revival of Learning, and it is unlikely (although I would be glad to be told the contrary) that wide-screen versions of *Measure for Measure, Coriolanus*, or *The Winter's Tale* will be coming any time soon to a theater near you, but it beats another movie about helicopters blowing up.

Doubtless there are thoroughly prosaic reasons for the momentary surge, having more to do with the random convergence of financing and marketing possibilities than with some cultural moment of reckoning. In a marketplace hungry for any pretested public domain property with instant name recognition, Shakespeare clearly has not altogether lost his clout, although his near-term bankability will certainly depend a great deal on the box office receipts of Kenneth Branagh's textually uncompromising four-hour *Hamlet*. In the meantime singular opportunities have been created, not to recapitulate but to reinvent.

Reinvention has always been the function of Shakespeare in performance. It could have turned out otherwise: If the English Civil War had not disrupted the line of transmission, or if the post-Restoration theater had not rejected the plays except in heavily revised form, we might have something more in the nature of Kabuki or Peking opera, a fixed tradition of gestures and voicings, with ritual drumbeats and trumpet flourishes marking the exits and entrances. Of course, there have always been productions—more a few decades back than now, perhaps—that inadvertently produced just that effect, of watching an ancient play in a foreign language as it moved through its foreordained paces.

In the face of such displays audiences often tended to shut down. A brilliant Shakespearean parody in the 1960 English revue *Beyond the*

Fringe hilariously summed up everything that has ever made Shakespeare in performance more burden than delight: the mellifluous rote readings gliding incomprehensibly over gnarled syntax and thickets of argument, the versified rosters of the history plays sounding like nothing so much as medieval shopping lists ("Oh saucy Worcester!"), the bawdy uproariousness and farcical mugging designed to disguise the fact that even the actors didn't get the jokes.

That parody, with its evocation of a lost era of complacent pageantry, came to mind while watching the recent production by Jonathan Miller (as it happens, one of the creators of *Beyond the Fringe*) of *A Midsummer Night's Dream* at London's Almeida Theatre. Here was the driest possible reimagining of a play capable of being smothered in ornate fancies: a *Dream* without fairies or fairy bowers, without even a hint of woodland magic or, indeed, of woodland. Miller recasts the play as a thirties comedy of precise class distinctions, where the mortals—Theseus as lord of the manor, Hermia and Helena as bright debs pursued by young fashion plates of inspired fatuousness, Bottom and company as workingmen recruited from the local pub—are indistinguishable from Oberon as a somewhat tattered aristocrat, Titania as a sleek hostess out of a Noel Coward play, Puck and the other fairies as reluctant butlers inclined to be surly in their off-hours. Mendelssohnian echoes are displaced by "Underneath the Arches" and some snatches of ready-made dance music. In place of palatial pomp and natural wonderland, there is an unchanging set (designed by the animation specialists the Quay Brothers) consisting of rows of receding glass fronts, like an abandoned arcade, and permitting endless variations on the entrances and exits in which the play abounds.

Although some English critics felt that Miller had cut the heart out of the play by his policy of deliberate disenchantment, he seems rather to have demonstrated that the enchantment lies elsewhere than in light shows or acrobatics. Instead of magic, he gives us the accoutrements of thirties drawing room comedy, appropriately enough in a retrospective culture for which thirties comedy, whether *Private Lives* or *Bringing Up Baby*, serves as a gossamer substitute for more substantial magic. By a similar process of analogy, Shakespeare's hierarchies of courtiers and mechanicals and nature spirits are mimicked by the gently graduated hierarchies of the English class system in a later phase, the great chain of being linking landed gentry to their groundskeepers and socialites to their chauffeurs. The pastoral sublime of *Dream* is transmuted into the terms of a more recent version of pastoral, the weekend country-house party as imagined by P. G. Wodehouse or Agatha Christie.

The net effect is not to do violence to the play, but to give it another text to play against, a visual and behavioral text compounded of fragments of thirties movies, plays, popular songs, magazine covers, a hundred tiny rituals and breaches of etiquette. It is a way of measuring distances: Shakespeare's distance from the Athens of Theseus, the distance of the 1930s from the 1950s, and our distance from all of those times. To put *Dream* through this particular wringer—reimagining every line precisely as if someone else (W. Somerset Maugham? Terence Rattigan?) had written it, so that Theseus's prettiest set pieces become exercises in obligatory speech-making, and Oberon's evocations of herbs and flowers are delivered with a cosmopolite's distaste for mucking about outdoors—turns out to be a way of forcing out some of its bitterer aftertastes.

The celebration already anticipates the incipient hangover; as soon as the play ends, Theseus and Hippolyta will settle into a loveless marriage, and the young lovers will begin to realize that their lives will not improve on the mysteries of the vision they have just woken from. The hilarity of a good feast, with *Pyramus and Thisby* for entertainment, may in fact be as good as it is ever going to get. The play needs only itself to confirm that the magic is real; the production adds the somewhat waspish acknowledgement that it is also unattainable outside the theatrical moment.

"Shakespeare, more than anyone else," writes Miller of this production, "recognized that the stage is a place in which blatant pretense is a perfectly satisfactory alternative to miraculous illusion." By eliminating decoration, by favoring the matter-of-fact social function of the language over its poetry, Miller lets us see *Dream* in skeletal form. Nothing essential is lost because the play turns out not to be about fairies any more than it is about weekend country-house parties in the 1930s. If it is about anything it is about the music of thought, which is why William Hazlitt considered the play intrinsically unstageable. Indeed, it may well have been unstageable in 1816 when, at Covent Garden, Hazlitt saw it "converted from a delightful fiction into a dull pantomime. . . . Fairies are not incredible, but fairies six feet high are so."* Perhaps—and wouldn't it be odd if it were so—the art of performing these plays to their fullest advantage is only now being invented.

But where, and for how many, they will be performed remains a question. It is a long way from the familial intimacy of the Almeida—with its audience and actors exquisitely attuned to each other, and a seating capacity one-tenth of Shakespeare's own playhouse (three hundred against the Globe's three thousand)—to the wider and colder world of multiplexes and cable television and the megastores in which the shiny video boxes containing *Hamlet* and *Twelfth Night* will have to compete on equal terms with *Mars Attacks!* and *Beavis and Butt-head Do America*. It's a world that's hard on old material, even as it pays lip service to what is "vintage" or "immortal"; where the earlier Shakespeare films are apt to turn up under rubrics such as Nostalgia or Classic Hollywood, and a phrase like "timeless classic" is just as likely to be applied to *Abbott and Costello Meet the Mummy* as to *Henry V*.

Shakespeare movies have never exactly been a genre in the same sense as cowboy pictures or musicals. There have never been enough of them, for one thing; although the record books cite astonishing numbers of adaptations, most turn out to have been made in the silent era. As for the filmmakers who have seriously explored the stylistic possibilities of Shakespeare adaptations, the list is very small: Olivier, Welles, Kurosawa, Polanski, and a few others. In any event it's something of a genre apart; there are regular movies, and then there are Shakespeare movies.

Kenneth Branagh, who kicked off this particular cycle of Shakespearean revival with his 1989 *Henry V,* challenged the distinction. With a defiance worthy of the victor of Agincourt he demonstrated that Laurence Olivier's Shakespeare films of the forties and fifties, and the performance style they embodied, could no longer be regarded as definitive. He also undertook to make a genuinely popular movie, against odds stiffer than those Olivier faced, at a moment when more than ever before Shakespearean language had to fight for a hearing. *Henry V*

*William Hazlitt, *Characters of Shakespeare's Plays* (Chelsea House, 1983), p. 95.

played at the local multiplex alongside *Honey, I Shrunk the Kids* and *Indiana Jones and the Last Crusade,* and it was obvious that Branagh was prepared to meet that competition on its own ground.

Yet for all its superficial indications of pop refurbishing—Derek Jacobi's playing the Chorus in modern dress and wandering among the trappings of a movie studio, or Branagh's Henry striding, to the accompaniment of strident electronic wheezing, into a medieval council chamber framed to look as much as possible like the inner precincts of *Star Wars'* Darth Vader—the new *Henry V* gave signs of an almost purist agenda. To a degree unusual in Shakespeare movies, one had the impression of having actually sat through a production of the play. Branagh restored many scenes—Henry's entrapment of the traitorous English lords, his threats of massacre at Harfleur, the hanging of his old companion Bardolph—that would have detracted from Olivier's single-minded depiction of heroic national effort (although even Branagh could not bring himself to include the English king's injunction to "cut the throats of those we have").

What was most strikingly different was the level of intimacy at which Branagh's film was pitched. The Olivier version of 1944 clearly occupied a niche quite separate from the other films of its moment, delivering in clarion tones a classical language inspiring but remote. For Branagh this was no longer an available choice. The continued power of *Henry V* was not to be taken for granted; what for Olivier had been a universally recognized (if far from universally enjoyed) cultural monument now had to defend itself.

The chief point of Branagh's direction was to keep the language in front of the audience at all times, with Derek Jacobi's clipped, almost haranguing delivery leading the way. The job of the actor was to clarify, line by line and word by word, not just the general purport of what the character was feeling, but the exact function of every remark, as if some kind of match were being scored. Abrupt changes of vocal register, startling grimaces and seductive smiles, every actorly device served to maintain awareness that absolutely every moment had its singular thrust, and thereby to keep the audience from being lulled into an iambic doze. The result was a more pointed, even jabbing style, a tendency to deflate sonority in favor of exact meaning, while at the same time giving the meter of the verse a musician's respect, and the rhetorical substructure a lawyer's questioning eye.

As I first listened, in that same multiplex, to the accents of *Henry V*—"But pardon, gentles all,/The flat unraisèd spirits that hath dared/ On this unworthy scaffold to bring forth/So great an object"—transmitted in Dolby Stereo, an unanticipated excitement took hold. It didn't matter that I could read those words anytime, or pop a video of the Olivier film into the VCR. The thrill was to hear them in the multiplex, in that public space from which the possibility of such language had been essentially barred. Here was real home-cooked bread, water from the source. It was possible to imagine that the strangers around me shared a similar unarticulated longing for a strain of expression that the culture seemed programmed to withhold.

2.

Everyone who subscribes to cable television has had the experience of switching rapidly from channel to channel and hearing at every stop the same tones and inflections, the same vocabulary, the same messages; a language flattened and reduced to a shifting but never very large repertoire of catchphrases and slogans, a language into which advertisers have so successfully insinuated their strategies that the consumers themselves turn into walking commercials. It is a dialect of dead ends and perpetual arbitrary switch-overs, intended always to sell but more fundamentally to fill time: a necessary substitute for dead air. Whether in movies or television dramas, talk shows or political speeches or "infotainment" specials hawking hair dyes and exercise machines, the homogenization of speech, the exclusion of anything resembling figurative language or rhetorical complexity or any remotely extravagant eloquence or wordplay or (it goes without saying) historical or literary allusions of any kind whatever, becomes so self-evident that the only defense is that winking tone of *faux* inanity of which the ineffable "whatever" seems to be an ironic acknowledgment. By contrast the dialogue in the old Hollywood movies unreeling randomly night and day—*The Road to Rio* or *The Falcon in San Francisco* or *The File on Thelma Jordan*—seems already to partake of some quite vanished classical age: How soon before it, too, needs footnotes?

Nothing leads from or to anything; the show rolls on because it isn't time for the next show yet. It is talk without any but the most short-term memory, as if language were not to be permitted its own past, a state of affairs which makes language in some sense impossible. In this context Shakespeare assumes an ever-stranger role as he becomes the voice of a past increasingly less accessible and less tractable, the ghost at the fast-food feast. If in translation Shakespeare can remain our contemporary, in English he carries his language with him, a language by now almost accusatory in its richness when compared with the weirdly rootless and impoverished speech of Medialand. "I learn immediately from any speaker," wrote Emerson, "how much he has already lived, through the poverty or the splendor of his speech."* But there is no telling what a four-hundred-year-old man will be saying; the older he gets, the more it changes, and we no longer know if we really want to hear everything. It is like peering into a flowerpot full of twisted vines and splotched discolored lichen surviving improbably from some ancient plot.

It is absurd that Shakespeare alone should have to bear this burden, as if the whole of the European past rested in him alone, but that's only because nearly everyone has already been cosigned to the oblivion of the archives. We aren't likely to get (speaking only of the English tradition) the Geoffrey Chaucer movie, the Edmund Spenser movie, the John Webster movie, the John Milton movie, the William Congreve movie, the Laurence Sterne movie, or even the Herman Melville movie; and the Bible movies, when they appear, owe more these days to the cadences of *Xena: Warrior Princess* than to those of King James. (One of Orson Welles's last and most quixotic film projects was a movie of *Moby-Dick* consisting of himself, in close-up, reading the novel against an empty blue background). Shakespeare has to stand, all by himself, for centuries of expressive language erased by common consent from the audiovisual universe which is our theater and library and public square.

If Shakespeare movies are to be worth making at all, they can hardly duck the language. It isn't simply that the language cannot be handled gingerly or parceled out in acceptably telegraphic excerpts; the words must be entered, explored, reveled in. Syntax must be part of screen

*Ralph Waldo Emerson, "The American Scholar," in *Essays and Lectures* (Library of America, 1983), p. 62.

space. (The new sensitivity of recording technology, with its potential for communicating an awareness of depth and distance, serves admirably toward that end.) How refreshing it proves occasionally to reverse the primacy (not to say tyranny) of the visual, that fundamental tenet of filmmaking textbooks.

Disregard this problem of language and the upshot can be something like Baz Luhrmann's high-speed, high-concept *William Shakespeare's Romeo and Juliet*. There is no real reason why Luhrmann's updating could not have worked; the whole mix, complete with automatic weapons, hip-hop cadences, religious kitsch, and teen sex, could have added up to the kaleidoscopic excitement obviously intended. As it is, the compulsive cleverness of the postmodernization—Friar Lawrence sending his message to Romeo by Federal Express, members of the Capulet and Montague gangs sporting CAP and MON license plates—keeps undercutting the teen pathos to the point of parodying it. However amusing Luhrmann's conceits of characterization (Lady Capulet as blowsy Lana Turner wannabe, Mercurtio as drag queen), they seem to have strayed in from his more charming debut feature, *Strictly Ballroom*.

It's the skittish handling of the language, though, that reduces Luhrmann's film to little more than a stunt. While he gets a bit of mileage from the accidental intersections of Elizabethan with contemporary usage (as when his gang members call each other "coz" and "man"), any speech longer than a few lines just gets in the way, and the effect all too often is of sitting in on the tryouts at a high school drama club. The Shakespearean text begins to seem like an embarrassment that everybody is trying to avoid facing up to; Luhrmann would have been better off dropping the dialogue altogether and hiring Quentin Tarantino to do a fresh job. There are many ways to get Shakespeare's language across, but trying to slip it past the audience as if it might pass for something else isn't one of them.

Of course it's possible to think of Shakespeare outside of language altogether (especially if you're Russian or Japanese): as inventor (or repackager) of endlessly serviceable fables, a choreographer of bodies on a stage, a visual storyteller whose most celebrated moments (Hamlet leaping into Ophelia's grave, Macbeth confronting Banquo's ghost at the feast) can be reduced to dumb show. It would be perfectly possible to stage the plays in pantomime without losing their structural force. This is the Shakespeare who is the inexhaustible font of ballets and engravings, musicals and comic books.

A remark by Grigori Kozintsev, the director of Russian versions of *Hamlet* and *King Lear*, pretty well sums up the orthodox "cinematic" view on filming Shakespeare:

> The problem is not one of finding means to speak the verse in front of the camera, in realistic circumstances ranging from long-shot to close-up. The aural has to be made visual. The poetic texture has itself to be transformed into a visual poetry, into the dynamic organisation of film imagery.*

This is an unexceptionable precept for a director working in a language other than English, and one need only turn to Kurosawa's *Throne of Blood* or *Ran*, or Aki Kaurismäki's *Hamlet Goes Business* (filmed on location in a succession of unbelievably sterile Helsinki office suites), to see it put sublimely into practice. But when a Shakespeare film is made in the English language, the unavoidable problem is precisely one of finding means to speak the verse in front of the camera. No way to sidestep the embarrassment of poetry, even if it is a term by now so fraught with difficulties that some contemporary academics in their discussions of Shakespeare prefer to enclose it in quotes, an awkward relic of superannuated discourse.

The Kozintsev doctrine has been carried through by one English-language director, of course. The Shakespeare films of Orson Welles triumph over the sheer inaudibility of much of their dialogue through an idiosyncratic vocabulary of spaces and masks. *Othello* is more like a symphonic poem inspired by the play than the play itself: but what a poem. Welles proceeds by analogies. Shakespeare's language is *like* the waves dashing against the walls, is *like* the cage in which Iago is hauled laboriously to the ramparts, is *like* the glimmers and shadows with which the frame is irrigated. Even the few brief surviving scenes

---

*Quoted in *Shakespeare and the Moving Image: The Plays on Film and Television,* edited by Anthony Davies and Stanley Wells (Cambridge University Press, 1994), p. 56.

of Welles's unfinished TV film of *The Merchant of Venice* (shown in Vassili Silovic's documentary *Orson Welles: The One-Man Band*) instantly create a distinct universe, as Shylock, making his way into the Venetian night, is hounded by silent ominous bands of white-masked revelers, a commedia dell'arte lynch mob.

The long-deferred restoration of the currently unseeable *Chimes at Midnight*—a film whose visual splendor is matched only by the inadequacy of its soundtrack—will I am sure confirm it as the best (and most freely adapted) of Welles's Shakespeare films. When it came out in the late sixties, its elegiac note was drowned out by the more belligerent noises of the moment. Welles described it as a lament for the death of Merrie England—"a season of innocence, a dew-bright morning of the world"*—as personified by Falstaff, but it could as easily be seen as a lament for Welles, for the kind of movies he wanted to make and no longer could, and beyond that for Shakespeare as he receded however gradually into an unknowable past.

In lieu of lament, Al Pacino's *Looking for Richard* proffers jokes and exhortations, backtalk and man-on-the-street interviews and off-the-cuff commentaries. Pacino intervenes in his own partial production of *Richard III* to question and elaborate, almost in the same way a puzzled member of the audience might be tempted to: What's going on? Who is this Margaret? The *Richard III* scenes themselves—including some very strong work by Kevin Spacey, Winona Ryder, and others—are so freshly conceived that it seems a pity not to have done the whole play; Pacino looks as if he could give us yet another kind of Shakespeare movie. His Richard is far scarier than Olivier's or the somewhat campy Mosleyite portrayed by Ian McKellen in Richard Loncraine's recent film version, a real killer especially when he's suffering verbal assaults in silence. It's all the more jarring to revert to the present and the jovial sparring of actors among actors; but that back-and-forth movement makes this one of the best movies about the acting life. Actors here are the true scholars, the ones who mediate between the text and the world, a secret order of preservationists keeping alive what elsewhere

*Quoted in Orson Welles and Peter Bogdanovich, *This Is Orson Welles*, (HarperCollins, 1992), p. 100.

is only mummified. We are left with the implication that the players know things the scholars have forgotten, and that they are joyful in that knowledge.

It is not precisely joyfulness, and certainly nothing like glee, that is exuded by Trevor Nunn's melancholic adaptation of *Twelfth Night*; or if so it is a joy sufficiently muted to accord with prevailing moods that range from Chekhovian-autumnal to Beckettian-wintry. The tone is set by Ben Kingsley's Feste, conceived rather scarily as a prophetic beggar lurking in the background and seeing all, a figure whose intimations of latent violence and mad wisdom suggest that Lear's fool has been grafted onto Olivia's. The revels of Sir Toby and Sir Andrew are played with excellent flair while at the same time evoking a downbeat *Last Tango in Illyria*. At every turn we are given to see how the comedy is about to slip into the realm of the tragedies, the shipwreck into that of *Pericles*, the duel into that of *Hamlet*, the wronged Malvolio into a figure of vengeance capable of destroying the whole household.

That said, Nunn's film succeeds beautifully in its chosen course. It is for the most part superbly played, although Helena Bonham Carter is somewhat lacking in the haughty disdainfulness required of Olivia: her surrender to love isn't enough of a humiliation, and so fails to echo the far harsher humiliation of her steward. Imogen Stubbs by contrast is a tough and wary Viola who keeps the film focused on the real risks and terrors of someone cast up in hostile territory. The sadistic tormenting of Malvolio, always the trickiest passage to negotiate, is here allowed to play itself out into the exhaustion, moral and physical, of the tormentors. When one sees *Twelfth Night* back-to-back with *Hamlet* (as it may well have been written), it is hard not to think of the plays as mirror images, a comedy that just barely avoids being tragedy and a tragedy that tries against all odds to be a comedy.

This *Twelfth Night*, like Branagh's *Hamlet*, is set in a mythical nineteenth century which seems to stand vaguely for the whole European past, as if that were as far back as we could go without suffering hopeless disorientation. Despite the clothes and the furniture, neither film has a particular nineteenth-century feel; it's more a question of meeting the seventeenth century halfway, settling on a space which is neither quite our own world nor quite Shakespeare's, inventing a historical era which—like the period in which cowboy movies take place—never quite happened. We want urgently to step outside of history but have perhaps forgotten how.

Finally—speaking of risks—there is Branagh's *Hamlet*, a movie on which he appears to have gambled his whole career. If this one doesn't fly, who knows when we shall see another of his Shakespeare films? On the one hand, the film pertains to the universe of high-concept marketing: a seventy-millimeter epic (the first such in Britain for twenty-five years) with sumptuous sets, an all-star cast with cameo appearances in the manner of *Around the World in 80 Days* (Jack Lemmon, Robin Williams, Billy Crystal, and Charlton Heston, not to mention the Duke of Marlborough, all assume minor roles), and a four-hour running time complete with an intermission to bring back memories of the early sixties heyday of blockbuster filmmaking, the days of *Spartacus* and *Lawrence of Arabia*.

Branagh has another concern, however: his desire to respect against all odds the integrity of Shakespeare's text, and this puts his movie paradoxically closer to such resolutely marginal projects as Eric Rohmer's *Perceval le Gallois* (1978), in which Chrétien de Troyes's twelfth-century courtly romance is recited to the accompaniment of quasi-medieval stage effects, and Jacques Rivette's *Jeanne la Pucelle* (1994), which in recounting the career of Joan of Arc restricts itself to the language of the earliest chronicles. (Branagh's version actually is completer than complete, since it conflates the First Folio text with the extensive passages that appear only in the Second Quarto, thus producing something longer than any known version of the play.) The word—or more precisely Shakespeare's words—is the life of this film, to which everything else, Blenheim Palace, Billy Crystal, FX, SurroundSound, is incidental.

The result might be pedantic except that Branagh isn't a pedant, although his passion has its pedagogical side. In order to resolve the contradictions of his approach he has to resort to a kind of aesthetic violence which can easily be misread as vulgarization: the horror-movie visuals (the blade piercing Claudius's head, the ground splitting open), the sometimes schmaltzy musical underscoring. The resort to such tactics has rather the effect of restoring a necessary vulgarity which other films have tended to polish. As in his previous adaptations but even more deliberately, Branagh undertakes to clarify the literal meaning by any means necessary. The silent movies he has concocted featuring the career of Fortinbras and the death of Priam function as footnotes, supplying a visualization which in a stage production would be left to the audience. This is the first *Hamlet* in which Old Norway (not to mention Hecuba, Priam, and Yorick) actually figures as a participant.

Branagh's decision to present the play uncut was a brilliant one, however one may differ with one detail or another of his execution. The differences are of more than scholarly concern; the narrative rhythm is transformed, and Hamlet himself, while no less central, concedes a good deal more ground to those around him. The sententious digressions, contests of wit, and theatrical recitations—the repetitions, the circuitous approaches toward a point of negotiation, the interruptions and side chatter and discussions of urgent diplomatic affairs— these are what give the flavor of the milieu, without which *Hamlet* appears to take place in an abstract void. The full *Hamlet* has a different specific gravity, a density which makes it seem like the first great English novel, a Renaissance novel like such roughly contemporaneous Spanish works as the *Celestina* of Fernando de Rojas or the *Dorotea* of Lope de Vega, unplayably long narratives in dialogue form, interspersed at times with songs and poems. It works with time in a more expansive and open-ended way, sharing the ceaseless discursiveness and purposeful sprawl of Rabelais or Montaigne.

With all the rests restored, it becomes possible to look beyond the intrusive shocks of the plot and get a feeling for the life they have interrupted. In general, modern productions, and most especially modern film productions, cut to the plot line, as if the rest of it were bothersome persiflage. We pare Shakespeare down to streamline him, bring out "meanings" that we have planted there. Driven by an obsession to bring things into sharp focus, we simplify. *Hamlet* is a much more interesting and surprising work—and, with its roundabout strategies and gradual buildups and contradictions of tone, a more realistic one— when all of it is allowed to be heard, and it is bold of Branagh to have gambled on this more ambitious dramatic arc.

Olivier's Hamlet, steeped in that marriage of Romanticism and Freud which is film noir, threads a lone path among expressionistic shadows and wreaths of mists before returning to confront the Others.

In Branagh's interpretation, Hamlet is one among a crowd of powerfully differentiated figures who play against each other as much as against him. He is a disturbing element in the midst of a very busy and brightly lit Renaissance court. Even "To be or not to be" is staged here as a two-character scene (or, more exactly, a three-character scene): While Branagh faces himself in a mirror (it is the mirror-image who is seen speaking), we see him also from the viewpoint of the hidden Claudius. This is a *Hamlet* in which Rosencrantz and Guildenstern function for once as central characters. The convergence of that pair and Polonius with the simultaneous arrival of the players and the recitation of the Hecuba speech (superbly done by Charlton Heston's Player King, with just enough restrained hokum to identify him as an actor) is allowed all its complexity.

Branagh can be forgiven every failed touch—even the 360-degree pans (presumably intended to prevent visual stasis) which sometimes make it look as if the inhabitants of Elsinore are all on Rollerblades, even Hamlet's absurd final swing from the chandelier into the lap of the dying Claudius—for having maintained an essential lightness, the verbal quicksilver at the heart of it. For all the sometimes athletic action, this *Hamlet* is strung on its language. The words *are* the play, unfolding in a space open enough to give scope to its unruly energies.

Dostoyevsky Behind a Camera

BY GARRY WILLS

O liver Stone makes movies out of the day's headlines. That is usually a prescription for the shallow or the ephemeral. A dozen or so conspiracy films came out after President John F. Kennedy was killed, but only one continues to nag at people's minds. Movies about sex and drugs in the sixties are painful to watch now, but *The Doors* has survived. Stone with some of his movies seemed to be writing future headlines, as when *Wall Street* and *Talk Radio* anticipated later developments. Newspapers can have trouble keeping up with him.

How do Stone's timely things stay fresh in a culture that devours its past, forgetting it daily? There is a feel for timeless narrative patterns in Stone's work, connected with his film-school training in the genres. *JFK*, for instance, is a mystery story. The prosecutor's speech (which runs for more than half an hour) is like William Powell's gathering of all the suspects to go over evidence in the final reel of a *Thin Man* film. *Wall Street* is *Father Knows Best*, a tale as ancient as the Prodigal Son

FROM *ATLANTIC MONTHLY*

and as commercially sturdy as the Andy Hardy series. *The Doors* tells the story of an artist torn between a good woman (his muse) and an evil woman who destroys him.

Natural Born Killers takes movies like Buster Keaton's *Sherlock Jr.* and Woody Allen's *Purple Rose of Cairo* and stands them on their heads. In those films people escape into movie dreams, mingling with the celluloid figures. In *Killers* the images leap off the screen to swallow up their viewers. Movies themselves are the monsters that devour the world.

People tend not to notice that Stone relies on such film clichés, because he imports into them not only newspapers from below but also a mysticism from above. He is constantly suggesting cosmic show-downs behind or beyond the newsy events and the genres. Improbable martyrs and gurus haunt the screen—the saintly photographer in *Salvador*, the Dionysiac Elias in *Platoon,* Ingmar Bergman figures of Death in *The Doors* and *Natural Born Killers*.

This mixture of apparently disparate materials—scandal and spiritualism, current events and eternal recurrences—is not promising on the face of it, but Stone arranges his scripts in a three-tiered system that gives layers of meaning to the stories he tells. Above the current events is an ordinating pattern taken from cinema typology. And above those types is a "war in heaven" of clashing spiritual principles.

Where have we seen this three-tiered approach before? Who else took plots out of trashy news reports, used the narrative conventions of melodrama, and topped the confection with the gaunt monks and foolish seers of an idiosyncratic religiosity? Dostoyevsky, too, has been accused of a bogus spirituality—as when Vladimir Nabokov denounced his characters for "sinning their way to Jesus." Dickensian plots and Victorian clichés (the good-hearted prostitute, for example) are his equivalents of Andy Hardy sentiment in Stone's work. But both men set this material ablaze with fierce energies.

Dostoyevsky's three tiers are evident in a work like *The Demons.* This story of radical plotters was taken from contemporary politics (in surprisingly accurate detail). But its complex elements are unified around the generic story of a doomed Byronic hero (which made Dostoyevsky first call his novel *The Life of a Great Sinner*). Finally, high in the sky over this local tale, the fate of Russia is being decided in a struggle with the demons who possess the great sinner, Stavrogin. Exorcised from Stavrogin, devils rush into his accomplices—as demonic spirits were driven into swine at Gadara, according to the Gospel of Saint Luke, from which Dostoyevsky takes his novel's epigraph.

That is the kind of storytelling that Stone is up to in *Natural Born Killers*. The script he began with, by Quentin Tarantino, is a shocker from our TV culture, the tale of a true-crime program that promotes the careers of the young serial killers Mickey (Woody Harrelson) and Mallory (Juliette Lewis). The TV host, Wayne Gale (Robert Downey Jr.), is the main character in Tarantino's little fable of media sensationalism; the killers have no psychic history at all. Stone provides a whole new layer of narrative, using the archetypal "they made me a criminal" pattern. As Bonnie and Clyde were the crippled cripplers of others (Clyde impotent and lame, Bonnie the victim of a despotically puritanical upbringing), Mickey and Mallory were victimized by violent parents in their childhood. But where Bonnie's father was repressive, Mallory's was leering and sexually aggressive. In flashbacks she remembers the killing of her parents as a sitcom like *Married with Children*. Mickey's physically threatening parents are also remembered in flashbacks, which make him feel guilty for his father's suicide. Their police stalker, Jack Scagnetti (Tom Sizemore), also carries the guilt of his mother's death (she was killed by the Texas Tower mass murderer); his dreams actually mingle with Mickey's.

Mickey and Jack are mirror images of each other, prey and hunter—Jack even kills a prostitute in order to enter into Mickey's mind. But then Stone imposes his top layer of spiritual meaning on the story, taking Mickey onto a plane entirely beyond Jack. Mickey and Mallory try to escape the media-polluted world of their upbringing by a return to nature—marrying each other above a huge canyon, seeking wisdom in the desert. They encounter a Native American shaman whose hogan has no TV, no newspaper, no telephone—just a great opening through the roof into heaven. Violence has scarred the shaman, as Mallory finds when she picks up a picture of his son, killed in Vietnam. But he has conquered his demons, just as he tamed the snakes in his desert home. He tries to drive the demons from Mallory; but Mickey, dreaming of his father's death, kills the shaman in his stupor. Mallory shouts "Bad! Bad! Bad!" at him, at a loss for a moral language to convey what she is only dimly aware of: "You killed life." The tamed snakes come alive with punitive hissings and bite the two. They seek a cure but don't find it, since they have been infected with tragic knowledge, and—as Stone says of this sequence—no pharmacy has an antidote for that.

After their capture and trial, Mickey and Mallory communicate their new awareness to each other, even though they are kept in separate cells. Tarantino's script had no room for such growth in the characters. In fact, Tarantino's Mickey, acting as his own attorney at the trial, kills a witness on the stand. Stone filmed that scene but did not use it, because it denied the changes wrought in Mickey by the shaman. Mickey's next violence will be against Jack and the prison warden, who have planned to kill him in a rigged escape attempt. But before that Wayne, the TV host, is given a live interview with Mickey. As the show progresses and Mickey denounces the institutionalized violence of our society, the devils go out of him into the listening prisoners—just as the demons of Stavrogin entered the nihilists around him. The apocalyptic riot that brings down the prison is a cleansing destruction of the system, like the healing ordeal that Dostoyevsky envisioned for his Russia.

Stone's movie, it is said, is too violent to be an indictment of violence—as Dostoyevsky was too complicitous in Stavrogin's beautiful destructiveness. But Stone's violence is stylized, done in the form of trashy media: comic-book wounds, bullets frozen in air, movies within movie-poisoned brains.

That a study of violent fantasies is taking the form of fantasy becomes clear in the garage scene where Mallory imagines that the man at the gas pump is Mickey. Mallory is angry because Mickey, in the predesert days, has proposed a sexual threesome with a female hostage. Imagining the attendant pumping gas into her car as Mickey raping the nonexistent hostage, she throws herself back on the hood of a sports car, to which she beckons the attendant to be killed. The blending of cars with sex and violence has been a staple of the advertising world for most of this century, but no commentary on the phenomenon has had the biting wit of this sequence—crowned when Jack Scagnetti, intuiting Mallory's body in the lines of the car, strokes it erotically.

Yet this whole garage sequence is done with no nudity, no pornography in the presentation of the advertising world's pornographic strategies. In fact, there was no nudity in the film's theatrical release, and only one topless shot, of the prostitute Jack kills, in the director's cut (standard fare for R-rated films). There is no drinking in the film, no homosexuality in the vicious prison, no drugs but the mushrooms Mickey takes in the desert. This is a world *all and only* violent, except for the interlude of peace at the shaman's hut. It is a world given over to demons, and the demons inhabit the media. Bob Dole denouncing the media was a piker next to this film, which makes his point a thousand times more forcibly.

It is true, nonetheless, that Stone brings an excess of rage to his work, not unlike Mickey's. That is because he, like Mickey, feels betrayed by his parents and their world. Though he was shunted to boarding schools in his boyhood, and to his grandparents in France for the summer, Stone never suspected that his parents' marriage was a sham covering up their affairs with other partners—not, that is, until his father's ex-secretary called him at boarding school to say that his father and mother were getting divorced and could not be reached by him. This disillusioning shock, delivered when he was sixteen, was followed by another when he was seventeen—the assassination of President Kennedy. He told his biographer, James Riordan: "To see his candle snuffed out so early and viciously was such a shock. I had no faith in my parents' generation after that." When I asked Stone if it is fair to say that the divorce and the assassination worked together to make him feel that his world was coming apart, he said, "Yes, that's fair." Later, when he examined the circumstances of Kennedy's death, he found that all was not as it had seemed: "My life was like that, uncovering what was *really* going on between my mother and my father—they were not *really* lovers."

So disoriented was Stone by such blows that he gave up on Yale after a year and went to Vietnam as an English teacher in the Catholic school system. After his return to America he buried himself ("like Dostoyevsky," he says) in writing his version of *Underground Man*. Rejection of the novel by publishers drove Stone to despair, and he volunteered to go back to Vietnam as an infantryman. "I was suicidal, though I would not pull the trigger on myself." After he was wounded twice in Vietnam, his death wish took him back to the front for a second time—but he returned to America, and to film school at New York University, with the materials he shaped later into *Platoon*.

There are no politics in *Platoon*, nothing about communism or dominoes or empire—just the grind and panic of war and the rub of frightened men against one another. The story pattern that Stone imposes on this is the clash of two leaders in a crisis situation—Mr. Christian against Captain Bligh on the *Bounty*, Odysseus against Agamemnon at Troy, Corporal Thomas against Sergeant Stryker in *Sands of Two Jima*. Stone draws directly on *Sands*, giving his Sergeant Barnes (Tom Berenger) John Wayne's slogans: "Saddle up! Lock and load!" Like Wayne, Barnes can boast, "I *am* reality."

Barnes is less vulnerable even than Wayne's character, who is killed by the enemy in *Sands*. The men in *Platoon* recognize that "the only thing that can kill Barnes is Barnes." Pitted against Barnes, the war god, is Sergeant Elias (Willem Dafoe), who is not opposed to the war—indeed, he had found an eerie serenity in the midst of his efficient killing. Barnes thinks that Elias has relaxed too much into a war that sickens Barnes to ruthlessness—Elias must be killed for the good of his own followers. Over the plot mechanics Stone has imposed the idea of a suffering Dionysus taken from Nietzsche and from Stone's study of Greek tragedy at NYU. Elias accepts death with the smile of Dionysus in Euripides' *The Bacchae*—a play Stone drew on and refers to in *The Doors*. In *Platoon*, Chris Tayler (Charlie Sheen), torn between "two fathers," has to become Barnes in order to destroy Barnes. He goes back to America with Elias in his heart but Barnes in his gut.

The student movie that Stone made in Martin Scorsese's class at NYU was unconsciously a preview of *Platoon*. Stone filmed himself as a Vietnam vet trying to purge the Barnes in him, going out to nature (the film changes from black and white to color) to shed his medals and bathe in cleansing waters, communing with his Elias side.

The search for a father is carried on in most of Stone's work. It is both private and public, reflecting the betrayals of his teens. This explains the fierce personal heat with which Stone engages public issues. Dostoyevsky drew on a similar private-public shock, undergone in his teens, when he lost his father. While Dostoyevsky was at engineering school, guilty over the funds he was draining from his father's struggling estate, the farm's serfs murdered the father for his stinginess—or so Dostoyevsky was given to believe (later evidence threw doubt on the matter). The public issue was the political discontent of the serfs. Dostoyevsky became, overnight, a champion of their liberation, because he felt he had forced them to desperation by the competing financial demands he placed upon his father. The tangled guilt of the Karamazovs was born (in part) of this experience.

Stone's feelings about his own father, Louis Stone, a New York stock analyst, are clearest in *Wall Street*. Charlie Sheen, as Bud Fox, is again torn between a commanding figure and a more humane one—the stock manipulator Gordon Gekko (Michael Douglas) and his own father, a union leader. Though the Andy Hardy pattern makes Fox see that his father's values are more important, forcing him to destroy Gekko (as Tayler destroyed Barnes), the Dionysian energy of Gekko has made him the hero of applicants to business schools and of the financial columnist for *National Review* (who writes under the pseudonym Gekko). Gekko is humanized by his love for his son (played by Stone's son Sean), his taste in art (better than that of his arty mistress), and his desire to get back at the Ivy League WASPs who tried to keep this City College product out of their clubs. Louis Stone—who changed his name from Silverstein, went to Yale, and repressed his writing talent in order to climb in the financial world—was a Gekko who failed and needed no destroying. But it is the act of forgiveness under the indictment that brings Gekko to life in *Wall Street*. Those who thought it a mere attack on Reagan's era of greed missed the conflicts within Stone's own sympathies. He does not tell simple stories.

Yet he is constantly accused of doing that. Because he takes on serious topics, he is called a "message" director. But it is hard to see a political message in, say, *Platoon*. What would it be? That one must become a Barnes to defend an Elias—thus undercutting the point of defending Elias? Stone is also said to be obsessed with conspiracies, though his one conspiracy film, *JFK*, is so inclusive in its condemnation of everything but an implausibly pure John Kennedy and a ludicrously virtuous investigator, Jim Garrison (Kevin Costner), that the real conspiracy seems to be life itself. It was a touching if loony idea to turn the hard-drinking and womanizing Garrison into a kind of Atticus Finch, straight out of *To Kill a Mockingbird*, a poster boy for family values.

Family is the crucial link between public and private in Stone's work—as it was the nexus for his own sense of betrayal at home and, with Kennedy's assassination, in the country. In *Born on the Fourth of July* and *Heaven and Earth* mothers first send their sons to war and then reject what they become there. Parents terrorized the two who become terrorists in *Natural Born Killers*. In *Nixon,* Hannah Nixon cripples her son emotionally, far more than his father, Frank, abuses him physically.

The reaction to *Nixon* is a good example of the errors people fall into when they read Stone in an ideological way. Some took his movie as a political attack on Nixon, the way they took *Wall Street* as a political attack on Reagan. There is a minor role for conspiracy in *Nixon*—but Nixon (Anthony Hopkins) is more the victim of a Cuban-CIA tie than its mastermind. What matters in *Nixon* is the extended rethinking it gives to *Citizen Kane*. The connections to that film were noticed by reviewers but treated as mere addenda or ornaments stuck onto the tale extraneously. In fact the attempt to fathom the mystery of a mysteryless man has not been done better since the Welles classic. Both Kane and Nixon are incapable of intimacy. In the scene where Kane's mother gives him away to a guardian, the boy thrusts his sled between himself and the guardian. After that he is never seen embracing anyone, not even his wife or mistress. How he can manipulate people while distancing himself from them is the intriguing puzzle never solved by the movie. Nixon's panicky circling away from Pat (Joan Allen) as the camera pursues him is as affecting as his few pathetic lunges toward intimacy—the delusion that he found common ground with the protestors at the Lincoln Memorial, and his drowner's way of pulling Kissinger (Paul Sorvino) down with him into desperate prayer.

Nixon is really the story of two Nixon generations, of Hannah and Frank, of Pat and Dick—and of the latter pair's inability to escape the former. Nixon is a victim of shattered family values, as surely as is Mickey in *Natural Born Killers*. The difference between them is that Mickey can find release into the higher world of the shaman. When Nixon turns to his mother's religion of fear, it does not free him from self-imprisonment but locks the bolts tighter. The tragedy of Nixon is that the path to transcendence is sealed off by the false sanctity of his mother, who uses religion to control and stunt him.

Here is the deepest paradox of Stone's career. At a time when the religious right is attacking movies in general and him in particular, Stone is one of the few filmmakers who regularly treat religion in a serious way. Some refuse to consider his religious thrashings important, because (like Dostoyevsky's) they take exotic form—the religion found in and beyond excess, the Dionysiac serenity-in-violence of Elias, the Bacchic ecstasy of Jim Morrison, the Native American shamanism of *Natural Born Killers,* the saintly quest for truth by the photographer John (John Savage) in *Salvador,* the universal forgiveness of the Buddhists in *Heaven and Earth.* But these reflect serious preoccupations in Stone's life—he has been meditating with a Buddhist master for years. And they reflect an age-old strain of religion that finds those deeply engaged in life's conflicts more capable of vision than are the complacent. It is a truth the Christian right can find in its own Gospels: "Verily I say unto you that the publicans and the harlots go into the kingdom of God before you" (Matthew 21:31). Nabokov might say that Stone's characters are "sinning their way to Buddha," but that is often the story of religion when it is real. When it is unreal, it becomes a temptation and a trap—not only the Christianity of Hannah Nixon but also the Judaism of the host in *Talk Radio,* who uses a lie about his ties with Israel to manipulate his audience. What is being attacked here is not Christianity or Judaism but the distortion of each for purposes of human domination.

If the secular saint Jim Garrison is totally unconvincing, it is because *JFK* alone of Stone's films has no complex character at its center. That, not the wacky theories it airs, is its real artistic failure. On the other hand, the photographer in *Salvador* is one of the few modern saints on film. A scene that reflects from an opposite pole the empty prayer of Nixon and Kissinger is that in which the morally despicable correspondent in *Salvador* (James Woods) clasps the hands of the dying John and accepts a higher sense of calling from him. (The scene reflects an earlier clasping of muddy hands, when the correspondent gave a dead church worker his own ring.)

In one of several interviews I have conducted with Stone, I said that I think of him as a moralist. At first he took it as an insult: "A moralist? You'll have to defend that." I meant that he engages issues with moral urgency. It is the difference between the script of an ironist (Tarantino) and the passionate film that Stone made of *Natural Born Killers.* Stone eventually accepted the "accusation" if it meant not that he tells others how to live but that he makes his characters try to give a responsible account of themselves. The selves being assessed are complex. Charlie Sheen's characters in *Platoon* and *Wall Street* contain both Elias and Barnes, both Gekko and Bud Fox's father. Mickey in *Killers* contains both the demons of his father and the shaman who fights demons. The heroine of *Heaven and Earth* (played by Hiep Le) contains two entirely different worlds, East and West, and wrestles them to a mutual forgiveness.

Heaven and Earth resists ideological reductionism. The heroine is violated more by the Viet Cong than by the French or the Americans, and the American husband she takes (Tommy Lee Jones) is more the victim of his own culture than an inflicter of it on others. She ends up realizing that a failure to forgive aggression is a deeper form of aggression, a yielding to the demons coming out of one's enemies. She reaches a sense of binding compassion like the vision of cosmic harmony at which Alyosha arrives in the foul world of the Karamazovs, or like Prince Myshkin's transcendence through suffering in *The Idiot*. This is not your ordinary two hours' traffic of the screen. It is more like what writers aspired to when they hoped to write the great American novel. Great novels are now being written with the camera—at least when Stone is behind the camera.

Jane Campion's Shining: Portrait of a Director

BY KATHLEEN MURPHY

*O*nly a filmmaker who possesses the hubris to imagine that art and moral adventure matter could have composed *The Portrait of a Lady* in the densely telling hues and uncompromising forms Jane Campion has achieved. To start with, the novel's author has always been rated as a "hard read," even in the days when reading wasn't rare. Henry James *works* every word, every phrase, every description or discourse, so that you must travel his narratives attuned to minute changes in social/spiritual weather and the moral and psychological reverberations of every bit of small talk. For lack of attention to dangerous undergrowth, a life, or a soul, can be shattered in his "civilized" minefields.

Campion's *The Portrait of a Lady* largely manages to recast James's exquisitely wrought prose, his interior epiphanies and apocalypses, into dialogue, images, and performances that explode in slowest, utterly devastating motion. Like James's hard reads, this brilliant, difficult

FROM *FILM COMMENT*

film demands close concentration and committed effort on the viewer's part. The novel's central metaphors (sun and shadow, house and garden, nature and artifice), resonating dialogue, and actors—aspiring or fallen angels—are authentically animated, without cinematic disguise or distortion, on Campion's canvas.

Campion chronicles the journeys of women into terra incognita with passionate conviction, making their quests as emblematic of the human condition as any Adam's. In this, she's been on the same track as Henry James, who loved to plunge (and vicariously plunge with) his brave Daisy Millers and Isabel Archers into refining—or fatal—"European" experience. Also in the Jamesian tradition, Campion's heroines may be armed with self-destructive or even killing innocence. In *The Piano*, Holly Hunter's silent émigré makes a kind of self-sufficient identity/sexuality of her speaking art. She's not unaware that her single-minded consecration to her instrument is a come-on, separating the men from the boys, crudely speaking. When she's brought to earth by Harvey Keitel's half-Caliban (and symbolically castrated by her jealous husband), she lets her art drown and gets reborn as happy wife and piano teacher.

An Angel at My Table, Campion's adaptation of the autobiographies of author Janet Frame, begins by looking down on a fat baby girl lying on her back in the grass. Then we see her toddler's feet, unsteadily navigating a meadow. Finally we wait—with the camera—for a chubby little girl topped by an explosion of frizzy red hair walking down a long road, straight toward us. When Janet Frame arrives, she takes one look into the camera—the world? The future?—and, terrified, runs back the way she came. By film's end, when the Australian writer finally makes her way home again, she has bitten deep, often painfully, into life, the imagination, even madness. Campion's camera puts a period to her journey by rounding the curved side of a very small, snug trailer to look in at Frame at rest and in virtual motion: writing, wombed in warm, golden light.

The hypnotic prelude to Campion's *The Portrait of a Lady* begins in darkness, murmurous with the dreaming voices of young girls: ". . . the best part of a kiss is the moment just before . . . we become addicted to being intertwined . . . finding the clearest mirror, the most loyal mirror . . . when I love, I know he will shine that back to me." Her camera gazes down into a grove where a sorority of lovely Mirandas lies about in innocent abandon, their bodies curved like silver fish in a sea of grass. Then, in a series of shots in black and white alternating with color, Campion's hieratic virgins undulate slowly or stand still, always gazing out at us with the provocative serenity of brave new souls. These vestals in modern dress point the way—the film's title is literally inscribed on the flesh of a woman's hand—into the film proper, the nineteenth-century pilgrim's progress of Isabel Archer, New World Candide.

Campion makes us see—with really stunning support from Nicole Kidman—Isabel Archer as both eligible virgin and the bright, double-faced spirit of idealism that humankind perennially projects. Narcissus as much as Diana, she embarks on a quest for her "most loyal mirror"— for wisdom as much as love—through four very different men of the world. Campion shows her as distaff knight, courageously tracking enlightenment, imagining life into art; as a chaste voyeur blind to complexity, willing be deflowered only by dead men; and as an Eve whose free will is illusory, a temporary luxury provided not by God but money.

Archer's odyssey ranges from heaven to hell on earth, from a garden rich with summer's green-gold promise into blighting experience and back again, to a white and frozen home base, hard ground to cultivate. But, in perhaps the cruelest sense, *nothing* happens in *The Portrait of a Lady*. A woman's world simply ends, winding down to wasteland: dead zero. Not by accident, as *Portrait*'s innocent abroad launches into her world tour, she pockets an ominous "ticket," a scrap of paper on which is written NIHILISM.

Our first portrait of Isabel closes in on her fiercely blue eyes brimming with tears as she turns down a proposal from wealthy Lord Warburton (Richard Grant): "When I'm touched, it's for life," the young man vows feelingly. (*Touch* and the prelude to touching, *nearness,* verbally and visually implode throughout *Portrait,* tagging the courage of passionate proximity and stone-cold possession.) This eminently desirable young woman is a guest at Gardencourt, the exquisitely appointed and landscaped English estate that houses her aunt (Shelley Winters, surprisingly good) and uncle (John Gielgud), the Touchetts. Seated among lush green leaves and molten sunlight, red-haired Isabel seems herself a bright flower, one that shrinks from plucking. The curving limb that embraces Isabel, now so much like an Edenic benison, becomes, by *Portrait*'s wintry end, a black, no-exit barrier.

Campion's precisely right to open on Isabel's laser-blue gaze, for this Eve is all eyes—they're the loci of her appetite, her avid curiosity: "I want to get a general impression of life . . . there's a light that has to dawn," she tells her uncle, her bright face shining out of a frameful of darkness. It does not yet occur to Isabel, in the ruthless purity of her innocence, that epiphanies may cast terrible shadows.

In these early scenes, Isabel's heart-shaped, flyaway red hair recalls Janet Frame's unbound coiffure, electrified by a passionate, open imagination. Later, as a member of Gilbert Osmond's (John Malkovich) coven—with his mistress Madame Merle (Barbara Hershey) and Pansy (Valentina Cervic), the exotic Venus flytrap Osmond and Merle have crossbred—Isabel's hair, styled in complex coils, darkens, signifying her new grasp of artifice and the occult. In the barely illuminated airlessness of her Roman home, Isabel is expected to move to a puppetmaster's design or be still, a rich objet d'art useful as investment, decor, or sexual lure.

Referring to a feature of one of Lord Warburton's many homes, Isabel's "I adore a moat" are the first words we hear from a Miranda so jealous of her virgin zone she refuses every hands-on surveyor. She flees Warburton, through an arch of greenery, across a vast verdant lawn where the family sips ritual tea. As she passes, her consumptive cousin Ralph Touchett (finely expressed by Martin Donovan) takes her in, following her progress with intense interest. A little dog drags at her flying skirts, and as she catches it, the frame slants slightly so that her shadow, holding up the animal, falls on the green.

Much of Isabel's itinerary and fate are foreshadowed—literally— in this English Eden, where nature as lush topiary art frames the Touchetts' quietly cultivated way of life. Taking flight from potential largesse—emotional and financial—Isabel imagines herself to be perfectly free to choose where and if she will touch down. Campion closes in on Isabel's skirts again and again in the film, as incremental refrain, measuring the decline of these beating "wings" from strong purposeful motion into aimless, futile flight.

The little dog that nips at the beautiful dreamer's heels at Gardencourt is animal life, energy from below that demands attention. Less positively, the dog prefigures Gilbert Osmond, Isabel's "small," bestial husband-to-be—variously hairy-faced, braying ass and snouting pig, who makes Merle "howl like a wolf" (though in fact her name's a poetic form of "blackbird"). Osmond later shockingly humiliates the Eve he's bell-jarred by deliberately tripping her up as she flees him, keeping her down by stepping on her skirts.

Tilting to frame that momentary stain on Gardencourt's lawn, Campion's camera signs the beginning of Isabel's slow descent into an "unfathomable abyss," inked in the blackness of Madame Merle's gloved hand spidering obscenely over Pansy's stomach; the grounded shadow of a parasol during Osmond's subterranean "rape" of Isabel; the line of shade that, by her father's decree, bars Pansy from a sunlit garden. Campion will later look down on a Roman park studded with trees moated by colorful flower beds. As animated aristos stroll the circular paths, shades of Joseph Cotten and Teresa Wright attend Isabel as she insists she hasn't "the shadow of a doubt" about the probity of the serpent on her arm.

Caspar Goodwood (Viggo Mortenson), the American admirer who has pursued Isabel to Europe, comes from good adamic stock; sunny open ground, he's physically passionate and single-minded in his affections. Down from the Touchett estate to London, in the first stage of Isabel's descent from garden to prison, a fleeting glimpse of a corset hanging suggestively on the back of the door of our adventurer's little bed-sitting room sets the tone for Goodwood's visit. Crowding her into a corner, her least talkative lover braces his arms on the walls that hem her, hardly able to resist touching her. "You don't fit in," she cries. She thinks she means in some large social scheme, but it's the plaint of a virgin, afraid of the pain—and pleasure—of penetration.

Every time Goodwood touches her, at almost ritual intervals throughout *Portrait,* Isabel recoils as if afraid she'll catch fire. She can't take this man in through her eyes, her mind alone; he is too large, too lively for her. As he leaves her room, rebuffed once more, he momentarily holds her chin in his palm. Afterwards, she touches herself in the same way and goes under, as though set off by some posthypnotic suggestion. Her eyes soft and unfocused, she rubs her face against the fringed hanging of her four-poster like a cat in heat. Wojiech Kilar's sensual music pulses as she trances out in carnal pleasure; Warburton, Touchett, and Goodwood snake about her body, caressing her until, suddenly startled, she shakes the men off and they decorporealize. It's a scene out of Coppola's *Dracula* (scored by Kilar), but even in fantasy, Isabel remains in control and intact.

In James, American Adams transplanted into the hothouse of Europe often grow into passive voyeurs; the refined, sexless inertia of a Ralph Touchett or Gilbert Osmond may signal an aesthetic or diabolical bent. The Gardencourt invalid who registered Isabel's frantic retreat from Warburton soon plays beneficent angel by "making" his young cousin, that is, by arranging for her to be rich enough to follow the "requirements of her imagination." Ralph Touchett looks forward, he tells her, to "the thrill of seeing what a young lady does who has refused" an English lord.

Ralph might be James, loosing his engaging young heroine into the world, eager to see where she will take him and his novel. Isabel and her ironically named cousin are *Portrait*'s truest soul mates. Platonic lovers happy to *see* and *imagine*, to apprehend and chew over life as if it were a complex masterpiece to be appreciated by earnest digestion. Their *Rear Window* symbiosis combines stillness and motion, invalid impotence and unfettered action. Pumping a friend of Isabel's about his cousin's treatment of Caspar Goodwood, Ralph inquires hungrily, "Was she cruel?" Campion cuts to a chilling shot of this consumer's nail clicking on a glass that imprisons a buzzing hornet.

Campion divides her *Portrait* with a superbly visualized scene between Ralph and Isabel, one that conjures up Buñuel's *Tristana* and *Belle de Jour,* along with Hitchcock's *Vertigo.* Isabel enters, distractedly, at the bottom of the frame. Inclining up frame-left is a wall of arched, moltenly yellow stable doors. Two great ebon horses stand against the slant of golden wood. The effect is surreal, a Buñuelian dream-image hot with sensual simile. But this Belle is blind; she does not blaze until she's inside the dark stables, her red hair thinly haloed by filtered sun, her face and body shaded blue by tinted windowlight. Isabel has just engaged to marry Gilbert Osmond; her vibrant warmth and color is already contracting toward the cool, hard, still "marble" he will make of her. (Stone and porcelain simulacra mark Isabel's descent into museumed life: lovers sleeping side by side on sarcophagi; the chubby marble hand of her dead child; Pansy's rosier, verboten suitor, diminished to a little doll hidden harmlessly at her breast.)

In the stables, Ralph Touchett grieves for the bright bird, now tethered by a sterile collector, he has ridden with such vicarious pleasure: "You were not to come down so easily, so soon. It hurts me as if I'd fallen myself." Isabel's been his Madeleine, an ideal he can cherish and pursue in his imagination; like Hitchcock's Scotty in *Vertigo,* Ralph doesn't want to "touchett," has no taste for a flawed woman of flesh and blood. A vampire of small but fastidious appetite, he has "made" his Eve for something finer than Osmond's debasement. As Isabel pleads her case against his "false idea," Ralph and the camera recede from her. She grows smaller in our eyes, as though her image has been released from his focus, to fall away into a void.

Their reunion comes in the penultimate moments of the film, in *Portrait*'s single scene of something like sexual consummation. The woman we've seen only in postures of sexual passivity or flight climbs into bed with the dying Ralph, frantically caressing and kissing a body already going cold. Their climax is his death, signaled by his hand falling uselessly away from her cheek. As he passes, he admonishes her to keep him in her heart—"I'll be *nearer* than I've ever been." (In a preceding, twinning scene, Osmond has come at Isabel as she beats her forehead against a door in despair, brutally pinning her with his body and firmly holding her valuable face from harm: "You are nearer to me and I am nearer to you than ever," gloats her curator.) In death, Ralph Touchett's spirit finally enters his beloved's body in perfect Platonic possession.

From the moment at Gardencourt when Madame Merle sirens Isabel down to her with voluptuous Chopin, images of the young woman who puts such arrogant faith in her islanded identity begin to be doubled, distorted and dissolved. In her Dantean journey, Isabel's eyes are opened to her own self-delusions, and to the ugly, convoluted reality behind the "vivid images" she has made of Merle and Osmond.

At the start of Campion's superb concatenation of horror movie, fairy tale, and refashioning of Eve's mythic Fall, Isabel winds down the stairs of an ancient Roman villa to fetch up in a round subterranean chamber—half mausoleum, half museum. Set at intervals in this strange room's ceiling are grilled openings; weak light falls through air dense with old debris, so that barred rectangles punctuate Isabel's path. Osmond materializes out of the shadows, twirling the parasol she's left behind. It snaps with unpleasant papery sounds, like the rushing of bats, and he uses it like Mesmer's hypnotic wheel. The two circle each other, like wary animals maneuvering for better ground, but Isabel's eyes are locked on his. We've seen him work Madame Merle with the most expert hand—"Every now and then I'm touched," he mocks his earlier conquest as he brutally disengages: Isabel hasn't a prayer against his snaky intensity. Much later, even as he lashes her with hateful verbal contempt, Isabel leans helplessly in toward his mouth, her eyes "stupefied" with longing.*

As Osmond declares the precise nature of his love—"I offer *nothing*"—Campion's camera rushes toward the couple around a curve of wall, past a skull set in old stone. The motion takes your breath away: Something like death has passed. The frame tilts to show the shadow of Isabel's parasol at the lovers' feet. Osmond seals their unholy bargain with a Judas kiss, swallowing her mouth with a prostitute's practiced, perfectly timed sensuality—and slides away into the dark. No Miltonic Satan vital with glamour and active evil, Isabel's ravisher is a lesser devil, a cold collector of fortunes. He has seduced her into a world of pimps and promoters, where manipulation of bodies and souls is his vulgar art.

"I'd give a good deal to be your age again . . . my dreams were so great . . . the best part is gone . . . and for *nothing*," confides Madame Merle, the dark sister who has preceded Isabel into Gilbert Osmond's soul-killing embrace. Nothing, out of James by way of Campion, is

*By means of a radical stylistic trope, Campion makes us see that the nature of Isabel's stupefaction is sexual, moral, and aesthetic. The primitively shot and imagined silent movie—"My Journey"—that follows hard upon Osmond's seduction is equal, lurid parts *Son of the Sheik* and Hitchcock's *Spellbound*, with a little *Caligari* thrown in for good measure. Jerkily, it segues from the comic, speeded-up motion of Isabel and her friend Henrietta sliding from side to side on the deck of a rocking ship; to Isabel costumed and veiled in Bedouin garb courtesy of a studio wardrobe department, abroad in exotic locales more back-projected than real; through the plateful of Daliesque beans that open like mouths or vaginas to groan Osmond's "I love you absolutely"; to a climactic plunge down into feverdream and final swoon in sheikland. Flashing on her own eyes and mouth, the bearded orifice of her demon lover and his hand splayed on her naked stomach (as she's seen Merle's brand Pansy's front), Isabel finally falls, naked, into the whirling wheel of a sideshow hypnotist. Is this Osmondian projection the "light that has to dawn" so anticipated by Isabel in the greenhouse of her imagination?

arrived at through the profoundest of passions, an awful violence practiced as perfectly deliberate, often quite public atrocity. In *Portrait's* last act, Campion frames Gardencourt in long shot, its beautiful stonework and ivy bleakly rimed in ice, as old Aunt Touchett creaks her way across the snowy lawn, clutching her walker. "Is there really no hope?" Isabel pleads, referring to Ralph's illness. With grating, indifferent finality, Shelley Winters's voice speaks a wider epitaph: "None whatsoever. There never has been."

I haven't said enough about the character of Madame Merle, played magnificently by that peerless Magdalene, Barbara Hershey. As the dark lady of *Portrait,* she is a truly tragic figure, because she has far more self-awareness and a larger vision than Isabel may ever attain—she chooses sin with her eyes open. Two images from the film, two sides of Merle: In the first, she and Isabel walk along a series of pedestals displaying classically monumental human parts in marble—a huge hand here, a gigantic foot there. Merle sits down in front of an heroic male torso, its genitalia backing her in the frame—as she unmasks for Isabel, confessing her role as procuress and trying to cozen Osmond's wife into pandering for Madame Merle's own daughter.

Later, at the dim convent where Osmond has locked Pansy up for being insufficiently commercial, Campion's camera passes Isabel's face in close-up, left of frame, to focus in on Madame Merle, who holds a little doll wrapped in waxed paper. Her glib social spiel, about paying a call on the lonely Pansy, stutters to a halt with her nearly whispered "a little dismal"—apt epigraph for her life and her child. This *mater dolorosa* is backed by a crucified Christ, painted on the wall behind her, but Isabel can't see that. Even in the rain outside, when a bedraggled Merle tries to touch her with "I know you are very unhappy, but I am more so," our unforgiving fundamentalist slides her carriage window shut between them, effectively making nothing of the woman who is perhaps her clearest mirror.

At film's end, Campion reprises the circling dance in Osmond's underground chamber, this time with Isabel and Caspar Goodwood, on the very site—now a wintry wasteland—where, as a green girl, she refused Warburton. But as the passionate Goodwood holds his upraised hands to either side of her face—as though afraid to catch hold of her—Isabel literally pants with fear, rounding against his offer of earthly happiness like a trapped animal. "Why go through this ghastly form?" her good angel cries out, referring to her marriage. "To get away from you," comes her terrible, perverse reply.

Fleeing Goodwood, Isabel follows her earlier route, but now Gardencourt's grounds are cold and unpromising. The whole weight of *Portrait* has slanted slowly, inexorably from summer down through seasons of dismal rain into this wintry whiteout, scrawled with the meaningless calligraphy of dead branches. We watch her dark skirts flash over the snow, as though Ralph Touchett's once high-flying soul knew to what significant South she was heading—but her advancement is herky-jerky, slowed by step-printing. Through the manor's windows, we can see a warm haven of golden candlelight, the color of home in the final shot of *An Angel at My Table*. In close-up, Isabel's hand turns on the doorknob. Then, her back to shelter, bleak landscape before her, our bright angel simply runs down, freeze-framed like some lost Galatea. In *Portrait*'s brave, hard-won ending, Campion's Eve—neither home nor exiled, but pinned in some deadly zone between—gazes out at nothing.

Warren Beatty

BY GEORGE PLIMPTON

*F*or some time now I have been sitting by the phone, waiting to hear from Warren Beatty. He is in New York making his film *Dick Tracy*. He knows "my work," as they say in Hollywood. I had a small role in his film *Reds*. I know exactly what he is going to say when the phone rings and he is on the other end. He is going to say, "Is this the man who has never had an olive?"

It is a kind of ritual between us. I once told him that, to my knowledge, I had never eaten an olive. Very likely I have had part of one, in a salad, perhaps, but I have never knowingly eaten one; I have never reached into an empty martini glass and popped one of the things into my mouth.

Warren has the most astonishing powers of recall. He remembers my telephone number in New York when the exchange was Lyceum. So when he telephones and I answer, he doesn't say, "Hello, it's War-

FROM *THE PARIS REVIEW*

ren," or whatever. He asks, "Is this the man who has never had an olive?"

I always reply by asking, "Warren, is that you?" which is nonsensical, since who else would call up and start asking about olives?

I have known him for years—not well, of course, because there is something quite ephemeral about Warren: He materializes briefly, like a face at the window, and then disappears for years at a time. Nothing is more typical of this than my experience with him on *Reds*. I happened to be staying as a guest at Hugh Hefner's Playboy Mansion in Holmby Hills. Coming up from the grotto swimming pool late one night, I discovered Warren apparently asleep on the floor of the foyer just by the front door. I found out later that he had just returned from the Soviet Union, where he had been trying (unsuccessfully, it turned out) to get the Russians to let him film *Reds* on location—specifically in Leningrad, where the October Revolution took place in 1917. Some extensive carpentry work was being done on his house; he had arrived at Hefner's—a face in the window—looking for a room for the night.

So there he was, lying on the marble floor, with his head on a knapsack. I looked down at him, and before his eyes snapped open and he brought up the business about the olive, I said, reversing the usual order of our ritual, "Is that you, Warren?"

He opened his eyes and immediately said, "Wiggen. Henry Wiggen." At this time I had no idea what he was talking about. It turned out that Henry Wiggen was a character in the screenplay of *Reds*—a rather obnoxious gentleman who runs a magazine called *The Cosmopolitan* and has dishonorable intentions toward Louise Bryant, played by Diane Keaton. In the mansion that night none of this was described. Warren—and I don't think he ever moved his head from the knapsack—simply said he now had me in mind for a small part (Wiggen), and could I come that summer to London, where *Reds* was to be filmed?

Of course, of course, I said. I was enormously pleased. At the very least it proved the old Hollywood adage that it was simply a question of being in the right place at the right time—Lana Turner "discovered" at the counter in Schwab's drugstore. A door had been opened on a whole new career!

But then a few months went by, and nothing happened. No contracts arrived. No script. Not a word from Warren. I began to think that he'd had second thoughts. Perhaps he had discovered that my main acting experience had been at an all-boys school in New England when I was cast as a "young widow" in a drama called *Seven Keys to Baldpate* almost entirely because of my ability to scream. There were tryouts and I had won.

Then one day early that summer I was sitting in my New York apartment and the phone rang.

"Is this the man who has never had an olive?"

"Is that you, Warren?"

It was, and he had called to say that he had Diane Keaton with him and that he wondered if he could drop around to introduce her, since we had a couple of scenes together.

Of course, of course. I went to the kitchen and mixed myself a gin and tonic. The two of them arrived. Warren had the script with him in black covers. The presence of the two seemed to diminish the size of the apartment. I noticed the windows weren't washed. A small tear in the living-room carpet suddenly seemed a foot in diameter. We chatted rather aimlessly, I thought, not about *Reds,* but about the hot weather and how Warren's house was coming along and whether Diane liked baseball, and it occurred to me during all this that they were *staring* at me. What was important was not whether I could act, but whether I *looked* like Henry Wiggen.

Sure enough. After ten minutes or so, Warren said they had to be on their way.

"Well, don't you want me to read?" I asked.

"It doesn't really matter," Warren said.

"Well, I'm so glad you dropped in," I said as I took them to the door.

The apartment seemed to reestablish its proportions after they had left. The sun shone brightly through the windows. I picked up the cat and began speaking to it. "What do you suppose," I said, "Warren meant when he said it didn't matter?"

The phone rang. It was Warren. This time he didn't say, "Is this the man . . ." He was calling from his limousine. He said, "Diane and I have been talking it over, and we think it's best if we heard you read."

"You want me . . . to *read.*"

"We're on our way back," Warren said.

Of course, of course. Well, there it was, I thought, as I hung up the phone. My limitations as an actor would be immediately evident. I could cancel London, I told the cat, as part of my summer plans.

The scene Warren wanted me to read involved a rendezvous in a hotel tearoom with Diane Keaton, who, as Louise Bryant, is aspiring to be a writer. She is showing Wiggen some of her work, but he, though the editor of *The Cosmopolitan*, is more interested in her: His manner is oily.

Diane Keaton sat opposite me on the sofa. It was startling to have such a famous face close at hand and to have it behave very much like any other face. One is inured to the still photographs of the famous looking out from magazines and newspapers: It was as if a storefront mannequin had come to life. Her eyes—copper green and speckled in the sunlight—blinked. Her mouth moved. "Mr. Wiggen, I brought some stories . . ."

"How nice," I said archly.

We went over the lines a few times. Suddenly, Warren leaned forward out of his chair and took the script from me.

"All right," he said, "*now* do it."

"But, Warren, I don't know the lines. You haven't given me a chance to memorize them."

"Don't worry about the lines," he said. "You've read them enough to know what sort of character you are. Go ahead."

I repeated the lines as best I could remember them. Then I improvised. Would she be interested in going to Coney Island and riding on the Swan Boat in the Tunnel of Love? What was her favorite cocktail? Did she like to have *lots* of them? I reached for her hand. My voice took on a curious, unctuous whine.

"That's fine," Warren said. He stood up.

"Do you want me to try another approach?" I asked anxiously.

"It doesn't really matter," he said.

I am poor with dates. It may have been a few months or even a year later. Time is of small consequence in anything involving Warren. I had almost forgotten *Reds* and Henry Wiggen. I was in Monte Carlo with the Grucci fireworks family. We were there competing for the fireworks championship of the world, which indeed the Gruccis eventually won. The phone rang in my hotel room. Through the static of a long-distance call I heard a voice saying, "Is this the man who has never had an olive?"

"Is that you, Warren?" I shouted.

It was, and he was telling me the dates I would be required to be in London.

So I went and performed. I wore a high turn-of-the-century collar and a watch chain and looked very dandified. Warren, who also directed the film, took more than thirty takes of our scene in the hotel tearoom. I went to the opening night in New York. The searchlights outside the theater pointed straight up. My scene was early in the film. During the intermission Paul Newman came by and said, "Hey, not bad."

It was the way he said "hey" that was especially pleasing—slightly surprised, as if I had performed a kind of conjuring trick. It pumped me up.

Indeed, afterward it occurred to me that at the Academy Awards an Oscar should be given for the best performance by someone from another "discipline" who hasn't the slightest idea how to act. From my own field I can think of Norman Mailer, who played Stanford White in *Ragtime;* Jerzy Kosinski, who played a party intellectual in *Reds;* John Irving in *The World According to Garp;* and Kurt Vonnegut, who runs up as Rodney Dangerfield's teacher in *Back to School.*

So I continue to keep an ear out for the phone. The rumor is that a lot of the actors in *Dick Tracy* wear rubber masks to better resemble the grotesque characters from the comic strip—B. B. Eyes, Flat Top. I wouldn't mind that. Anything to keep my hand in as a member of the Screen Actors Guild. Firing a machine gun from a window. Being zapped by someone and failing backward in a heap. I'm perfectly willing to resurrect the scream from *Seven Keys to Baldpate.*

The phone rings. It is someone I don't know from Bear Stearns. Or Shearson Lehman Hutton. Or Solomon Brothers. They invariably give their names and ask, "How are you this morning?" They have extremely interesting financial proposals. Can I spare them a moment? No, I say. I am waiting for a phone call.

Honoring the Difficult

BY ALICE WALKER

To create today is to create dangerously. Any publication is an act,
and that act exposes one to the passions of an age that forgives
nothing. Hence the question is not to find out if this is or is not
prejudicial to art. The question, for all those who cannot live
without art and what it signifies, is merely to find out how, among
the police forces of so many ideologies (how many churches, what
solitude!), the strange liberty of creation is possible.
—ALBERT CAMUS

Since my book *The Color Purple* was filmed ten years ago, I have been asked innumerable times about my opinion of the result. I have found it one of the most difficult questions I have ever tried to answer. For many years I began my response by talking about the headache I got the first time I saw the film. Peter Guber, a producer,

FROM *THE SAME RIVER TWICE*

had warned me that on first viewing, I might be shocked. I was to be grateful for the warning. I saw the film in a huge theater with only two other people, and everything about it seemed wrong, especially the opening musical score, which sounded like it belonged in *Oklahoma!* After reciting this experience I would launch into my tale about buying the magic wand that I took to the premiere in New York City, and how, thanks to its magical powers, and a packed theater of enthusiastic viewers all sobbing and guffawing in my ear, I was able to critique the film for its virtues rather than its flaws. Sometimes I would simply say, "I love the film." Other times I would say, "I have mixed feelings." Occasionally I would say, "It is a child with at least three parents: It looks like all of them." Most frequently I said, "Remember, the movie is not the book."

It has taken me a while to realize that attempting to respond honestly to this question has kept me from examining the ones I've continually asked myself: "What did I learn from this extremely thrilling, challenging, and ultimately liberating experience? How was I changed during this period in my life? In what ways did my personal life and the filming of my book connect, so that looking back I am able to chart real learning, satisfaction, suffering, and growth?" I was late getting around to these questions because from the moment word went out that there would be a movie, it was attacked by people who loathed the idea. The attacks, many of them personal and painful, continued for many years, right alongside the praise, the prizes, the Oscar award nominations. I often felt isolated, deliberately misunderstood and alone. This too is the writer's territory; I accepted it with all the grace and humor I possessed. Still, there is no denying the pain of being not simply challenged publicly, but condemned. It was said that I hated men, black men in particular; that my work was injurious to black male and female relationships; that my ideas of equality and tolerance were harmful, even destructive to the black community. That my success, and that of other black women writers in publishing our work, was at the expense of black male writers who were not being published sufficiently. I was "accused" of being a lesbian, as if respecting and honoring women automatically discredited anything a woman might say. I was the object of literary stalking: One black male writer attacked me obsessively in lecture, interview, and book for over a decade, to the point where I was concerned about his sanity and my safety. In the country north of San Francisco, where I had always sought peace and renewal, I regularly found myself the target of hostile, inflammatory comments by the editor and publisher of the local paper. Because I was the only black woman resident in the community, I was highly visible and felt exposed and vulnerable. This feeling prevented my working at the depth of thought at which I feel most productive. I eventually sought temporary refuge in Mexico, where I was able to work in peace. By then I had grown used to seeing my expressions taken out of context, rearranged, distorted. It was a curious experience that always left me feeling as if I had ingested poison.

Of all the accusations, it was hardest to tolerate the charge that I hated black men. From infancy I have relied on the fiercely sweet spirits of black men; and this is abundantly clear in my work. Nor did these spirits fail me as I sought to stay on my path to health, wholeness, truth, and creativity. Bob Marley, Ron Dellums, Nelson Mandela, Black Elk, Jesse Jackson, Randall Robinson, James Baldwin, Crazy Horse, Langston Hughes, and a host of black and red men living and dead walked with me. As did the spirits of Walt Whitman, Leo Tolstoy, John Lennon, and Howard Zinn. But even more important, I felt close to, and always affirmed by, the black male spirit within myself. This spirit's indomitable quality is fierceness of emotion, tenderness of heart, and a love of freedom so strong that death is easily preferable to imprisonment of any kind. Out of respect, I worked hard to reassure my nephews, uncles, brothers, friends, and former lovers that the monster they saw being projected was not the aunt, niece, sister, woman who loved them. I was not guided or accompanied by the spirits of black men who embarrass and oppress us, or by those of assorted "gangsta" rappers for whom the humiliation and subjugation of women is the preferred expression of masculinity: I feel no regret for this.

What the question about my response to the film could not address, I realized only belatedly, was the hidden trauma I endured during its creation, of which these attacks were only a part, trauma not always noticeably connected to the making of it. The reason the question itself seemed so exasperating was because I knew a comprehensive response would be long. It would not be simple. It would be, in order to have meaning for me, about deeply painful issues that were literally the "behind the scenes" struggles of one of my life's most complex public events.

For instance: At the time the movie was being made, I thought that I, and my mother, were dying.

In the beginning, at the end of the seventies, my mother had small strokes that left her barely marked, but shortly after *The Color Purple* was written in 1981 she suffered a major one. I flew to Georgia to see her and to consult with my family and her doctor about what should be done. Her X rays showed carotid arteries so blocked with cholesterol that almost no oxygen was getting to her brain. Though this blockage was removed, she remained largely paralyzed. There followed many months of trying to make life better for her, a temporary, hopeful period when she felt well enough to make the journey out to California to visit me. As I had suspected, she loved the redwoods, the ocean, the hills, and valiantly lurched along, leaning on my arm, her face radiant; but then, ultimately, there was a decline brought on by many smaller "afterstrokes." For over a decade, until her death in September 1993, my mother was completely incapacitated physically. She had not read *The Color Purple* before her stroke, beyond the first few pages, though it was deliberately written in a way that would not intimidate her, and other readers like her, with only a grade school education and a lifetime of reading the Bible, newspapers, and magazine articles. Because of her inability even to sit up in bed, she would never be able to read it.

From the moment I realized my mother would never again be the woman I knew, something fell inside of me. It did not fall with a crash, but was rather a slow, inexorable collapse. There was a strong green cord connecting me to this great, simple-seeming, but complicated woman, who was herself rooted in the earth. I felt this cord weakening, becoming a thread. My legs seemed to be going out from under me. My heart felt waterlogged. My spirit lost its shine. My grief was kind enough to visit me only at night, in dreams: As I felt it wash over me, I did not care that I might drown. I knew that, awake, the unshed tears of rage and irremediable loss I was suffering would surely kill me. I had only known my mother as active, heroically so, and strong. This does not mean she was never sick; she was, from time to time. But she was never one to lie in bed past seven in the morning, even after her eight children were out of the house for good. After raising all of us, and being a full-time worker and housewife, she was often up at dawn managing her house and garden, honoring her religious obligations, and hastening to her duties to her friends. She was strong-hearted.

Which, indeed, she remained. Her doctor marveled that even though the rest of her body failed to obey her most minor wish, her heart remained that of a lion. This was also true, amazingly, of her spirit. Eventually, all that was left of my mother was her smile, radiating out of a body that already seemed, in her bed, settled into its final resting place. There was not a day, all those years, that I did not feel the emptiness left by my mother's absence, particularly as she gradually lost the ability to talk, beyond a slurred greeting, which, true to her spirit, she slurred cheerfully.

I loved the way my mother talked, which was always fresh, honest, straight as an arrow describing anything. When I sat on the set of *The Color Purple*—and as controversy raged even over whether my characters "degraded" black folk speech—it was this kind of speech that I tried to make sure the actors expressed. For me the filming of my book was a journey to the imagined and vastly rearranged lives of my mother and father and grandparents before I was born (among other things); it was a re-created world I hoped desperately my mother would live long enough to enter again through film. I used to amuse myself, on the set, watching Steven work, and thinking of the gift he was preparing for a woman he had never seen.

My own trial was different from my mother's, but coincided with and to an extent echoed portions of it.

It is my habit as a born-again pagan to lie on the earth in worship. In this, I imagine I am like my pagan African and Native American ancestors, who were sustained by their conscious inseparability from Nature prior to being forced by missionaries to focus all their attention on a God "up there" in "heaven." Unknown to me, however, sometime during the late seventies and early eighties, the earth tired of people, worshipers or not, taking her for granted. I was bitten by three of the ticks that cause Lyme disease. I pulled off the ticks casually, as I had done all my life, and thought no more about it, although I later noticed the marks on my stomach, large, red bull's-eyes. I felt soreness and swelling. I did not even realize I was sick for most of 1983, even though my mood swings, always precipitous because of PMS, became increasingly dramatic. I found myself one day ranting at an old friend whose ineffectual efforts to colonize me and my work—she insisted in public gatherings and in private that she comprehended the significance of both me and my work far better than I did—suddenly became intolerable (I'd suffered uncomplainingly for years). I noticed I was always tired.

It was not until I flogged myself onto a flight to China, where I hoped to exchange ideas with Chinese women writers, and once there found it a challenge even to think, that I realized something was very wrong. Pictures of me from that trip show a gray, puffy-faced woman, much older and heavier than I would later be, pitched blankly toward the camera. On the train from Shanghai to Hong Kong I began to hemorrhage. By the time I reached Hawaii, I was barely able to put one foot in front of the other. By the time I reached California, I ached in every muscle and joint. I couldn't raise my arms; I could barely move my legs. My eyes ached. My ears. I felt a weariness so profound, it disturbs me to remember it. Though the pain for the most part left, eventually, the weariness and weakness remained. For the next three years I would require a walking stick to keep me upright. And in fact the one memorable item I purchased in China was an elaborately carved dragon-headed cane.

In the early eighties nobody knew about Lyme disease. There was, however, a rumor about something else that eventually became known as Chronic Fatigue Syndrome; I latched on to that, desperately needing some label to define what was happening to me. It was known to be a condition that afflicted mainly women, women who were active politically and socially, women who were "creative." I read that most of these women spent their days weeping and depressed, scared and often unable to move. It had no cure (and still doesn't), though Lyme disease does—if caught early. I went to doctor after doctor, but there was, as far as they could see, nothing wrong with me.

It felt exactly as if I were being attacked from the inside at the same time I was being attacked from the outside. Would I survive it? I thought not. And then, just when I was feeling this, my partner of many struggling but overall happy years informed me that because I had been "distracted by my work and sexually inattentive" he'd had an affair a year or so earlier with an old girlfriend from the past. Having felt more secure in our relationship over time, I'd had no inkling of this, and had blissfully helped plan our future as if it were assured. I felt completely foolish and naive. Though we were in a committed, monogamous relationship, which I, after many hesitations, honored, I did not blame him so much for the infidelity. I recognized that our bond was complicated by my need to live in my own space most of the time, by my periods of creative and/or depression-driven moodiness. It was also complicated by my bisexuality, which my partner joked about—"I am alcoholic, you are bisexual, we cancel each other out"—but which caused both of us a degree of anxiety. I knew he often wondered if I really loved him, and for how long. At times my deep love of and reverence for women felt like ambivalence to both of us.

It was the timing of his confession that sent me reeling. Although his revelation came before there was public awareness of AIDS, I worried there might be a connection between his infidelity and my inexplicable illness. As my trust dissolved along with my health, I became horribly conscious of my vulnerability: I began to make arrangements to leave the relationship. My partner, however, blamed his behavior on alcoholism, a disease that had caused us much suffering before. He was someone whose sweetness, intelligence, love of the moon, and refusal to be inducted into the Vietnam War I cherished, someone I deeply loved. He was also a person who would try to do what he said. I stayed. But in fact the relationship had lost its numinousness, especially sexually: without a sense of the sacred in our physical connections I began to slowly starve. Though we continued together for many more years, and though he tackled and successfully overcame not only his addiction to alcohol but other addictions as well, what remained of the life we'd constructed together was only its shell.

I also stayed because I was too weakened and confused by my illness, and by my mother's illness, to make such a painful break. The humiliation of being in this position with a black man, at a time when I was being publicly and venomously accused of "attacking" black men, was especially enervating. These accusations seemed singularly crass and simpleminded, but they found their target just the same.

In a filmed interview around that time my partner, looking embarrassed but determined, bravely talks about the pain of envying my success, and of our struggle to talk out and understand his feelings so that I would not be sabotaged by his behavior without even knowing it. But I had, by then, already been sabotaged. In this film I am studying my partner as he speaks with a look of horror, for I am fearful he will speak of his affair as an example of his undermining behavior, and I feel trapped to still be trying to stay with him and not be ashamed. This is the feeling of being deep in the messy stuff of women's secret lives, that place from which unscathed survivors are so rare.

Because she was a black woman of humor and spunk, I had responded affirmatively to Elena Featherston's request to make a film about my life during this period of illness. I still had no idea what was wrong with me. Nor was I even able to talk about it, since it had no name. I still leaned on a stick everywhere I went. I think I wanted a witness, through this film. (Reading through my journal from that time I am amazed at how upbeat I sound, with remarkably little mention of my fear. I just omitted any mention of health. Occasionally I admitted to being *tired*. I seemed to focus most of my attention on present and former relationships with lovers, teachers, and siblings: I wrote often about my father. Not knowing what is wrong with you is silencing, even to yourself.) Always chronically short on funding, the filming of *Visions of the Spirit* (an ironically apt title) took nearly four years to complete. It is clear to me at least how sick I was the first years I was filmed in the countryside and at my writing shack in Mendocino. There is a heavy, stoic quality of resignation that reminds me of those days when it took everything I had simply to sit upright and respond to Elena's questions. I can see that I was somewhat better, not as puffy or as absent, when she filmed me a couple of years later on the set of *The Color Purple*, and that by the end of the film the puffiness is gone, my color is normal, and I have begun the long journey back to myself. I will always be grateful to Elena for providing this record, though the first time I viewed her film I saw mostly my own and my mother's suffering and went into mourning for my mother's lost strength, my own weaknesses and failures. My mother, in Elena's film, is typically happy to be alive, though she can move neither foot nor arm, and though there seems little possibility she ever will again. By then she had seen the film of *The Color Purple*; she was carried to the theater on a stretcher in an ambulance. She liked it very much. She said it reminded her of her mother's life.

My mother was less frightened of movies than of books; seeing the characters of *The Color Purple* in the familiar way she'd always seen movie characters soothed her, as did feeling the overwhelming acceptance of the movie by the people in the audience. I understood that part of her resistance to having my book read to her was based on things she had heard about it, or been told. She must have had terrible fears about what I had created, given the vehemence of some of the opposition; but that she could see even a glimmer of her mother's life in our film deeply comforted me.

She adored her own mother, Nettie, whose name I gave to the character most longed for, most consistently loved and missed, in my story. In real life her mother, unlike Nettie who goes to Africa, never went anywhere, and was battered unmercifully by my grandfather. She died, still sweet, but broken, when I was two. A lament of my weeping mother—"My mother was *good*, and he still mistreated her!"—has haunted my life. I am sitting next to my mother in Elena's film, trying gallantly to put up a good appearance, and not to mention to her or to my sister that my own legs and arms are a little hard to move. For with my mother's collapse I have suddenly become "the strong one." Certainly the primary one to be counted on financially, however extended that long haul might be.

When I think of Steven Spielberg's "version" of my book, my first thought is of Steven himself. His love of and enthusiasm for my characters. His ability to find himself in them. I also think of what he says about me in Elena's film: He says that I am "other worldly." That I always seem to be somewhere else. That there is something "apparitional" about me. That I am "very haunting." When I saw this I realized that perhaps Steven intuited that I was extremely fragile as our film was being made, walking some days as if in a dream; as, perhaps, many of the cast and the crew also sensed. For even though I was present on the set every moment I could drag myself up from my couch, I was also not there. As I watched each scene unfold I felt more like a spirit than a person. Sometimes a couple of the male characters would move my director's chair to a new location, with me in it. Whoopi and Oprah, Danny and Akosua, Margaret, Desreta, and Willard, carried on splendidly; I sat under a tree and offered speech lessons and tarot readings, painfully conscious of my fuzzy thinking and blotchy skin, my soul-deep exhaustion and an almost ever-present nausea. I was unequal to the task of pointing out to Steven every "error" I saw about to be made, as my critics later assumed I should have, or even of praising the exquisite things he constantly thought up, which moved me to tears each evening as we watched "dailies." This pained me; I felt it an unexplainable and quite personal failing.

My inability to speak up further prostrated me. I was moved by the way the actors themselves often saved the day, and of how receptive Steven was to them. I was amazed to see how true to the characters Oprah and Margaret played Sofia and Shug; and how incredibly *sweet* and gracious they were as themselves. I cheered inwardly to see Whoopi stand toe to toe one day with Steven and insist that Celie would not age the way he was envisioning her, but would look more like colored women do as they age. A matter of posture and gait, not of wrinkles and a white wig. Because Oprah reminded me of my mother as she was when I was small, I could barely resist sitting beside her as I worried about what was wrong with me and about my mother, and putting my head in her lap. Of all the women in the cast Oprah was most loving and protective toward my daughter, Rebecca (at fifteen the youngest production assistant on the film), spending time with her on the set and inviting her to visit in Chicago. Days when I could not be there I considered Oprah the "aunt" whose presence meant Rebecca would feel "looked out for," more at home.

Throughout the filming Quincy Jones was the older brother/father/beloved figure everyone responded to with simple adoration, longing, and love. Though I would never like the *Oklahoma!*-sounding opening score, I would help choose the music for the rest of the film, and it would feel right. The song "Sister," written by Quincy, Rod Temperton, and Lionel Richie, which I immediately imagined as a signal of affirmation that women could hum to each other coast to coast, is an immeasurable gift to the bonding of women. And, because men of a certain kind wrote it, it includes them, necessarily, in that bonding. In Elena's film Quincy "sees," affirms, and praises me with an abandon unknown to me previously. This "seeing" of what I am as an artist and a person was to heal some of the pain I felt when other black men attacked me. It also served to remind me that I and my work could be loved without envy—creative "distraction" could be recognized and honored—and that I did not have to fear, as I sometimes did, that there were no black men who were healed enough to value the truth of my work. Or to publicly affirm it.

Although I have wanted to publish this book for a number of years—as a record of this process, which I consider especially useful for women, anyone who is fascinated by film, and people of color—I have hesitated. I certainly could not attempt it while my mother was alive. Even after her death it is painful to dwell on her over-a-decade-long immobility; there was the task, as well, of seeking to understand, and not be hurt by, the not-so-noble parts of her that her sickness sometimes revealed, and my efforts to "forget" those parts, while attempting to address them in my art. Nor could I put my relationship with my former partner into perspective while still sharing a life with him. When I finally began to get well again, and leave the relationship, I experienced a return of energy, of clarity and groundedness in reality, that I'd missed for a long time. A gift of a well-earned, just, separation. I was also aware that throughout all my struggles, my feelings at various times to the contrary, I had never been truly alone. Always with me was the inner twin: my true nature, my true self. It is timeless, free, compassionate, and in love with whatever is natural to me. This was the self that came in dreams, to be pursued in the essays I was writing at that time. And as always the sight of trees, the scent of the ocean, the feel of the wind, and the warmth of the sun were faithful to me. In fact, as my body became less dependable over the three years I was most ill, my spirit became more so; my sense of humor sharpened, and I frequently had dreams, visions, and spiritual revelations of extraordinary power. There was developed in me a spontaneous way of knowing that seemed more like remembering than learning. There were things I just suddenly seemed to know, about life, about the world. As if my illness had pushed open an inner door that my usual consciousness was willing to ignore. I found myself in easy contact with the ancestors, a condition I relish, and I seemed to spend long, delightful seasons in a time before this one. I recorded some of these experiences in my book *Living by the Word,* and in the novel I wrote after *The Color Purple, The Temple of My Familiar.*

I understand that, oddly, the experience of making a film of my work, as bewildering and strange as any labyrinth, and as unpredictable as any river, was an initiation into the next, more mature, phase of my life. Harsh criticism, especially when it is felt to be unjust, is at first very painful. After that, there is numbness. After that, as Emily Dickinson wrote about grief, "there is the letting go." I discovered that "the letting go" is actually a state that can be survived, lived in, and treasured. I am a different, more flexible and open person now than I was before. Slower. More maternal about the world. Both more committed and more detached: I recognize solitude as my most necessary private room, yet I now find I am *always* glad, eventually, to welcome guests. I know now that my religion is love and that I practice it by hugging, something I did spontaneously from babyhood. My mother used to tell me, with an incredulous expression, "You would always go to just anybody!" Perhaps I was initiated, via collaboration on the film, into how such trust could feel as an adult. I admit that, as in a fairy tale, when suddenly in the midst of my peaceful life there comes an unexpected knock at the door, I am happy to go off in strange conveyances with odd people I've never met before; this suits the wondrousland quality of life to which I was apparently born attuned.

Certainly much that concerned me before, does not. I lost what attachment I had to the image others might have of me, since I learned decisively that this is an area over which I have little control. I was called "liar" and "whore" and "traitor" for no other reason than that people who have been made to depend on the approval of the powerful grow afraid of criticizing themselves, because the powerful may hear, amplify their distress, and hold them up to censure and ridicule. The powerful can also manipulate people, and pass horrible, repressive laws, based on the negative images that are permitted to proliferate. This is the reality. And yet, until we can criticize ourselves, and feel safe doing so, there is no hope of molding better values in our children, or of increasing the respect we feel for ourselves. I am not interested in being a role model, or in fulfilling the expectations of others. I know I am of most use to others and to myself by being this unique self: Nature, I have noticed, is not particularly devoted to copies, and human beings needn't be either.

During my time on the labyrinthine river of high-risk collaborative creativity, private illness and public praise and censure, everything I understood as a child was reinforced. The world *is* magical; there *are* good people in it. *Inherent in life is fun.* What I may never know is why my initiation involved tick bites and illness and Steven Spielberg. Nor do I need to know. To me the world seems filled with an endless stream of miracles and wonders; some feel better than others, but I am amazed by them all.

At the heart of the most mysterious labyrinth lives the greatest mystery. Because I followed love and joyous curiosity through the twists and turns of the labyrinth, because I managed not to be turned back, or battered too disastrously by the boulders rising up in the river, I did find all the women in *The Color Purple*, who together are the sacred feminine that, because of the accessibility of film, can be beamed across a world desperate for its return. They also suggest infinite possibilities for women, and for myself. Womanist women. I also found Quincy and Steven, two green and supple men; also much longed for by the world. But even more calming to my heart, I found again the old imperfect sinner and pagan I love so much, my grandfather. Surely doing his part, after a sorely misguided youth spent in dissipation, confusion, and cruelty, to represent, as a grandfather, an old man, the sacred masculine. It broke my heart that so few people were able to really see him, in the much maligned character of Mister. But *irregardless,* as he used to say (meaning, *in spite of everything*: an "incorrect" word I carry with me everywhere; it is on my license plate), there he sat at the end of the day, the end of the film, the end of the journey, in the small wooden chair he sat in for so long it began to look like him. Waiting. For me to finish taking him completely apart, for me to share his failings with all the world, for me to understand him as well as a granddaughter can. For me to know that my love and appreciation of his life is even more sturdy than my grief. Waiting for me to bring him back home, back inside my heart, secure, in myself. Unlike Danny Glover, who played Mister in the movie, my grandfather was small, and, as an old man, decidedly impish. I always understood there were layers and layers of him: To think of him reduced to one layer, and that of brutality, was a torture I survived only because I knew he would understand it was my intention to render him whole. I felt no condemnation from his spirit.

I especially have wanted to publish the script I wrote for the film. I read in magazines after the film opened that I started a script but couldn't finish it. This would have been, it was said, like "giving birth to the same baby." I started a script, under conditions of debilitating illness, single motherhood, betrayal, and nearly unbearable grief, and I completed it to my own satisfaction. It was, however, not the script that Steven loved. It was quieter than the one by Menno Meyjes, which was filmed, and which I was happy to find I liked a lot. There was not so much music in mine. It was clear the women loved each other. It was clear that Shug is, like me, bisexual. That Celie is lesbian. Do I regret my version of my book was not filmed? I have accepted that it wasn't. But to balance this experience, I have felt a need to share what I did attempt.

What I discovered in any event was interesting. An old idea: You really cannot step into the same river twice. Each time it is different, and so are you. Though it hurt to see in Spielberg's film that Celie ceases to be a writer, which she is to her very soul, when I had sat down to re-create her, it bored me to make her a writer, and so I too thought of something else. When people criticized the movie for not being more true to the book, I understood how difficult it is for a creative person to stick to one way of doing things. Though why Harpo keeps falling through the roof, among other odd inventions; why it rains inside the juke joint, I will never understand. Perhaps Harpo is Steven, falling down the stairs of his life at the time, breaking his bones against his parrot's cage, needing to rattle his own. Or maybe Steven assumed Harpo was named with Harpo Marx in mind. He wasn't.

When I read my script, I see that in some ways it is also different from the book. What I have kept, which the film avoided entirely, is Shug's completely unapologetic self-acceptance as outlaw, renegade, rebel, and pagan; her zest in loving both women and men, younger and older. When Shug says in the book *The Color Purple*, "I believe God is everything that is, ever was, or ever will be," she is saying what I too believe; she is also quoting Isis, the ancient African goddess, a precursor of the Virgin Mary, mother of Christ, although I did not know this at the time. I have also kept Celie's grasp of the concept that what is holy is the whole thing, not some thing above it or beyond it, not something separate from herself; as well as her complete bafflement that there could be anything wrong with loving another woman. Especially a woman so loving, brave, and sweet-smelling as Shug. And that the earth itself produces all the wonders, along with the sorrows, anyone could want. I have kept Albert's awakening to the fact that *it is attention to the details of tenderness* that supports and encourages life, which he learns under the guidance of a child.

After nearly three years of feeling almost dead, I decided I would live as if I were really alive. I heaved myself onto yet another plane and went to Custer, South Dakota, where Dennis Banks, a Native American I believed in, was on trial for defending himself and other Indians against the FBI, the contemporary cavalry of the federal government. I was still so weak that I spent most of the time outside the courthouse lying on the ground. Only dogs and children approached me, and the drumming of nearby Buddhist nuns and monks kept my pulse going.

But it was that journey that marked the clear beginning of my return to health. My decision to continue to live as myself, regardless of how tedious it might be to get around. Later on, I would read that what I had done was exactly what a person with Lyme disease should do: something that seems impossible. Apparently such behavior is a kick to the immune system. I would one day run into Dennis Banks again, as we delivered medicines to the children of Cuba, and I would tell him what he, a bound prisoner in South Dakota, had done for me; he would tell me that the copy of *The Color Purple* I managed to slip him during the trial was the only reading matter he had, and that in prison, that same copy passed from hand to hand among the prisoners until it fell apart. Knowing I must have been stung by the harsh criticism of the character Mister, Dennis said: "There's a little bit of Mister in all of us." We rejoiced to find ourselves connecting on hard and often amazing paths through life, held each other, banged on the ceremonial drum he always carries and prays with, and thanked the Universe we had survived.

If one factors in the time difference between Georgia and California, my mother died on my father's birthday. That is, in any event, when she died for me. Knowing how deeply she loved him and that he loved her as much, for all their struggles and failings, made me feel this was a special message to me about loving and healing, about remembering and honoring the love. When I think of my parents—my father died in 1973—both of them are green. Both rooted in the earth. Both faithful to their love of Nature, the beauty of the seasons, the magic of this heaven we are in. My mother was given a splendid farewell ceremony, to which hundreds of people came. Generations of children, other than her own, she'd raised. People of all ages she'd inspired, encouraged, helped. There was an endless cortege, pickup trucks filled with the flowers she loved. My daughter and I stood beside her coffin and thanked her for the blessing her life had been to us. We asked her as well to take our greetings and our thanks to a long list of other warriors of good who had preceded her into the spaciousness. Since my mother's burial, according to my sister who visits her grave regularly, the entire cemetery has been carpeted, in each season, with flowers. I am not surprised.

My former partner is someone who has for many years counseled other men and boys about the physical and emotional violence they inflict on women and children, and on other boys and men, and about how this behavior destroys everything: families, communities, relationships, and themselves. We have known each other all our adult lives, since I was a student at Spelman College, in Atlanta, and he was a student at Morehouse, across the street. We were lovers for thirteen years and friends for thirty. The dramatic way that "success" strikes in America is extremely stressful and destructive of certain areas of a relationship. Perhaps, this being so, there is no way we could have survived as a couple. On the other hand, I accept that I am of a particular character, prone to distraction and content to think of my body and my sexuality as my own; my autonomous behavior need not invite betrayal, sabotage, or attack. At least we were able, after staying together and steadily working our way toward the next honest place for us, to separate with increased humility before the imponderables of coupledom, whatever its status and configuration, and with vastly reduced rancor and pain. We are able still to talk, to joke, to laugh and go on walks together; we are hopeful of honoring both the difficult and the good, and especially that place where they meet.

Contributors' Notes

Peter Bart is the editor of *Variety* and *Daily Variety.*

David Bogle's books include *Brown Sugar* and *Toms, Coons, Mulattoes, Mammies, and Bucks: An Interpretive History of Blacks in American Films.*

Edward Field's most recent book, *Counting Myself Lucky, Selected Poems 1963–1992,* won a Lambda Award. He wrote the voice-over for the Academy Award–winning documentary film *To Be Alive.*

Bonnie Friedman's books include the collection of essays *Writing Past Dark.* She is a former teacher at Dartmouth College and the University of Iowa, whose work appears frequently in our country's leading journals and collections.

Stephen Fry's most recent book is the novel *The Hippopotamus.* He is also the author of The *Liar,* a novel; *Paperweight,* a collection of articles, stories, and essays; and the screenplay *The Confederacy of*

Dunces. He has starred in several films, including *Peter's Friends* and *IQ.*

Libby Gelman-Waxner's movie writings have appeared monthly over the past five years in *Premiere* magazine.

Albert Goldbarth's most recent books include *Across the Layers: Poems Old and New* and *Adventures in Ancient Egypt.* He is the Distinguished Professor of Humanities at Wichita State University.

Daniel Harris writes regularly for *Harper's, Salmagundi,* and *Newsday.* His work has also appeared in *The New York Times Magazine, The Nation,* and *Best American Essays,* among many leading magazines and anthologies.

Evan Hunter (a.k.a. Ed McBain) is the author of the best-selling "87th Precinct" series of mystery novels, including, most recently, *Nocturne, Ice,* and *Best Hope.*

Barbara Maltby is a contributing editor at *American Scholar.*

Kathleen Murphy is writer in resident with the Film Society of Lincoln Center.

Geoffrey O'Brien's books include *The Phantom Empire,* a book about movies. He is the executive editor of the Library of America.

Gerald Peary is a film columnist and critic for the *Boston Phoenix.* He is a professor of film and journalism at Suffolk College and teaches film studies at Boston University.

John Powers is the author of *The Last Catholic in America, Do Black Patent Leather Shoes Really Reflect Up?* and *The Unoriginal Sinner,* among other books. His awards include two Emmy Awards for writing.

Jill Robinson's seventh book is the novel *Star Country.* Her work has appeared in *Vogue, The New York Times Magazine,* and *Cosmopolitan,* among other leading journals in America and Europe.

Martin Scorsese has directed many of our country's most distinguished and original films, including *Mean Streets, Taxi Driver, Raging Bull, Goodfellas,* and *The Last Temptation of Christ.*

Mark Singer's books include the novel *Funny Money* and *Mr. Personality,* a collection of essays. He has been a staff writer for *The New Yorker* since 1974.

Susan Sontag's most recent works are a novel, *The Volcano Lover,* and a play, *Alive in Bed.* Her new novel, *In America,* will be published in 1998.

Alice Walker's novels include the Pulitzer Prize–winning novel *The Color Purple* and, most recently, *Possessing the Secret of Joy.* She is also the author of several poetry books and the memoir *Anything We Love Can Be Saved.*

Garry Wills's many books include the Pulitzer Prize–winning *Lincoln at Gettysburgh: The Words That Remade America* and, most recently, *John Wayne's America: The Politics of Celebrity.* He is the former Henry R. Luce Professor of American Culture and Public Policy at Northwestern University.

Isabel Wilkerson is a senior writer at *The New York Times* and currently a visiting professor of journalism at Princeton University. Her essay in this collection was written with research assistance from Craig Rose.

Notable Movie Writings of 1997

ABOUT THE EDITOR

George Plimpton's books include the best-selling biographies *Edie* and, most recently, *Truman Capote*. His other books include the celebrated *Paper Lion, Shadow Box,* and *Bogey Man.* Founder and executive editor of the international magazine *The Paris Review,* Mr. Plimpton is a frequent contributor of essays, profiles, and articles in our country's most distinguished journals, often about some of the most engaging and influential events and leaders of our time. Plimpton has appeared in several films, including the Academy Award–winning movies *Reds, Nixon,* and *When We Were Kings,* and, most recently, *Good Will Hunting.*

ABOUT THE SERIES EDITOR

Jason Shinder's books include the poetry collections *Every Room We Ever Slept In* and the forthcoming *Among Women.* He has edited several anthologies, most recently *Lights, Camera, Poetry: American Movie Poems,* a New York Public Library Best Book Award winner. Founder and director of the YMCA National Writer's Voice, a network of literary arts centers at YMCAs nationwide, and New Century Films and Public Literature, Shinder teaches in the MFA writing programs at Bennington College and the New School for Social Research. His forthcoming books include *Tales from the Couch: Writers on the Talking Cure* and the annual resource edition *First Books.*

(continued from page iv)